# SHERLOCK HOLMES, ESQ. AND JOHN H. WATSON, M.D.

*An Encyclopædia of Their Affairs*

# Sherlock Holmes, Esq.
# and John H. Watson, M.D.

*An Encyclopædia of Their Affairs*

By Orlando Park

*Northwestern University Press*
1962

Open access edition funded by the National Endowment for the Humanities/Andrew W. Mellon Foundation Humanities Open Book Program.



Orlando Park. Sherlock Holmes, Esq. and John H. Watson, M. D.:
An Encyclopedia of Their Affairs.
Evanston, Ill.: Northwestern University Press, 1962.

ISBN 978-0-8101-3967-1 (paper)
ISBN 978-0-8101-3968-8 (ebook)

Printed in the United States of America

Original edition LCCN 62-17805

To Thomas Baird

*who was often surprised but never at a loss*

# Preface

About thirty years ago I read *The Hound of the Baskervilles.* It made a lasting impression. From this account I read backwards and forwards through the affairs of Mr. Sherlock Holmes and Dr. John H. Watson. During one of the re-readings I began to take notes. Later these latter were found to be too short or too incomplete, and some ten years ago a systematic analysis was undertaken. The present compilation is incomplete in that all matters are not set forth, but a sizable proportion is accumulated here. There is good reason for this course. In the first place, "much more grist has actually been gathered than has come through the mill" (William Rose Benét, *The Reader's Encyclopedia* [Crowell Co., 1948], p. vi) . Second, the material that follows is intended to answer questions, but also to stimulate curiosity—in short, to suggest that those who have not had the experience of reading the exploits of Holmes and Watson should do so as soon as feasible.

There are many problems posed in their long association, and some of them have not been answered satisfactorily as yet. Even distinguished Holmesians are not always in agreement. Possibly this is why they are distinguished. Then there are lesser things—*e.g.,* why is there so much said about violins and dogs and almost nothing about pianos and cats?

Opinion will differ in degree or kind, but to me there are three critical events in the saga. First, the solidification of Holmes's hobby of detection into an occupation whereby he might earn a living. Trevor, Senior, was the critical factor here. Victor Trevor was young Sherlock's only close friend at college, and he invited Sherlock to his home in Norfolk, near Langmere in the Broads. Victor's father was impressed by Sherlock's ability to reason objectively and to intuitively put his finger on the solution of a problem having to do with human frailty. He congratulated the young man on his powers, and this led Holmes to substitute occupation for pastime, to make a living out of the science of detection. This new purpose is recorded in Holmes' first case, *The Gloria Scott.*

Second, the bringing together of Holmes and Watson. Watson, recovering indifferently from a shoulder wound and enteric fever, was back from India, looking for cheaper lodgings in London. He ran into his former dresser of hospital-training days, young Stamford, at the Criterion Bar. The two went on for lunch at the Holborn, and Stamford recalled that another acquaintance, Holmes, wanted to share living costs with someone in chambers at 221B Baker Street. After lunch Stamford took Watson to meet Holmes. The result of this meeting is historic, and for seventeen years (opening sentence in the *Veiled Lodger*) the two were more or less associated with each other in the prevention of crime and the hunting down of wrongdoers. I am aware of the interesting discrepancy between Watson's stated "seventeen years" of collaboration with Holmes and a longer span which can be deduced from a study of the published cases. In fact, I have spent many a happy hour working on a chronology of the saga. But this has been done by others, and probably will be done again. It is not my present task. Watson said seventeen years, and I prefer to be canonical in this matter. Their momentous meeting takes place in the opening of their first collaboration, *A Study in Scarlet.*

Third, Watson's first marriage. This was in the memorable account of *The Sign of the Four,* in which Watson meets, woos, and becomes engaged to blonde, blue-eyed Mary Morstan. They marry later, and this affects the course of quite a few incidents directly or indirectly in the saga.

The present work is based upon the two-volume Memorial Edition of 1931, *The Complete Sherlock Holmes* by Sir Arthur Conan Doyle, published by Doubleday, Doran & Company. In this edition the British spelling is retained, which accounts for such words as "Honourable" in the following text where cases and characters are involved.

Several items of information may assist in the use of my alphabetical guide. Definite and indefinite articles are not used in the entries except in direct quotations. In several of the cases there is a story within a story. Such internal stories, *e.g.,* "The Country of the Saints" within *A Study in Scarlet,* do not bear directly on the action and are largely disregarded, since this present book deals with the participation of Holmes and (usually) of Watson. To avoid repetition and to save space, **H** stands for Holmes, and **W** stands for Watson. In this I have followed the example of Sir Winston S. Churchill in his 1932 *The Unknown War,* in which a similar method of substituting capital letters for the names of the principal generals of the German and Austrian armies is used with effect. Where they constitute a main entry, published cases appear in capital letters, and unpublished cases are preceded by an asterisk.

Finally, I express my gratitude to the distinguished Holmesian, Mr. Vincent Starrett, who took time to examine in detail the manuscript of this book.

My labor will have its best result if it stimulates others to read and re-read the adventures of Holmes and Watson and enjoy them. To do otherwise were to miss a measure of happiness.

ORLANDO PARK

# Sherlock Holmes, esq.
# and John H. Watson, M.D.

*An Encyclopædia of Their Affairs*

# A

**Abbas Parva.** Berkshire village where the Ronder circus caravan stopped for the night en route to Wimbledon (*Veiled Lodger*).

**Abbey Grange.** Kent home where Sir Eustace Brackenstall was murdered. Stanley Hopkins wanted to consult **H** there (*Abbey Grange*).

ABBEY GRANGE, ADVENTURE OF THE. Winter's end, 1897. Sir Eustace Brackenstall had been killed. Inspector Stanley Hopkins asked for **H. H** investigated but let the killer go free because he felt that Captain Crocker was justified.

***Abbey School.** **H** could not go at once to Tuxbury Old Place with James Dodd, for he was clearing up the "Abbey School case," as **W** called it. This was the case in which the Duke of Greyminster was so deeply involved (*Blanched Soldier*).

***Aberdeen.** There was a case here that was similar to the *Adventure of the Noble Bachelor, q.v.* (*Valley of Fear*).

**Aberdeen.** Inspector Alec MacDonald was brought up here (*Valley of Fear*).

**Aberdeen Shipping Company.** In Fresno Street. Mrs. St. Clair had a parcel waiting for her here (*Man with Twisted Lip*).

**Aberdonian accent.** Inspector Alec MacDonald had it (*Valley of Fear*).

***Abergavenny murder.** This case was up for trial (*Priory School*).

***Abernetty family.** A dreadful business first brought to **H's** notice by a seeming trifle (*Six Napoleons*).

***Abrahams, old.** It was not feasible for **H** to leave London while old Abrahams was in such terror of being murdered (*Lady Frances Carfax*).

**Achmet.** Untrustworthy servant of the rajah. The rajah sent his most precious jewels (the Agra Treasure) in a steel box with Achmet to Agra Fort. Achmet was murdered by Dost Akbar (*Sign of Four*).

**Acton.** County magnate near Reigate in Surrey. His house was broken into, but the paper was safe with his solicitors (*Reigate Puzzle*).

**ADAIR, HILDA.** Sister of Ronald. Lived with Ronald and mother at 427 Park Lane (*Empty House*).

**ADAIR, HONOURABLE RONALD.** Second son of Earl of Maynooth. Living in London with mother and sister at 427 Park Lane. Formerly engaged to Miss Edith Woodley. Played cards with Colonel Moran. Murdered by Moran. **H** thought that Adair had caught Moran cheating at cards. Moran captured for the murder and for attempted murder of **H** (*Empty House*).

***ADAMS.** He was the chief suspect in the Manor House case. Mycroft thought that Sherlock was not up to it, but **H** told his brother that he had solved it and that Adams was the man (*Greek Interpreter*).

***ADDLETON TRAGEDY.** This happened in 1894 (*Pince-Nez*).

**ADELAIDE.** Australia. Mary Fraser brought up here (*Abbey Grange*). Henry Peters (*alias* Dr. Shlessinger) hailed from here (*Lady Frances Carfax*).

**ADELAIDE-SOUTHAMPTON LINE.** **H** felt that the next move was to inquire here (*Abbey Grange*).

**ADLER, IRENE.** To **H** she was always *the* woman. Born in New Jersey in 1858. A contralto, with experience at La Scala, and Prima Donna of the Warsaw Imperial Opera. Met King of Bohemia at Warsaw, and once a photograph was taken with them together. Retiring from her operatic career, she came to Briony Lodge, Serpentine Avenue in St. John's Wood, London. The king wanted the photograph, but Irene would not give it to him. By a ruse **H** trapped her into revealing where she had hidden the photograph. She disguised herself as a boy and accosted **H** later. She married Godfrey Norton with **H** present as a disguised witness. When the Nortons departed England, she left **H** a letter and the king a photograph of herself. The latter **H** asked for and received from the king (*Scandal in Bohemia*).

**ADMIRALTY, THE.** Decided that the "Gloria Scott" was lost at sea (*Gloria Scott*). The Admiralty was buzzing like an over-turned bee-hive (*Bruce-Partington*).

**AFGHANISTAN.** **W** wounded at battle of Maiwand, *q.v.* First time **H** met **W**, he noted to latter's mystification that **W** had been here (*Study in Scarlet*). **W's** army life in this country had made him used to packing quickly (*Boscombe Valley Mystery*). **W** was in pain from a Jezail bullet in his leg in his Afghan campaign and noted this pain "a few weeks" before his marriage (*Noble Bachelor*). **W** refers to his Afghan experiences when he attended Colonel Hayter (*Reigate Puzzle*). Twisted Henry Wood came to this country and then returned to the Punjab (*Crooked Man*). **W** tried to interest Percy Phelps in this country (*Naval Treaty*).

AFRICA. Dr. Sterndale was about to leave for this continent when he was recalled by Mr. Roundhay (*Devil's Foot*). Sahara King was from northern Africa (*Veiled Lodger*). Cf. South Africa and West Africa.

AGAR, DR. MOORE. Harley Street specialist who advised **H** to rest or have a complete breakdown (*Devil's Foot*).

AGATHA. Milverton's housemaid. **H** becomes engaged to her, and this results in the watchdog's being locked up nights (*Milverton*).

AGRA. Indian city where Jonathan Small came when Abel White's plantation was burned in the great mutiny. The fort was held against rebelling native troops, and it was here that Small and his three companions buried Achmet and the Agra Treasure; here too they were all four imprisoned for murder (*Sign of Four*).

AGRA TREASURE. Obtained by Major John Sholto and Captain Arthur Morstan. Stated to be worth £500,000 by the finder of the treasure, Bartholomew Sholto. Treasure recovered from Jonathan Small (cf. "Aurora"), and **W** takes it to Mary Morstan. The treasure chest, of Benares metal-work, was forced by **W** and Mary and found to be empty. Jonathan Small threw the Agra Treasure into the Thames (*Sign of Four*). Peter Jones refers to this treasure case (*Red-headed League*).

AINSTREE, DR. According to **W**, the greatest living authority on tropical disease. Cf. Sir Jasper Meek (*Dying Detective*).

AIR-GUN. 1. Made by the blind German, Von Herder, to Moriarty's order and used by Colonel Moran in attempted assassination of **H**. The weapon is in the Scotland Yard Museum (*Empty House*).

2. Made by Straubenzee, in the Minories, for Count Sylvius, apparently for the same purpose as above (*Mazarin Stone*).

AKBAR, DOST. One of the Four and foster brother of Abdullah Khan. Akbar traveled north with Achmet, who bore the Agra Treasure, and he was author of plan to kill Achmet and take the treasure. Akbar murdered Achmet (*Sign of Four*).

ALBEMARLE MANSION. Kensington. Mr. Melville lived here (*Wisteria Lodge*).

ALBERT DOCK. London. Lestrade boarded the "May Day" here and arrested Jim Browner (*Cardboard Box*). **H** discovered here that the "Lone Star" had sailed down the Thames, homeward bound (*Five Orange Pips*).

ALBERT HALL. Carina was singing here, and **H** felt that he and **W** had time to dress, dine, and hear her sing (*Retired Colourman*).

ALDERSGATE. **H** and **W** got off the Underground here (*Red-headed League*).

ALDERSHOT. **H** and **W** admired the hills en route to Winchester (*Copper Beeches*). **H** and **W** were in this area on the 11:10 from Waterloo station (*Crooked Man*).

ALDGATE. Station on London Underground where Mason found the body of Cadogan West (*Bruce-Partington*).

ALDRIDGE. Lestrade compared him in size to Jim Browner, whom he arrested on the "May Day" (*Cardboard Box*).

ALEXANDRIA. Ionides made special cigarettes here for Professor Coram (*Pince-Nez*). N. Garrideb preferred the ancient coins of Syracuse (*Garridebs*).

ALEXIS. The true love of Anna, Professor Coram's wife in Russia. Alexis was sent to Siberia on his exposure by Sergius, *alias* Professor Coram (*Pince-Nez*).

ALGAR. **H** asked him to send the answers to the police station (*Cardboard Box*).

ALGERIA. Count Sylvius had shot lions here (*Mazarin Stone*).

ALICE. Maid to Hatty Doran (*Noble Bachelor*).

*"ALICIA." This cutter sailed into a patch of mist, and both ship and crew vanished. This is an unfinished case, and the data are in **W**'s dispatch box in Cox bank (*Thor Bridge*).

ALLAHABAD. Edmunds, a Berkshire constable, later was sent here (*Veiled Lodger*).

ALLAN BROTHERS. Chief land agents of Esher. They had rented Wisteria Lodge to Aloysius Garcia or his agent (*Wisteria Lodge*).

ALLARDYCE'S BACK SHOP. Here **H** tried to transfix a pig by a single blow of a spear and failed (*Black Peter*).

ALLEGRO. Flora Millar was a *danseuse* here (*Noble Bachelor*).

ALLEN, MRS. House servant to Mr. and Mrs. John Douglas (*Valley of Fear*).

ALMANAC. See Whitaker's.

ALPHA INN. It was near the British Museum (*Blue Carbuncle*).

ALTAMONT. *Alias* of **H** when he was chief espionage agent for Von Bork and a bitter Irish-American (*Last Bow*).

*ALUMINUM CRUTCH, SINGULAR AFFAIR OF THE. This case was pre-Watsonian, but the record exists, for it was briefly exhibited to **W** (*Musgrave Ritual*).

*AMATEUR MENDICANT SOCIETY. The Society had a luxurious club in the lower vault of a furniture warehouse. **W** recorded the case in 1887 but has not given the data to the public so far (*Five Orange Pips*).

AMATI. **H** noted the difference from a Stradivarius violin (*Study in Scarlet*).

AMAZON RIVER. Maria loved J. Neil Gibson near this river, and later she loved him in British woods in Hampshire (*Thor Bridge*).

AMBERLEY, JOSIAH. He murdered his wife and Dr. Ernest, then threw their bodies in a well (*Retired Colourman*).

AMERICA. Henry Baskerville came here in his teens from a South Coast Devonshire cottage and grew up chiefly in Canada. He was called to England to inherit Baskerville Hall (*The Hound*). John Douglas and his wife were from America (*Valley of Fear*). So were Mr. and Mrs. Francis Hay Moulton (*Noble Bachelor*).

AMERICAN EXCHANGE. In the Strand. Letters addressed to E. J. Drebber and to Joseph Stangerson were found in the pockets of E. J. Drebber, dead at No. 3 Lauriston Gardens (*Study in Scarlet*).

AMES. Butler to Mr. and Mrs. John Douglas (*Valley of Fear*).

AMOY RIVER. In China. The Blue Carbuncle was found in this river (*Blue Carbuncle*).

AMSTERDAM. Count Sylvius told Merton that Van Seddar could have the stone cut up into four pieces by Sunday (*Mazarin Stone*).

ANDAMAN ISLANDS. Captain Morstan had many curios from these islands in his luggage at Langham Hotel. Mary Morstan told **H** and **W** that Major Sholto and Captain Morstan, her father, had commanded the troops in these islands. An Andaman Islander, Tonga, murdered Bartholomew Sholto at Pondicherry Lodge. Cf. Blair Island (*Sign of Four*). **W** recalls the pursuit of the Andaman Islander (*Pince-Nez*).

ANDERSON. Friend of Baldy Simpson and Godfrey Emsworth. Killed near Buffelsspruit in Boer War (*Blanched Soldier*).

ANDERSON. Village constable of Fulworth. He hoped to solve the death of McPherson and receive credit—at least he did not want to have censure from Lewes (*Lion's Mane*).

ANDERSON MURDERS. **H** recalled these murders in North Carolina as similar to the Baskerville case (*The Hound*).

ANDOVER. **H** noted a case here in 1877 that paralleled Mary Sutherland's case (*Case of Identity*).

ANERLY ARMS. Norwood hotel where McFarlane spent the night (*Norwood Builder*).

ANGEL, HOSMER. *Alias* of Mr. Windibank, stepfather of Mary Sutherland (*Case of Identity*).

ANGLO-INDIAN CLUB. Col. Sebastian

Moran was a member (*Empty House*).

**ANNA.** After her betrayal in Russia by her husband, she came to Yoxley Old Place in England to get the documents from Professor Coram that would free her lover, Alexis, in Siberia. At Yoxley she killed Willoughby Smith (*Pince-Nez*).

**ANSTRUTHER, DR.** Physician who took care of **W**'s practice while **W** joined **H** (*Boscombe Valley Mystery*).

**ANTHONY.** Manservant at Merripit House. **H** thought that his name was "Antonio," that he knew the way through the Grimpen Mire, and that he fed the dog when Jack Stapleton was away (*The Hound*).

***Anthropological Journal.*** **H** has published two monographs on the human ear in this periodical (*Cardboard Box*).

**APACHES (AMERICAN).** They were reported to have killed Francis Hay Moulton (*Noble Bachelor*).

**APACHES (PARISIAN).** Crippled Le-Brun in Montmartre (*Illustrious Client*).

**APPLEDORE TOWERS.** Fifteen minutes' walk from Church Row, and the home of Milverton. **H** burgled Milverton's safe, burned the contents, and **H** and **W** escaped from the grounds just in time (*Milverton*).

**AQUA TOFANA.** Alluded to in *Daily Telegraph*'s account of E. J. Drebber's murder (*Study in Scarlet*).

**ARABIAN NIGHTS.** Isadora Klein's drawing room according to **W** (*Three Gables*). **W** refers to them (*Noble Bachelor*).

**ARABS, STREET.** Cf. Baker Street Division of the detective police force.

**ARGENTINE.** An entry in J. H. Neligan's notebook (*Black Peter*).

**ARIZONA.** Francis Moulton prospected here (*Noble Bachelor*).

**ARKANSAS RIVER.** "A. H. Garrideb" bought land along this river, west of Fort Dodge (*Garrideb*).

**ARMITAGE, JAMES.** Legal name of Trevor, Senior. His use of the bank's money resulted in his being chained in the "Gloria Scott," bound for Australia (*Gloria Scott*).

**ARMITAGE, MR.** Of Crane Water, near Reading, and father of Percy (*Speckled Band*).

**ARMITAGE, PERCY.** He proposed marriage to Helen Stoner (*Speckled Band*).

**ARMSTRONG, DR. LESLIE.** Cambridge University Medical School faculty. **H** and **W** saw him over Godfrey Staunton's disappearance; he tried to throw them off the track, but Pompey traced the physician. In the end **H** and the physician were mutually at ease (*Three-Quarter*).

*ARNSWORTH CASTLE BUSINESS. **H** refers to this case to compare it with Irene Adler's secret of concealment (*Scandal in Bohemia*).

ASTON, BIRMINGHAM. "Howard Garrideb" had offices at Grosvenor Mansions (*Garrideb*).

"AS YOU VALUE YOUR LIFE OR REASON KEEP AWAY FROM THE MOOR." This warning message was sent to Sir Henry Baskerville at The Northumberland Hotel (*The Hound*).

*ATKINSON BROTHERS. Involved in the singular tragedy at Trincomalee in which **H** cleared up the case (*Scandal in Bohemia*).

ATLANTA. Mr. Munro said that Mr. Hebron and only child died here of yellow fever (*Yellow Face*).

AUCKLAND. New Zealand. Uncle Ned lived here and on his death left £100 a year to Mary Sutherland (*Case of Identity*).

AUDLEY COURT. Cf. Rance (*Study in Scarlet*).

"AURORA." Steam launch of Mordecai Smith. It was a trim boat, painted black with two red streaks and with the funnel black with a white band. **H** advertised for information on the missing boat in the *Standard*. **H, W,** and Athelney Jones chased the launch, which was driven aground by Smith and later hauled off and tied to the police launch (*Sign of Four*).

AUSTRALIA. John Trevor made his money here in gold (*Boscombe Valley*). James Armitage was to be sent here in the prison ship "Gloria Scott" (*Gloria Scott*). James Wilder left England to seek fortune here (*Priory School*). Lady Brackenstall was brought up here (*Abbey Grange*).

AYRSHIRES. According to Hall Pycroft, the stock was up 106¼ to 105⅞ (*Stock-Broker's Clerk*).

# B

**Backwater, Lord.** He recommended **H** to Lord St. Simon. He had an estate at Petersfield (*Noble Bachelor*) and a large training stable, "Mapleton," near Tavistock (*Silver Blaze*).

**Baden.** Lady Frances arrived by a circuitous route and put up at the Englischer Hof here (*Lady Frances Carfax*).

**Bagatelle, The.** Card club to which Ronald Adair belonged. Ronald's last game here was with Mr. Murray, Sir John Hardy, and Colonel Moran (*Empty House*).

**Bain, Sandy.** Sir Norbertson gave Lady Falder's favorite spaniel to Sandy and told him to take the dog to old Barnes (*Shoscombe*).

**Baker, Mr. Henry.** His hat and goose were lost at Googe Street and Tottenham Court Road (*Blue Carbuncle*).

**Baker, Mrs. Henry.** Her name was on the Christmas goose (*Blue Carbuncle*).

**Baker Street, 221B.** Home of **H** and **W** *circa* 1878 or 1879, "a couple of comfortable bedrooms and a single large airy sitting-room, cheerfully furnished, and illuminated by two broad windows" (*Study in Scarlet*). Professor Moriarty's gang set fire to these rooms (*Final Problem*). Later **H** and **W** looked across Baker Street, from Camden House, and saw their old quarters (*Empty House*). **H** and **W** could be back here for dinner (*Dancing Men*). Violet Smith called here (*Solitary Cyclist*). **W** came from his own rooms in Queen Anne Street to the old quarters (*Illustrious Client*). **W** came to visit **H** (*Mazarin Stone*). Since Holloway & Steele were closed, **H** and **W** returned home (*Garrideb*). **H** wired **W** to come here (*Creeping Man*). These rooms are specifically referred to by **H** or **W** (*Shoscombe; Retired Colourman; Priory School; Milverton; Six Napoleons; Three Students; Pince-Nez; Abbey Grange; Second Stain; The Hound; Valley of Fear; Cardboard Box; Bruce-Partington;* and *Lady Frances Carfax*).

**Baker Street Division of the detec-**

TIVE POLICE FORCE. Now and then six small, dirty "street arabs" were employed by **H.** Of this group Wiggins apparently was the leader (*Study in Scarlet*). **H** wired for them from the Great Peter Street post-office. Wiggins is still presumably in charge, but their ranks are increased to about twelve. **H** described the "Aurora" to them and wanted to know where the launch was (*Sign of Four*). One of this group, Simpson, kept an eye on Henry Wood (*Crooked Man*).

BAKER STREET IRREGULARS. See Baker Street Division of the detective police force.

BALDWIN, TED. American. *Alias* Mr. Hargrave, of the yellow overcoat and sawed-off shotgun. Killed by John Douglas of Birlstone Manor. Baldwin's body was foisted on the police as that of John Douglas. **H** was not deceived (*Valley of Fear*).

BALDWIN, THE. Card club to which Ronald Adair belonged (*Empty House*).

BALLARAT. Colony of Victoria, Australia. **W** stated he has seen excavations at Ballarat similar to those in the earth at Pondicherry Lodge, in converse with Mary Morstan (*Sign of Four*). **H** cleared the confusion about what son James thought he heard his father say as he died, *i.e.*, "a rat" was probably "Ballarat" (*Boscombe*).

BALLARAT GANG. See Black Jack.

BALMORAL, DUCHESS OF. She attended wedding of her son, Lord Robert St. Simon, and Hatty Doran (*Noble Bachelor*).

BALMORAL, DUKE OF. Children: Lord Robert St. Simon (second son); Lord Eustace (third son); Lady Clara St. Simon (*Noble Bachelor*). The duke was at one time secretary for foreign affairs (*Boscombe*). Iris, the duke's horse, came in third in the Wessex Cup race (*Silver Blaze*).

BALMORAL, LORD. Had an expensive afternoon at cards with Godfrey Milner, *q.v.* (*Empty House*).

BALZAC. Quoted by Hosmer Angel in letter to Mary Sutherland (*Case of Identity*).

BANK OF ENGLAND. According to "Killer" Evans, no one could tell the difference between one of Rodger Prescott's forgeries and a bill made by this institution (*Garrideb*).

BANNISTER. Soames's room servant at St. Luke's. He was onetime butler to Sir Jabez Gilchrist and had to help out young Gilchrist at St. Luke's (*Three Students*).

BARBERTON. South Africa? Hon. Philip Green made money here (*Lady Frances Carfax*).

'BARCAROLE.' See Hoffman (*Marzarin Stone*).

BARCELONA. Don Murillo, his two children, and the secretary escaped from San Pedro and arrived here in 1886 (*Wisteria Lodge*).

BARCLAY, COLONEL JAMES. Commanded at Aldershot. Royal Munster regiment. He died in his morning-room. He had betrayed Corporal Henry Wood in the Indian Mutiny (*Crooked Man*).

BARCLAY, MRS. NÉE NANCY DEVOY. She was almost tried for the murder of her husband but was saved by information supplied by Major Murphy, Miss Morrison, and Henry Wood. She was originally in love with Henry Wood, but her father favored James Barclay (*Crooked Man*).

BARCLAY SQUARE. Admiral Sinclair lived here (*Bruce-Partington*).

BARDLE, INSPECTOR. Sussex constabulary. Consulted with **H** on death of Fitzroy McPherson. **H** cautioned against premature action, said that he would know "In an hour—possibly less." **H** demonstrated that the killer was *Cyanea capillata* (*Lions Mane*).

BARELLI, AUGUSTO. Lived in Posilippo. His daughter, Emilia, married Gennaro Lucca (*Red Circle*).

BARITSU. Form of Japanese wrestling which **H** knew. This knowledge enabled **H** to slip from Moriarty's grip (*Empty House*).

BARKER, CECIL JAMES. Hales Lodge, Hampstead. Friend of John Douglas and mined with him in California. He lied to police at Birlstone Manor in order to help Douglas to represent the body of Ted Baldwin as that of Douglas. Later Cecil heard from Ivy Douglas that John Douglas, her husband, was lost overboard. **H** assured Cecil that Moriarty would be brought to justice eventually (*Valley of Fear*).

BARKER, MR. Amateur detective. **H** described him, jokingly, as his hated rival on the Surrey Shore. Barker and **H** cooperated in the Amberley case. **H** remarked that Barker had had several good cases to his credit; a police inspector said in reply, "He has certainly interfered several times" (*Retired Colourman*).

BARKING LEVEL. As for pool.

BARNES, JOSIAH. Proprietor of the Green Dragon inn at Crendall. Sir Robert Norbertson gave Lady Falder's favorite spaniel to him (*Shoscombe*).

BARNICOT, DR. Physician. Admirer of Napoleon; bought two cheap plaster busts of Napoleon from Morse Hudson, and both were smashed—one in his Kennington Road office and one at a smaller office of his on Lower

Brixton Road (*Six Napoleons*).

BAR OF GOLD. Opium den in Upper Swandam Lane ("The vilest murder-trap on the whole riverside"). Cf. Paul's wharf. Neville St. Clair took opium here. Hugh Boone had a room here (*Twisted Lip*).

BARROW, ANCIENT BRITISH. Involved in an 1894 case not yet written up by **W**, who said that this barrow contained something of singular interest (*Pince-Nez*).

BARRYMORE, ELIZA. Housekeeper to Sir Charles, and later to Sir Henry, Baskerville. Her husband, John, was butler, and her brother was Selden, the escaped convict (*The Hound*).

BARRYMORE, JOHN. Butler to Sir Charles, and later to Sir Henry, Baskerville (*The Hound*).

BARS AND RESTAURANTS. See restaurants.

BARTON, DR. HILL. *Alias* of **W** when he went to see Baron Gruner about the blue Ming saucer. Dr. Barton's card read 369 Half Moon Street (*Illustrious Client*).

BARTON, INSPECTOR. In charge of disappearance case of Neville St. Clair. He arrests Hugh Boone (*Twisted Lip*).

BART'S. London hospital where **W** was on duty and where young Stamford was his "dresser" (assistant) (*Study in Scarlet*).

BASIL, CAPTAIN. *Alias* of **H** (*Black Peter*).

BASKERVILLE, SIR CHARLES. Of Baskerville Hall, Devonshire. Made a fortune in South African speculation. Came to his inheritance in Devon, worried over the family legend, and was found dead near the Hall by Barrymore. Barrymore sent Perkins to fetch James Mortimer. It was reported that Sir Charles died of cardiac exhaustion (*The Hound*).

BASKERVILLE, SIR HENRY. Son of Sir Charles's younger brother. Came from Canada to inherit Baskerville Hall. James Mortimer brought Henry to consult **H** first. Henry had inherited £740,000 from Sir Charles. Later, **H** shot the phosphorus-painted hound of Jack Stapleton before it attacked Henry, but the shock was so severe he had to take a year's voyage with James Mortimer before recovery from the hound's attack and from the shock of knowing that Beryl Stapleton was not a sister of, but wife of, Jack (*The Hound*).

BASKERVILLE, HUGO. A black hound-like beast with blazing eyes and dripping jaws was recorded as having torn out his throat. **H** showed **W** that Hugo's portrait at Baskerville Hall looked much like Jack Stapleton (*The Hound*).

BASKERVILLE, JACK. *Alias* Mr. Vandeleur, *alias* Jack Stapleton, *q.v.* (*The Hound*).

BASKERVILLE, REAR-ADMIRAL. His portrait hung in Baskerville Hall. He served with Rodney in the West Indies (*The Hound*).

BASKERVILLE, RODGER. A close resemblance to Hugo Baskerville was noted. He fled to South America where he married and had one son, Jack, and died in 1876 of yellow fever (*The Hound*).

BASKERVILLE, SIR WILLIAM. Served under Pitt in House of Commons (*The Hound*).

BASLE. **H** felt that **H** and **W** should pass through this city (*Final Problem*).

"BASS ROCK." Ship of the Adelaide-Southampton Line (*Abbey Grange*).

BATES, MARLOW. Estate manager for J. Neil Gibson. Called on **H** to warn him of his employer (*Thor Bridge*).

BATHSHEBA. See Uriah.

BAXTER. **H** quotes him (*Boscombe*).

BAXTER, EDITH. Maid that brought Ned Hunter his supper (*Silver Blaze*).

BAYARD. King's Pyland stable was running this horse, and the favorite, Silver Blaze, in the Wessex Cup race (*Silver Blaze*).

BAYNES, INSPECTOR. Surrey constabulary. **H** felt that he would rise high in the profession since he had both instinct and intuition (*Wisteria Lodge*).

BAYSWATER BUS. Lord Mount-James came by bus (*Three-Quarter*).

"BE AT THE THIRD PILLAR FROM THE LEFT OUTSIDE THE LYCEUM THEATRE TO-NIGHT AT SEVEN O'CLOCK. If you are distrustful bring two friends. You are a wronged woman and shall have justice. Do not bring police. If you do, all will be in vain. Your unknown friend" (*Sign of Four*).

BEAUCHAMP ARRIANCE. Dr. Sterndale had a lonely bungalow in these woods (*Devil's Foot*).

BEAUNE. **W** had some of this wine with his lunch (*Sign of Four*).

BECHER, DR. Lived at Eyford with Colonel Lysander Stark (*Engineer's Thumb*).

BECKENHAM. **H** thought they should go here at once, after picking up Inspector Gregson (*Greek Interpreter*).

BEDDINGTON NO. 1. *Alias* was Pinner, Arthur or Harry (*Stock-broker's Clerk*).

BEDDINGTON NO. 2. Brother of Beddington No. 1. Forger and cracksman. Impersonating Hall Pycroft, obtained mouldings of locks at Mawson & Williams. He murdered the watchman but was captured by Sergeant Tuson and Constable Pollock (*Stock-broker's Clerk*).

BECKENHAM. The Myrtles, where Sophy was staying, was here (*Greek Interpreter*).

BEDDOES. Evans lived in Hampshire under this *alias* (*Gloria Scott*).

BEDFORD. In Bedfordshire. Tuxbury Old Park was near (*Blanched Soldier*).

BEDFORDSHIRE. Tuxbury Old Hall in Tuxbury Old Park was near Bedford (*Blanched Soldier*).

BEECHER, HENRY WARD. W had an unframed picture of him (*Resident Patient*).

BELFAST. Browner's ship, the "May Day," stopped at this port, and this was the first place that he could send the package of ears to Sarah Cushing (*Cardboard Box*).

BELGIUM. Since there was a treaty between England and this country, Von Bork felt that England would go to war regardless of the consequences (*Last Bow*).

BELGRADE. Trelawney Hope had a memorandum from here (*Second Stain*).

BELLAMY, MAUD. "Maudie" to Fitzroy McPherson, she was the Fulworth beauty and secretly his fiancée (*Lion's Mane*).

BELLAMY, TOM. Fulworth businessman, formerly fisherman, who commenced renting boats and bathing-cots, with his son William. His daughter, Maud, was a local beauty (*Lion's Mane*).

BELLAMY, WILLIAM. Son of Tom and helper in father's business (*Lion's Mane*).

BELLINGER, LORD. Twice Prime Minister of Britain. Came to consult **H** (*Second Stain*).

BELLIVER TOR. **W** saw this wild spot in late afternoon as he was going to Black Tor (*The Hound*).

BELMINSTER, DUKE OF. Lady Hilda Trelawney Hope was his youngest daughter (*Second Stain*).

BELMONT PLACE. **H, W** and Toby on trail here of murderers of Bartholomew Sholto (*Sign of Four*).

BENARES METAL-WORK. Cf. Agra Treasure chest.

BENGAL ARTILLERY. Major-General Stoner belonged to this outfit (*Speckled Band*).

BENITO CANYON. California. Where John Douglas and Cecil Barker had a successful mining claim (*Valley of Fear*).

BENNETT, TREVOR. Professional assistant to Professor Presbury, lived with him and was engaged to his daughter, Edith. He had a medical degree. Edith called Trevor "Jack." He consulted **H**, and **H** solved the problem why Roy, the devoted wolfhound, attacked his master (*Creeping Man*).

BENTINCK STREET. **H** was almost run down here. Moriarty at work? (*Final Problem.*)

BENTLEY'S. Private hotel in London, where the University of Cambridge rugger team stayed (*Three-Quarter*).

BENZ. 100-horsepower model belonging to Baron Von Herling (*Last Bow*).

BEPPO. Italian who made himself useful at Morse Hudson's shop and at Gelder & Co. He was captured while stealing a cheap plaster bust of Napoleon from home of Josiah Brown (*Six Napoleons*).

BERKELEY SQUARE. General de Merville lived at No. 104 (*Illustrious Client*).

BERKSHIRE. At one time the Roylott family lived in this county (*Speckled Band*). Eyford was in the county, and Colonel Stark asked Mr. Hatherley to see his machinery there (*Engineer's Thumb*). Abbas Parva, a village here, where the Ronder circus stopped for the night (*Veiled Lodger*). Scene of *Shoscombe Old Place*.

BERLIN. Baron Von Herling felt that Von Bork would be here within the week (*Last Bow*).

BERMUDA DOCKYARD. The true husband of the barmaid worked here (*Boscombe*).

BERNSTONE, MRS. Housekeeper of Bartholomew Sholto. She was arrested by Athelney Jones in connection with Bartholomew's murder but shortly released. Reported in the *Standard* (*Sign of Four*).

BERTILLON. **H** admired him and his system of measurements (*Naval Treaty*). James Mortimer annoyed **H** when he put Bertillon first and **H** second in detection (*The Hound*).

BERYL CORONET. A precious public possession of the Empire. Three beryls were missing, and Holder's son, Arthur, was arrested. **H** was consulted (*Beryl Coronet*).

BERYL CORONET, ADVENTURE OF THE. Mr. Holder consulted **H** in February on a missing piece of the coronet. **H** saved England from a scandal.

BEVINGTON'S. Pawn shop in Westminster. The Shlessingers were pawning Lady Frances' jewels here (*Lady Frances Carfax*).

BHURTEE. India. Where the 117th was stationed at the Mutiny outbreak. Corporal Henry Wood volunteered to break out and tell General Neill of their danger (*Crooked Man*).

BIBLE. **H** quoted this with reference to the betrayal of Henry Woods by James Barclay. The reference, **H** thought, was either Samuel I or II—it is Samuel II:11 (*Crooked Man*). It would not do as a basis for the cipher (*Valley of Fear*).

BIDDLE. One of the Worthingdon bank gang (*Resident Patient*).

BIG BEN. It was late, 7:35 A.M., as **H** and **W** rushed to the Shlessinger house in Poultney Square (*Lady Frances Carfax*).

BILL. Helper to Mr. Breckinridge (*Blue Carbuncle*).

BILLIARDS. See Thurston.

BILLY. Occasional page of **H** and **W** (*Valley of Fear*), and of **H** after **W** no longer lived at 221B (*Mazarin Stone*). He opened the door to Marlow Bates (*Thor Bridge*).

BIRCHMOOR. Small estate of Lord St. Simon (*Noble Bachelor*).

BIRLSTONE. Northern Sussex village where tragedy occurred (*Valley of Fear*).

BIRLSTONE MANOR HOUSE. In Sussex. Home of John Douglas (*Valley of Fear*).

BIRLSTONE RIDGE. **H** was told that the views from here over the Weald were remarkable (*Valley of Fear*).

BIRMINGHAM. **H** asks **W** to go with him to this city on behalf of Hall Pycroft (*Stock-broker's Clerk*). The senior Trevor's daughter died here of diphtheria (*Gloria Scott*). Steve Dixie was in training here at the time of young Perkins' death outside the Holborn Bar (*Three Gables*). Nathan had to go here to see "Howard Garrideb" (*Garrideb*).

*BISHOPGATE JEWEL CASE. Mr. Athelney Jones granted rather grudging acknowledgement of **H's** help in this case (*Sign of Four*).

BLACKHEATH. Mr. McFarland lived in Torrington Lodge here (*Norwood Builder*) **W** played rugby for Blackheath (*Vampire*).

BLACKHEATH STATION. **W** caught his train here for London from Lewisham (*Retired Colourman*).

BLACK JACK OF BALLARAT. *Alias* John Turner (*Boscombe*).

BLACKMAIL. Cf. *Milverton; Second Stain; Black Peter; Gloria Scott.* The Cunninghams were being blackmailed by their coachman, William Kirwan (*Reigate Puzzle*).

BLACK PETER. Nautical name for Captain Peter Cary, *q.v.*

BLACK PETER, ADVENTURE OF. July, 1895. Captain Peter Cary was harpooned. Stanley Hopkins arrested the wrong man. **H** supplied the right man in the person of Patrick Cairns.

BLACK SEA. Convict ships were being used as transport in this sea during Crimean War (*Gloria Scott*).

BLACK STEVE. Appellation of Steve Dixie, *q.v.*

BLACK SWAN HOTEL. In Winchester, on High Street. Violet Hunter wished to consult **H** here (*Copper Beeches*).

BLACK TOR. **W** saw the stranger here, and Mr. Frankland saw the boy who took supplies to **H.** Later **W** found **H** here, much to his consternation (*The Hound*).

BLACKWALL. As for pool.

BLACKWATER, EARL OF. His son was in the Priory School (*Priory School*).

**BLACKWELL, LADY EVA.** To be married to the Earl of Dovercourt, and blackmailed by Milverton. **H** came to the rescue (*Milverton*).

**BLAIR ISLAND.** Of the Andamans. Jonathan Small was finally imprisoned here, at Hope Town (*Sign of Four*).

**BLANCHED SOLDIER, ADVENTURE OF THE.** January, 1903. **H** was the narrator, for **W** had married and moved out. Godfrey Emsworth did not have leprosy after all.

**BLANDFORD STREET.** **H** and **W** en route to Camden House (*Empty House*).

**BLESSINGTON, MR.** *Alias* for Sutton. Became a patient in Dr. Trevelyan's house in Brook Street and paid the bills. He was murdered (*Resident Patient*).

**BLONDIN.** Possibly a constable on guard at Pondicherry Lodge after murder of Bartholomew Sholto (*Sign of Four*). Ingenious alternative suggestion is that Blondin was the great French rope-walker, since **H** was about to scale a roof (personal communication from Mr. Vincent Starrett).

**BLOOMSBURY.** Scene of action in death of Gorgiano, *viz.*, Great Orme Street and Howe Street (*Red Circle*). The Alpha Inn was located here (*Blue Carbuncle*).

**BLOUNT.** Fellow student of Sudbury, *q.v.*

**BLUE ANCHOR.** Probably non-existent. In Lewisham, where **H** felt **W** could have gotten the information about Dr. Ernest and the Amberleys (*Retired Colourman*).

**BLUE CARBUNCLE, ADVENTURE OF THE.** Countess of Morcar's blue carbuncle was in the crop of a Christmas goose.

**BLYMER ESTATE.** Mrs. Harold left it to Count Sylvius (*Mazarin Stone*).

**BOCCACCIO.** Pocket edition of the *Decameron* was carried by Enoch J. Drebber (*Study in Scarlet*).

**BOER WAR.** Had just concluded in January, 1903, when James M. Dodd consulted **H** (*Blanched Soldier*).

**BOHEMIA.** **W** was glad that "something connects with something." He was perplexed by a possible connection between an irate wolfhound and a visit to Bohemia (*Creeping Man*).

**BOHEMIAN.** After his own marriage, **W** so described **H's** living habits (*Engineer's Thumb*).

**"BOLTED."** **W** was to telephone this word to Baker Street rooms if Josiah broke away or returned to Lewisham (*Retired Colourman*).

**BOMBAY.** India. **W** landed here from England to join the Fifth Northumberland Fusiliers but had to follow to Candahar before finding them (*Study in Scarlet*).

**Bond Street.** At foot of Kennington Lane, **H**, **W**, and Toby on trail of the murderer of Bartholomew Sholto (*Sign of Four*). Madame Lesurier, milliner, was here (*Silver Blaze*). **H** and **W** passed time in picture galleries here before their 2 P.M. luncheon with James Mortimer and Henry Baskerville (*The Hound*).

"**Book of Life, The.**" Title of magazine article written by **H** on the science of detection. **W** read it and scoffed. **H** proved his point by explaining how he knew that **W** was an army doctor who had been wounded in Afghanistan. March 4, 1879? (*Study in Scarlet.*)

**Boone, Hugh.** Had room at Bar of Gold. A cripple and professional beggar with business spot on Threadneedle Street, in disguise. **H** demonstrated that he was St. Clair (*Twisted Lip*).

**Bordeaux.** France. Mr. Windibank's company had French offices here (*Case of Identity*).

**Borgias, Black Pearl of the.** **H** deduced its presence in the sixth bust (*Six Napoleons*).

**Borough, The.** John Clayton lived at No. 3 Turpey Street (*The Hound*).

**Boscombe Pool.** Charles McCarthy was found dead here by his son, James (*Boscombe*).

**BOSCOMBE VALLEY MYSTERY.** This happened in Herefordshire, near Ross. James McCarthy found his father dead. It was fortunate that **H** was called in.

**Boswell.** **H** said of **W** that he was "my Boswell" (*Scandal in Bohemia*).

**Bouguereau.** A painting at home of T. Sholto (*Sign of Four*).

**Bowery.** Gennaro Lucca saved Tito Castalotti from ruffians in this New York area (*Red Circle*).

**Bow Street.** **H** and **W** to police station here to see Hugh Boone (*Twisted Lip*).

**Brackenstall, Sir Eustace.** Dead, and Lady Brackenstall was not candid with **H**. **H** solved the case but, seeing the provocation for the crime, held his tongue except to **W** and Captain Crocker (*Abbey Grange*).

**Bradley's.** Oxford Street tobacconist which supplied **H** with strong shag and **W** with cigarettes (*The Hound*).

**Bradshaw.** **H** asked **W** to look up the trains to Winchester in this book (*Copper Beeches*).

**Bradstreet, Inspector.** B Division. On duty at Bow Street when **H** wanted to see Hugh Boone (*Twisted Lip*). Arrested John Horner (*Blue Carbuncle*). Called in by **H** (*Engineer's Thumb*).

**Brambletye Hotel.** Forest Row, Sussex. **H** and **W** had rooms here, and young Neligan came here to a ground-floor room on the day that Peter Cary was killed (*Black Peter*).

BRANDY. **W** gave Mr. Eccles some (*Wisteria Lodge*). **H** gave **W** some (*Empty House*).

BRAZIL. J. Neil Gibson looked for gold here (*Thor Bridge*).

BRECKINRIDGE. He sold Mr. Windigate, of the Alpha Inn, some geese in Covent Garden Market (*Blue Carbuncle*).

BREWER, SAM. Curzon Street moneylender. He was horsewhipped and nearly killed by Sir Robert Norbertson on Newmarket Heath (*Shoscombe*).

BRIARBRAE. In Woking. Percy Phelps lived here and wanted **W** to bring **H** (*Naval Treaty*).

BRICKFALL & AMBERLEY. Manufacturer of artistic materials. Josiah Amberley retired from junior partnership at 61 and bought The Haven, in Lewisham, Essex (*Retired Colourman*).

BRIONY LODGE. On Serpentine Avenue, in St. John's Wood. Home of Irene Adler in London (*Scandal in Bohemia*).

BRISTOL. James McCarthy spent three days here with his barmaid wife, who, learning that James was accused of murdering his father, told James that she always had had a husband in the Bermuda Dockyard (*Boscombe*).

*British Birds.* Volume offered to **W** by a disguised **H** (*Empty House*).

BRITISH BROKEN HILLS. Their stock went from 7 to 7-and-6 according to Hall Pycroft (*Stock-broker's Clerk*).

*British Medical Journal.* As for *Lancet* (*Blanched Soldier*). **W** was reading this journal after breakfast when **H** called on him at the house in Paddington where **W** had his practice (*Stock-broker's Clerk*).

*British Museum.* **H** first lived near here on Montague Street; see also Museum (*Musgrave Ritual*). Jack Stapleton was well known here and had described a species of moth (*The Hound*). The Warrens lived near here, on Great Orme Street (*Red Circle*).

BRIXTON. **H, W,** and Toby here on trail of murderers of Bartholomew Sholto (*Sign of Four*). The commissionaire lived at 16 Ivy Lane (*Naval Treaty*). The Shlessingers left Lady Frances at 36 Poultney Square (*Lady Frances Carfax*). Nathan Garrideb ended up in a nursing home here (*Garridebs*).

BRIXTON, LOWER. J. Davenport answered Mycroft Holmes's advertisement from here (*Greek Interpreter*).

BRIXTON ROAD. **H** and **W** took a taxi via this street to No. 3 Lauriston Gardens (*Study in Scarlet*). Mrs. Oakshott lived at No. 117 and sold geese to Mr. Breckinridge (*Blue Carbuncle*). **H** and **W** en route to

Shlessinger's house in Poultney Square (*Lady Frances Carfax*).

BRIXTON WORKHOUSE INFIRMARY. The Shlessingers brought Rose Spender from here to their Poultney Square home (*Lady Frances Carfax*).

BROADMOOR. **H** told Inspector McKinnon that in all probability Josiah Amberley would end up in this place rather than on the scaffold (*Retired Colourman*).

BROADS, THE. The Trevors lived in this area of Norfolk, at Donnithorpe, near Langmere (*Gloria Scott*).

BROAD STREET. **H, W,** and Toby came to water's edge at end of this street, where trail of murderer of Bartholomew Sholto ends. Cf. Mordecai Smith (*Sign of Four*).

BRODERICK & NELSON'S TIMBER-YARD. On Nine Elms Street, just past the White Eagle Tavern. This was the end of the false trail. Cf. Knight's Place (*Sign of Four*).

BROOKS. One of fifty men who had reason to kill **H** (*Bruce-Partington*).

*BROOKS. As for Woodhouse.

BROOK STREET. Dr. Trevelyan lived at No. 403 (*Resident Patient*).

BROTHER BARTHOLOMEW. See Bartholomew Sholto.

BROTHERHOOD, THE. This group was after Sergius, *alias* Professor Coram (*Pince-Nez*).

BROWN, JOSIAH. Bought a bust of Napoleon from Harding Brothers and had it stolen and then smashed by Beppo (*Six Napoleons*).

BROWN, LIEUTENANT BROMLEY. Officer at Blair Island, in the Andamans (*Sign of Four*).

BROWN, SAM. One of two policemen on the police launch in her chase after the "Aurora." Sam also went with **W** carrying the Agra Treasure chest to Mary Morstan's home (*Sign of Four*).

BROWN, SILAS. Manager of Mapleton, Lord Backwater's training stable near Tavistock (*Silver Blaze*).

BROWNER, JIM. Dropped first Susan, then Sarah, and married Mary. Steward of the "May Day." Later, at instigation of jilted Sarah, Mary and Alec Fairbairn were often together. Jim killed Mary and Alec and sent an ear of each to Sarah, but Susan got the package. **H** worked on this postal error, and Jim was arrested (*Cardboard Box*).

BRUCE-PARTINGTON PLANS, ADVENTURE OF THE. Third week in November, 1895. The submarine patents had been tampered with, and the late Cadogan West was suspect. **H** recovered the missing papers, and the villains were jailed.

BRUCE-PARTINGTON SUBMARINE. Ten of thirty patent papers were taken from Woolwich, but only seven were in Cadogan West's pocket. **H** recovered the missing plans by trapping first Colonel Walter and later Hugo Oberstein (*Bruce-Partington*).

BRUCE PINKERTON PRIZE AND MEDAL. Dr. Trevelyan got these for his monograph on nervous lesions (*Resident Patient*).

BRUNTON, RICHARD. Butler at Hurlstone Manor. Dismissed by Reginald Musgrave; murdered by Rachel Howells (*Musgrave Ritual*).

BRUSSELS. **H** and **W** spent two days here en route to Switzerland (*Final Problem*).

BUDA. There was a sample of Devil's Foot Root in a laboratory here (*Devil's Foot*).

BUDA-PESTH. **W** and **H** received a newspaper cutting from here (*Greek Interpreter*).

BUDDHA. At times **H** was so eager that he sat on the floor amidst the books, according to **W** like an image of Buddha (*Veiled Lodger*).

BUDDHISM OF CEYLON. As for Miracle Plays.

BUFFALO. After a period in Chicago, **H** joined a secret society in Buffalo as a step toward building his role as Altamont (*Last Bow*).

BUFFELSSPRUIT. Outside Pretoria, where Godfrey Emsworth was injured in the Boer War. (*Blanched Soldier*).

BULL. Inn at Esher in Surrey, where **H** and **W** put up while looking into murder of Aloysius Garcia (*Wisteria Lodge*).

BURBERRY. McPherson was found dead in his (*Lion's Mane*).

BURNETT, MISS. Governess to Mr. Henderson's two daughters. She is an English woman, about 40 years old. Don Juan Murillo had her husband murdered, and she joined the plot. *Alias* of Signora (Señora?) Victor Durango. She escaped with the help of John Warner and told all to **H** (*Wisteria Lodge*).

BURNWELL, SIR GEORGE. Friend of Arthur Holder, and a most undesirable person (*Beryl Coronet*).

BUSHMAN. James Mortimer, Sir Charles Baskerville, and friends spent many an evening discussing the comparative anatomy of the Bushman and the Hottentot (*The Hound*).

# C

**Cabinet, the.** Percy Phelps's uncle, Lord Holdhurst, was foreign minister in it (*Naval Treaty*).

**Cafe Royal.** Near here, on Regent Street, a murderous attack was made on **H** (*Illustrious Client*).

**Cairns, Patrick.** Harpooner under Captain Peter Cary of the "Sea Unicorn." He saw the Captain throw J. H. Neligan's father overboard in August, 1883. His attempted blackmail of the Captain ended in his killing Peter and in his subsequent arrest by Stanley Hopkins, on information supplied by **H** (*Black Peter*).

**Cairo.** **H** asked Mary Maberley if she would like to go here (*Three Gables*).

**Calcutta.** Dr. G. Roylott was in practice here (*Speckled Band*).

**Calhoun, Captain James.** Leader of the KKK gang that killed John Openshaw, and captain of the bark "Lone Star." He and his crew perished apparently when the ship broke up in an Atlantic storm (*Five Orange Pips*).

**California.** John Douglas was said to have made his money in gold fields here (*Valley of Fear*). Aloysius Moran had lived in San Francisco (*Noble Bachelor*).

**Cam.** **H** said that Dr. Armstrong would have to drive through here to elude Pompey (*Three-Quarter*).

**Camberwell.** Madame Charpentier's boarding-house was in Torquay Terrace, where E. J. Drebber lodged (*Study in Scarlet*). Mary Morstan was governess in home of Mrs. Cecil Forrester in Lower Camberwell (*Sign of Four*). **H, W,** and Toby here on trail of Bartholomew Sholto's murderers (*Sign of Four*). Mr. and Mrs. Windibank and Mary Sutherland lived at 31 Lyon Place (*Case of Identity*). **H** on two occasions sent money to Fred Porlock, in care of the post office here (*Valley of Fear*). Miss Dobney lived here (*Lady Frances Carfax*).

***Camberwell Poisoning Case.** 1887. **W** recorded this case, in which **H** wound the watch, but has not released it to the public (*Five Orange Pips*).

CAMBERWELL ROAD. A London haberdasher sold a hat to E. J. Drebber on this street (*Study in Scarlet*).

CAMBRIDGE UNIVERSITY. Percy Phelps went here on a scholarship (*Naval Treaty*). Willoughby Smith went here (*Pince-Nez*). Cyril Overton was at Trinity College here (*Three-Quarter*).

CAMDEN HOUSE. On Baker Street, where **H** and **W** watched (*Empty House*).

CAMFORD. The Chequers inn and Camford University were in this town (*Creeping Man*).

CAMFORD UNIVERSITY. At Camford. Here Professor Presbury taught physiology, and in time Roy, his devoted wolfhound, tried to kill him (*Creeping Man*). It is of interest to note that for **H** and **W** respectable events generally are associated with Cambridge and Oxford universities whereas the unorthodox behavior of Professor Presbury occurs at Camford. Colonel Sebastian Moran went to Oxford, it is true, but years before his moral decay (*Empty House*).

CAMPDEN HOUSE ROAD. Mr. Harker, journalist, had a bust of Napoleon stolen and later smashed in this street (*Six Napoleons*).

CAMPDEN MANSIONS. In Notting Hill. Louis LaRothiere lived here (*Bruce-Partington*).

CANADA. Henry Baskerville lived here (*The Hound*).

CANDAHAR. India. **W** reached here in safety and joined the Fifth Northumberland Fusiliers (*Study in Scarlet*).

CANNON STREET. Neville St. Clair returned from here, by the 5:14, bound for his home in Kent (*Twisted Lip*).

CANTERBURY. The Continental Express stops here (*Final Problem*).

CANTLEMERE, LORD. He doubted **H's** ability and disliked **H's** profession, and so **H**, while he recovered the stolen jewel, played a practical joke on him (*Mazanin Stone*).

CAPE TOWN. South Africa. Ivy Douglas cabled Cecil Barker from here that John Douglas was lost overboard on the "Palmyra" (*Valley of Fear*). James Dodd had a letter from Godfrey Emsworth from here (*Blanched Soldier*). Cf. Africa, West Africa.

CAPE VERDES. They were about 500 miles north of this area when Armitage and Evans were cut adrift (*Gloria Scott*).

CAPITAL & COUNTIES BANK. Neville St. Clair banked here (*Twisted Lip*). **H** used their Oxford Street branch (*Priory School*). Cadogan West used their Woolwich branch (*Bruce-Partington*).

Carbonari. The Red Circle, of which Black Gorgiano was a leader, was affiliated with this society (*Red Circle*). Cf. Vehmgericht.

CARDBOARD BOX, ADVENTURE OF THE. Three sisters: Susan, Sarah, and Mary. Mary marries Jim Browner. Jilted Sarah causes the murder of Mary and Alec Fairbairn by Jim Browner. (Note that paragraphs 3 to 19 of this case are identical with the same paragraphs of the *Resident Patient.*)

cardboard boxes. Mary Morstan received at least one fine pearl in such a receptacle (*Sign of Four*), and a pair of human ears of assorted sex came in one to Susan Cushing (*Cardboard Box*).

*Cardinal Tosca. His sudden death in 1895 was investigated by **H** at the express desire of the Pope. **W** has not given us this case (*Black Peter*).

*Carère, Mlle. Her step-mother, Mme. Montpensier, was accused of murdering Mlle. Carère. **H** successfully defended Mme. Montpensier, and her step-daughter was located living in New York and married. **W** has not seen fit to report this case (*The Hound*).

CARFAX, LADY FRANCES, THE DISAPPEARANCE OF. Only direct survivor of the late Earl of Rufton. She was last heard of from the Hotel National in Lausanne. She gave her maid, Marie Devine, £50 for a wedding gift and went to London with the Shlessingers, who almost murdered her. **H** and **W** saved her at the last possible moment (*Lady Frances Carfax*).

Carina. She was singing at Albert Hall, and **H** thought that **W** and he had time to dress, dine and "enjoy" (*Retired Colourman*).

Carleton Club. From here Sir James Damery wrote **H** for an appointment (*Illustrious Client*).

Carlo. Mastiff that guarded the grounds of the Copper Beeches at night (*Copper Beeches*).

Carlo. Spaniel. Hind quarters partially paralysed. The vet thought it was spinal meningitis, but **H** knew it was a case of experimental South American poisoning (*Vampire*).

Carlton. The Diogenes Club was nearby (*Greek Interpreter*).

Carlton Terrace. Presumably the German legation in London was located here (*Last Bow*).

Carlyle. Read by **H** and **W** (*Sign of Four*).

Carriton's. **W** said such a house name would be found about Lamberley (*Vampire*).

*Carruthers, Colonel. **H** was involved in the case of this fellow, and his evidence served to jail the Colonel. **H**, bored, was glad to have a new case to work on. **W** has not yet reported this case (*Wisteria Lodge*).

Carruthers, Mr. Home from Africa with Mr. Woodley, with news about Violet Smith's uncle. He proposed marriage to Violet and was rejected. Later shot Woodley, after latter illegally married Violet. Woodley lived, and Carruthers got off with a light sentence (*Solitary Cyclist*).

Carstairs. Miss Edith Woodley lived here (*Empty House*).

Cartwright. Young messenger in employ of Wilson, *q.v.* When **H** came to Baskerville Hall area, he brought Cartwright to add a set of acute young senses and to carry food and messages (*The Hound*).

Cartwright. One of the Worthingdon Bank gang, *q.v.* Another member of the gang, Sutton (*alias* Mr. Blessington), informed on his fellow-criminals, and on his evidence Cartwright was hanged (*Resident Patient*).

Cary, Captain Peter. Born 1845. Successful seal and whale fisher. Commanded steam sealer "Sea Unicorn" (1883) of Dundee. Retired 1884, to Woodlan's Lee, near Forest Row, Sussex. Puritan, intermittent drunkard, he had been feared by his crews. He was harpooned to his wall, and on **H's** investigation, Patrick Cairns was arrested (*Black Peter*).

Castalotte & Zamba. New York firm of fruit importers (*Red Circle*).

Castalotte, Tito. Senior partner of Castalotte & Zamba. Gennaro Lucca saved him from Bowery ruffians and, later, refused to molest him at behest of the Red Circle (*Red Circle*).

cataract knife. Used by John Straker in attempt to lame the favorite (*Silver Blaze*).

Catholic. See Roman Catholic.

Catullus. One of the books offered for sale to **W** by a disguised **H** (*Empty House*).

Caulfield Gardens. Kensington. Hugo Oberstein lived at No. 13. The backstair windows open on the Underground line, and the trains stop at Gloucester Road Station (*Bruce-Partington*).

Caunter. Elder boy in room where Lord Saltire slept (*Priory School*).

Cavendish, The. A card club to which Ronald Adair belonged (*Empty House*).

Cavendish Square. Dr. Trevelyan established in area, on Brook Street, by Mr. Blessington (*Resident Patient*). **H** and **W** left the cab in this area (*Empty House*).

Cawnpore. Indian city involved in Great Mutiny (*Sign of Four*).

Cedars, The. Home of Mr. and Mrs.

Neville St. Clair, near Lee, in Kent (*Twisted Lip*).

CENTRAL AMERICA. Don Murillo was a terror here (*Wisteria Lodge*).

CENTRAL PRESS SYNDICATE. The unfortunate Mr. Harker was in its employ (*Six Napoleons*).

CEYLON, BUDDHISM OF. As for Miracle Plays.

CHALDEAN LANGUAGE. **H** thought that it might be akin to certain Cornish linguistic roots (*Devil's Foot*).

CHANDOS, SIR CHARLES. Ames, the John Douglas' butler, had been with Sir Charles for ten years (*Valley of Fear*).

CHANNEL. **H's** place in Sussex had a view of this water (*Lion's Mane*).

CHARING CROSS. Mr. and Mrs. Norton left on the 5:15 for the Continent (*Scandal in Bohemia*). **H** thought he should be kicked all the way from The Cedars to Charing Cross (*Twisted Lip*). Mr. Melas and Mr. Latimer en route to Kensington (*Greek Interpreter*). Trains to Chatham, in Kent, from here (*Pince-Nez*). **H** and **W** en route to Kent (*Abbey Grange*). The warning message to Sir Henry Baskerville was postmarked Charing Cross post office (*The Hound*). Scott Eccles wired **H** from this post office (*Wisteria Lodge*). **W** had the bad news between here and the Grand Hotel (*Illustrious Client*). Bank of Cox and Co., in which **W** keeps dispatch-box of case records, is here (*Thor Bridge*).

CHARING CROSS HOSPITAL. Friends here presented a walking-stick to James Mortimer on the occasion of his marriage (*The Hound*). **H** is brought here when he is attacked near the Cafe Royal on Regent Street (*Illustrious Client*).

CHARING CROSS HOTEL. Message from Colonel Walter to Hugo Oberstein (in reality dictated by **H**) named this hotel as the meeting place, and Oberstein was captured (*Bruce-Partington*).

CHARLES AUGUSTUS MILVERTON, ADVENTURE OF. Murder of a blackmailer who lived at Appledore Towers.

CHARLES STREET. Clerks at the Foreign Office used this as a short cut (*Naval Treaty*).

CHARLES THE FIRST. Coins of this king were in the Hurlstone Manor House chest (*Musgrave Ritual*).

CHARLES THE SECOND. Sir Ralph Musgrave was his right-hand man (*Musgrave Ritual*).

CHARLINGTON. Violet Smith cycled between Charlington Heath and Charlington Hall woods. It was a lonely stretch of road (*Solitary Cyclist*).

CHARLINGTON HALL. Near Farnham. Rented by the odious Williamson, the unfrocked clergyman (*Solitary Cyclist*).

CHARPENTIER, ALICE. Daughter of Madame Charpentier and sister of Sub-lieutenant Arthur. E. J. Drebber aroused Arthur to anger by embracing Alice and asking her to "fly with him" in her mother's presence. Alice was of age (*Study in Scarlet*).

CHARPENTIER, ARTHUR. Sub-lieutenant in Her Majesty's Navy. Arrested by Inspector Gregson for murder of E. J. Drebber. Arthur had previously attacked Drebber for making improper advances to his sister Alice (*Study in Scarlet*).

CHARPENTIER, MADAME. Ran boarding house in Camberwell, where E. J. Drebber lodged (*Study in Scarlet*).

CHARYBDIS. See Scylla.

CHATHAM. In Kent, seven miles from Yoxley Old Place (*Pince-Nez*).

CHEESEMANS, LAMBERLEY. Sussex. Home of the Robert Fergusons, part of the house dating from 1670 (*Vampire*).

CHEQUERS. Inn in Camford that, according to **H**, serves above-average port (*Creeping Man*).

CHEQUERS. Inn in Lamberley, where **H** and **W** left their bags and drove to the home of Robert Ferguson (*Vampire*).

CHESTERFIELD. Reuben Hayes was arrested here for murder of Heidegger, the German Master (*Priory School*). Neville St. Clair's father was a schoolmaster here (*Twisted Lip*).

CHESTERFIELD HIGH ROAD. Near Priory School (*Priory School*).

CHESTERTON. **H** searched here (*Three-Quarter*).

CHIANTI. T. Sholto offered Mary Morstan a glass of it. Mary refused (*Sign of Four*).

CHICAGO, ILLINOIS. Cecil Barker had heard John Douglas talk of this city (*Valley of Fear*). **H** began his rôle of Altamont here (*Last Bow*). "A. H. Garrideb" made money in the wheat pit here (*Garridebs*). Abe Slaney was the "most dangerous crook in Chicago," according to Wilson Hargrave (*Dancing Men*).

CHILTERN GRANGE. Near Farnham. Mr. Carruthers persuaded Violet Smith to teach music to his daughter here (*Solitary Cyclist*).

CHINA. Mr. Jabez Wilson had a fish tatooed above his right wrist here (*Red-headed League*). The blue carbuncle was found on the banks of the Amoy River here (*Blue Carbuncle*).

CHIN CHINA COASTER. Jack Prendergast called the ship by this name (*Gloria Scott*).

CHINESE POTTERY. Baron Gruner was a recognized authority on the subject, and he doubted Dr. Hill Barton's (*alias* of **W**) *bona fides* (*Illustrious Client*).

CHINESE SAILORS. **W** repeated his message to Culverton Smith that **H** had contracted an Eastern disease while working on a case with certain Chinese sailors at Rotherhithe (*Dying Detective*).

CHISELHURST STATION. **H** and **W** en route to home of Sir Eustace Brackenstall (*Abbey Grange*).

CHISWICK. Josiah Brown lived in Laburnum Vale (*Six Napoleons*).

CHOPIN. **H** admired the way in which Norman Neruda played a piece by this musician (*Study in Scarlet*).

CHRISTIE'S. If pressed for a price, **W** was to suggest that this firm could give a valuation of the blue Ming saucer (*Illustrious Client*). Nathan Garrideb sometimes went here (*Garridebs*).

CHRONICLE. London newspaper. Cf. *Morning Chronicle.*

CHURCH OF ST. MONICA. In Edgware Road, where Irene Adler married Godfrey Norton (*Scandal in Bohemia*).

CHURCH ROW. **H** and **W** drove this far (*Milverton*).

CHURCH STREET. Stepney. Gelder & Co. was here (*Six Napoleons*).

C.I.D. Cf. Scotland Yard. **H** gave **W** a message for Youghal of this organization (*Mazarin Stone*). People in this organization were happy to obtain the Rodger Prescott forgery outfit (*Garridebs*).

CIPHER. See cryptology.

CITY AND SUBURBAN BANK. Coburg branch on the Strand (*Red-headed League*).

CITY, THE. Financial section of London. On their way to hear Sarasate play, **H** and **W** went through here and stopped to study Jabez Wilson's pawnshop in Saxe-Coburg Square (*Red-headed League*).

CIVIL WAR. **W** was introspective, and **H** broke into his stream of thought (*Resident Patient*).

CLAPHAM JUNCTION. **H**, **W**, and Colonel Ross en route to London (*Silver Blaze*). Mr. Melas caught the last train from here to Victoria (*Greek Interpreter*). **H** and **W** en route from Woking to London (*Naval Treaty*).

CLARET. **H** has a glass with some biscuits at case's end: "I never needed it more" (*Dying Detective*).

CLARIDGE'S HOTEL. London. After taking Von Bork to the police, **H** was to shave off his goatee and join Martha and others here (*Last Bow*). J. Neil Gibson wrote from here to **H** (*Thor Bridge*).

CLAY, JOHN. *Alias* of William Morris, *alias* of Vincent Spaulding, *q.v.* Grandson of a royal duke, with schooling at Eton and Oxford, he was, according to **H**, the fourth smartest man in London. He was captured by **H** while breaking into a bank vault (*Red-headed League*).

CLAYTON, JOHN. Cabby, No. 2704, who picked up a fare who claimed to be Sherlock Holmes (*The Hound*).

CLEFT TOR. Selden, escaped convict, signaled from hereabouts to Baskerville Hall (*The Hound*).

CLEVELAND, OHIO. Home of Enoch J. Drebber. A telegram from here—"J. H. is in Europe"—was found in a pocket of the murdered Stangerson by Lestrade. **H** wired Cleveland's chief of police concerning Drebber (*Study in Scarlet*).

CLUBS. Anglo-Indian; Bagatelle; Baldwin; Carleton; Cavendish; Diogenes; Nonpareil; Tankerville.

COAL-TAR DERIVATIVES. Research on these was done by **H** at the Montpellier Laboratory in this city in France (*Empty House*).

COBB, JOHN. Groom who drove Charles McCarthy to Ross (*Boscombe*).

COBURG BRANCH OF THE CITY & SUBURBAN BANK. John Clay and accomplice were foiled in their attempt to steal £30,000 in French gold from a vault by **H** (*Red-headed League*).

COBURG SQUARE. Jabez Wilson had a pawnshop here (*Red-headed League*).

COCAINE. **H** gave himself an injection of a 7% solution, and **W** remonstrated (*Sign of Four*). An occasional dose was used (*Yellow Face*).

COLD HARBOR LANE. Four-wheeler carrying **H**, **W**, and Mary Morstan en route to T. Sholto (*Sign of Four*).

COLDSTREAM GUARDS. Mr. Tangey, the commissionaire, formerly was of this regiment (*Naval Treaty*).

COLIN, SIR. Liberated Lucknow in the Indian Mutiny (*Sign of Four*).

COLLEGE OF ST. LUKE'S. 1895. **H** and **W** in residence at unnamed "great university" to allow **H** to pursue library research in early English charters. Consulted by Hilton Soames, tutor and lecturer of this college (*Three Students*).

COLONNA, PRINCE OF. The black pearl of the Borgias disappeared from his bedroom at the Dacre Hotel (*Six Napoleons*).

COLONNA, PRINCESS OF. She was much upset by the disappearance of the black pearl of the Borgias. She had a maid, Lucretia Venucci (*Six Napoleons*).

"COME AT ONCE IF CONVENIENT—IF INCONVENIENT COME ALL THE SAME." Wire from **H** to **W**, opening case of Professor Presbury (*Creeping Man*).

COMMERCIAL ROAD. Dorak, a Bohemian, kept a general store here, according to Mercer (*Creeping Man*).

COMPOSITORS, HANDS OF. See Holmes.

CONDUIT STREET. Listed in **H's** index

as address of Colonel Moran (*Empty House*).

*CONK-SINGLETON FORGERY CASE. As Lestrade left their quarters, **H** asked **W** to put the black pearl in the safe and take out the papers on this case. So far, the case is unrecorded (*Six Napoleons*).

CONTINENT. **H** and **W** go away for a "few days" (*Final Problem*).

CONTINENTAL EXPRESS. **H** and **W** were to meet in the second first-class carriage from the front, leaving Victoria station for France (*Final Problem*).

*Continental Gazetteer.* Used by **H** (*Scandal in Bohemia*).

CONTINENTAL WIRE SERVICE. **H** reminded **W** that he could get advice by this service (*Lady Frances Carfax*).

"COOEE." A usual call between Charles and James McCarthy, and probably between Charles McCarthy and John Turner (*Boscombe*).

COOK. Constable that heard John Openshaw call for help (*Five Orange Pips*).

COOK'S. Their local office at Lausanne told **W** that Lady Frances had gone to Baden (*Lady Frances Carfax*).

COOMBE TRACEY. L. L.'s letter to Sir Charles Baskerville was from this village (*The Hound*).

COPENHAGEN. E. J. Drebber and J. Stangerson had their luggage labeled from this city (*Study in Scarlet*).

COPPER BEECHES. Residence of Jephro Rucastle, near Winchester, in Hampshire (*Copper Beeches*).

COPPER BEECHES, ADVENTURE OF THE. The Jephro Rucastles overpay Violet Hunter as governess but desire that she cut her hair. Jephro is nearly killed by his own dog, Carlo.

COPTIC MONASTERIES. Professor Coram's treatise was on these establishments in Syria and Egypt (*Pince-Nez*).

*COPTIC PATRIARCHS. **H** was involved in the case designated by this name, and he asked **W** to start an investigation as to the whereabouts of Dr. Ernest and Mrs. Amberley (*Retired Colourman*).

CORAM, PROFESSOR. Lived at Yoxley Old Place, near Chatham, in Kent. An invalid, presumably, writing a book and employing Willoughby Smith as his secretary. Coram was an *alias* for Sergius. His Russian wife, Anna, killed Willoughby Smith in trying to get the documents that would free her true love, Alexis, in Siberia. **H** was at the top of his form in this case (*Pince-Nez*).

CORK-CUTTERS, HANDS OF. See Holmes.

CORNELIUS, MR. He received large checks from Mr. Oldacre. **H** felt that Cornelius and Oldacre were the same person (*Norwood Builder*).

CORNISH HORROR. See *Adventure of the Devil's Foot.*

CORNISH LANGUAGE. **H** felt that this might be akin to Chaldean and largely derived from Phoenician tin traders (*Devil's Foot*).

CORNWALL. As for Scotland (*Red-headed League*). Scene of action for *Adventure of the Devil's Foot.* Cf. Dawson & Neligan (*Black Peter*).

COROT. A genuine painting of his hung at T. Sholto's home (*Sign of Four*).

CORPORATION STREET. Temporary offices of the Franco-Midland Company were at 126B, in Birmingham (*Stock-broker's Clerk*).

COSTA RICA. Entry in J. H. Neligan's notebook (*Black Peter*). Beryl Garcia of this country married Jack Baskerville, son of Rodger (*The Hound*).

COUNTRY OF THE SAINTS. Background for Drebber, Stangerson, and Hope. Cf. Ferrier; also Hope (*Study in Scarlet*).

COVENT GARDEN. It was a "Wagner Night" here, and if **H** and **W** hurried, they might be in time for the second act (*Red Circle*).

COVENT GARDEN MARKET. Mr. Breckinridge had a large stall here and sold Mr. Windigate of the Alpha Inn some geese (*Blue Carbuncle*).

COVENTRY. Midland Electrical Company was located here (*Solitary Cyclist*).

COVENTRY, SERGEANT. Of the Winchester police, and he was happy to have **H** inquire rather than Scotland Yard. He hopes to get some credit (*Thor Bridge*).

COX & CO. BANK. Charing Cross. In a vault in this bank is a battered tin dispatch-box that belongs to **W.** It is crammed with data on **H's** cases, including the cutter "Alicia," Isadora Persano, and James Phillimore (*Thor Bridge*). Presumably, this dispatch-box also held the records about Professor Presbury, but these data *have* been published (*Creeping Man*).

COXON & WOODHOUSE. Stock-brokers, in Draper's Gardens (*Stock-broker's Clerk*).

C.P.R. **H's** suggestion was Canadian Pacific Railway (*Black Peter*).

CRANE WATER. Home of the Armitages (*Speckled Band*).

CRAVEN STREET. The Mexborough Private Hotel was here (*The Hound*).

CREDIT LYONNAIS. In Montpellier. Marie Devine cashed the last check, for £50, of her employer, Lady Frances (*Lady Frances Carfax*). **H** felt that Count Sylvius had forged a check here in 1892, but the Count said he was innocent (*Mazarin Stone*).

CREEPING MAN, ADVEN-

TURE OF THE. Early in September, 1903. Professor Presbury took primate preparations, behaved like an ape, and his devoted wolfhound, Roy, almost killed him. **H** intervened.

CREMONA. Violins (*Study in Scarlet*).

CRENDALL. Village three miles from Shoscombe Old Place (*Shoscombe*).

CREWE. Mrs. Roylott was killed in a railway accident near here (*Speckled Band*).

CRIMEAN WAR. Convict ships were pressed into service as troop transports in the Black Sea (*Gloria Scott*). The Royal Munsters served (*Crooked Man*). Mortimer, Professor Coram's gardener, was an "old Crimean man" (*Pince-Nez*). Admiral Green was in charge of operations in the Sea of Azov (*Lady Frances Carfax*).

CRIMINALS. This category is used loosely. It is not restricted to those people who have been apprehended in some crime, duly sentenced, and sent to prison or otherwise retired from action. Rather it lists those who have committed a crime or crimes. There is probably injustice in this listing. For example, the crime of Mr. Windibank seems greater than that of, say, Jefferson Hope. Such matters are controversial.

Adams
Akbar, Dost (one of the Four)
Baldwin, Ted
Baskerville, Jack (*alias* Mr. Vandeleur, *alias* Jack Stapleton)
Beddington No. 1 (*alias* Arthur Pinner, *alias* Harry Pinner)
Beddington No. 2 (brother of No. 1, impersonator of Hall Pycroft)
Beppo
Biddle (Worthingdon Bank gang)
Brooks
Browner, Jim
Cairns, Patrick
Calhoun, Captain James
Carruthers
Carruthers, Colonel
Cartwright (Worthingdon Bank gang)
Clay, John (*alias* William Morris, *alias* Vincent Spaulding)
Cunningham
Dixie, Steve (*alias* Black Steve of Spencer-John gang)
Dowson, Baron
Evans, "Killer" (*alias* James Winter, *alias* Moorecroft, *alias* John Garrideb)
Ferguson, Jack
Ferguson, Mr.
Gorgiano, Giuseppe (infamous title: Black Gorgiano)
Gruner, Baron Adelbert
Hayes, Reuben
Hayward (Worthingdon Bank gang)
Hope, Jefferson
Howells, Rachel
Hudson
Huret

Kemp, Wilson
Khan, Abdullah (one of the Four)
Latimer, Harold
Leonardo
Lopez (*alias* Lucas, *alias* Rulli)
Mathews
McGinty, "Bodymaster"
Merridew
Merton, Sam
Milverton, Charles Augustus
Moffat (Worthingdon Bank gang)
Moran, Colonel Sebastian (Moriarty organization)
Morgan
Moriarty, Professor (chief of the organization)
Murillo, Don Juan (*alias* Mr. Henderson, *alias* Marquess de Montalva)
Neligan, Senior
Oldacre, Jonas
Parker
Peace, Charlie
Peters, Henry (also "Holy" Peters, *alias* Dr. Shlessinger)
Pinner, Arthur (see Beddington No. 1)
Pinner, Harry (see Beddington No. 1)
Porlock, Fred (Moriarty organization)
Prescott, Rodger (*alias* Waldron)
Pritchard, Dr.
Randalls, the (father and two sons, *i.e.,* the Lewisham gang)
Ronder, Eugenie
Ross, Duncan ("Archie")
Selden
Sergius (*alias* Professor Coram)
Sholto, Major John
Singh, Mahomet (one of the Four)
Slaney, Abe
Small, Jonathan (one of the Four)
Smith, Culverton
Stark, Colonel Lysander
Staunton, Arthur H.
Staunton, Henry
Sterndale, Dr. Leon
Stevens, Bert
Stockdale, Barney (Spencer-John gang)
Straker, John (*alias* William Derbyshire)
Sutton (*alias* Blessington of the Worthingdon Bank gang)
Sylvius, Count Negretto
Tonga
Tregennis, Mortimer
Upwood, Colonel
Van Seddar
Venucci, Pietro
Wainwright
Walter, Colonel Valentine
Wild, Jonathan
Wilder, James
Williamson
Wilson
Windibank, James (*alias* Hosmer Angel)
Winter, Kitty
Woodhouse
Woodley, Jack

CRITERION BAR. W renews his acquaintance with young Stamford here (*Study in Scarlet*).

CROCKER, CAPTAIN. In command of the "Bass Rock" of the Adelaide-Southampton Line. He came to **H** and told all (*Abbey Grange*).

CROCKFORD, J. C. Elman, M.A., vicar of Little Purlington in Essex, was in this reference work (*Retired Colourman*).

CROOKED MAN, THE. A few months after **W** married Mary Morstan, **H** and **W** were called to Aldershot to look into the death of Colonel Barclay.

CROOKSBURY HILL. It was about here that Violet Smith first noted the cyclist that shadowed her (*Solitary Cyclist*).

*CROSBY. A banker who died terribly in 1894. It seems reasonably clear that his death was connected with the repulsive red leech (*Pince-Nez*).

CROSBY, MR. A banker, *circa* 1894 (*Pince-Nez*).

CROSS STREET. In Croydon. Miss Susan, not Miss Sarah, Cushing lived here (*Cardboard Box*).

CROWDER, WILLIAM. Gamekeeper for John Turner (*Boscombe*).

CROWN INN. In Surrey. Helen Stoner got a dog-cart and drove to Leatherhead, en route to consult **H**. **H** and **W** got a bedroom and sitting room here (*Speckled Band*).

CROYDON. See Cross Street.

CRYPTOLOGY. See *Adventure of the Dancing Men; Valley of Fear; Adventure of the Red Circle.*

CRYSTAL PALACE. Mr. Grant Munro took an hour's walk in the grounds here (*Yellow Face*).

CUBITT, HILTON. His wife, *née* Elsie Pattrick, was worried by the queer messages. Abe Slaney killed Mr. Hilton and was arrested by Inspector Martin (*Dancing Men*).

CUMMINGS, JOYCE. He was barrister for the defence of Grace Dunbar (*Thor Bridge*).

CUNARD LINE. The "Ruritania" was one of its ships (*Illustrious Client*).

CUNNINGHAM, MR. His place was burgled, and William, the coachman, was shot. Cunningham was a J.P. in this part of Surrey, near Reigate. He was impatient with **H** until he was charged with the murder (*Reigate Puzzle*).

CUNNINGHAM, ALEC. Son of Mr. Cunningham noted. Alec drew a revolver on **H** and was arrested for the murder of William Kirwan (*Reigate Puzzle*).

CURZON SQUARE. Mr. Henderson and Mr. Lucas escaped pursuit by entering a lodging-house on Edmonton Street and going out the back gate into this square, and eventually to Madrid (*Wisteria Lodge*).

CURZON STREET. Sam Brewer, moneylender, had his place here (*Shoscombe*).

CUSACK, CATHERINE. Maid to Countess Morcar (*Blue Carbuncle*).

CUSHING, MARY. Sister of Susan and Sarah. Married Mr. Browner in Liverpool. Killed by Jim Browner later, when, at instigation of jilted Sarah, Mary became friendly with Alec Fairbairn (*Cardboard Box*).

CUSHING, SARAH. Sister of Mary and Susan. Mr. Browner dropped Sarah and married Mary. She could not get along with Susan and so moved to New Street, Wallington. Sarah was responsible for Mary's and Alec Fairbairn's intimacy after Mary's marriage to Jim Browner and thus for the death of Mary and Alec at hands of Jim Browner (*Cardboard Box*).

CUSHING, SUSAN. Eldest sister, hence Miss Cushing, and thereby the package of ears sent by Jim Browner and meant for Sarah was received by Susan after Sarah had moved (*Cardboard Box*).

CUVIER, BARON. **H** compared his case reconstructions to those of the palaeontologist's reconstructions of fossils (*Sign of Four*).

*Cyanea capillata.* A giant sea medusa, described in J. G. Wood's *Out of Doors* and identified by **H** as the killer of McPherson and his dog (*Lion's Mane*).

*Cyclopides.* An insect that flew over path and was pursued by Jack Stapleton—thereby making possible a meeting of **W** with Jack's sister, Beryl. She mistook **W** for Sir Henry Baskerville (*The Hound*).

# D

DACRE HOTEL. The black pearl disappeared from Prince of Colonna's bedroom here (*Six Napoleons*).

*Daily Gazette*. **H** and **W** found the messages from "G" in the Agony Column. Later **H** found that the letter "G" stood for Gennaro Lucca (*Red Circle*).

*Daily News*. London newspaper in which Mycroft Holmes inserted an advertisement for the whereabouts of Paul Kratides and Sophy (*Greek Interpreter*).

*Daily Telegraph*. London newspaper (*Study in Scarlet; Copper Beeches; Norwood Builder*). Carried account of the double life of Eduardo Lucas (*Second Stain*). Oberstein used its Agony Column to get the secret documents (*Bruce-Partington*).

D'ALBERT, COUNTESS. Milverton was expecting her servant to call with her mistress' letters that could be used for blackmail. Instead he received another caller (*Milverton*).

DAMERY, SIR JAMES. (Colonel Damery). Consulted **H** in the case of Violet de Merville's infatuation for Baron Gruner (*Illustrious Client*).

DANCING MEN, ADVENTURE OF THE. **H** solves the death of Hilton Cubitt and secures the killer by cryptography.

"DANGLING PRUSSIAN, THE." **H** warned Von Bork that he should not cry out en route to London, since, if he did, his fate might furnish this new signpost for an English village inn (*Last Bow*).

DARJEELING. India. Henry Wood was taken here by the rebels in the Mutiny but escaped to the Afghan country (*Crooked Man*).

*DARLINGTON SUBSTITUTION SCANDAL. **H** referred to this case and compared it with Irene Adler's secret of concealment. So far **W** has not seen fit to record the case for the public (*Scandal In Bohemia*).

DARTMOOR. **H** felt he would have to travel here in connection with the disappearance of the favorite for the Wessex Cup (*Sil-

*ver Blaze*). James Mortimer lived in hamlet of Grimpen on the moor (*The Hound*).

DARTMOOR PRISON. Jonathan Small felt that he would end his days here (*Sign of Four*).

DARWIN, CHARLES. **H**, excited by the Neruda concert, tells **W** that Darwin claims that "the power of producing and appreciating it [music] existed among the human race long before the power of speech arrived" (*Study in Scarlet*).

DARWINIAN THEORY. As for Vehmgericht. The *Daily Telegraph* found this relevant to its account of E. J. Drebber's murder (*Study in Scarlet*). Cf. Malthus

DAUBENSEE. Switzerland. **W** felt that it was a melancholy place (*Final Problem*).

DAVENPORT, J. He answered Mycroft Holmes's advertisement in the *Daily News* (*Greek Interpreter*).

"DAVID." Mrs. James Barclay was heard to use this word in her dispute with James Barclay, by Jane Stewart, their housemaid. **H** explained to **W** later that it was a biblical reference to Colonel Barclay's betrayal. Cf. Bible (*Crooked Man*).

DAVOS PLATZ. A fictitious lady wintering here, and in advanced consumption, had presumably stopped at the Englischer Hof en route to Lucerne. **W** was told that she asked for an English physician, and he turned back to attend her, leaving **H** alone (*Final Problem*).

DAWSON. Servant of Abel White, killed in the Mutiny (*Sign of Four*).

DAWSON. Stable-boy at Mapleton (*Silver Blaze*).

DAWSON & NELIGAN. West country bankers. Their failure for the sum of £1,000,000 ruined half the county families of Cornwall. Neligan disappeared after the failure (*Black Peter*).

DAY'S MUSIC HALL. In Birmingham. Hall Pycroft was told to relax here (*Stock-broker's Clerk*).

"DEAR ME, MR. HOLMES. DEAR ME!" Note sent to **H** about two months after John Douglas was acquitted of killing Ted Baldwin. **H** felt that it was from Professor Moriarty to acquaint him with the death of John Douglas (*Valley of Fear*).

DE BRINVILLIERS, MARCHIONESS. As for Vehmgericht.

*Decameron*. See Boccaccio.

DE CAPUS, HUGO. He built part of the Birlstone Manor area during the first crusade (*Valley of Fear*).

DEEP DENE HOUSE. Jonas Oldacre lived here in Lower Norwood (*Norwood Builder*).

*De Jure inter Gentes*. Published by Philippe de Croy in Latin in 1642 at Liège. Owner's name was Guliolmi Whyte. **H** bought it second-hand (*Study in Scarlet*).

DELIRIUM. **H**, in one of his best performances, fooled even **W** by his appearance and behavior (*Dying Detective*).

DE MERVILLE, GENERAL. Of Kyber fame. His daughter, Violet, was threatened, and Sir James Damery asked for **H's** help. The General lived at 104 Berkeley Square (*Illustrious Client*).

DE MERVILLE, VIOLET. She lived with her father, General de Merville. *q.v.* **H** triumphed in her cause (*Illustrious Client*).

DENNIS, TOM. Husband of Sally (*née* Sawyer). They presumably lived at 3, Mayfield Place, Peckham (*Study in Scarlet*).

DEPTFORD REACH. As for pool.

DE QUINCEY. **W** remembers that Isa Whitney read this author—to his disadvantage (*Twisted Lip*).

DERBY. Mr. Hargrave was reported from here (*Valley of Fear*).

DERBY, THE. Shoscombe Prince, a promising colt, ran in this race. He won and paid £80,000 to his owner, Sir Robert Norbertson (*Shoscombe*).

"DERBYSHIRE, MRS." **H** noted that she had expensive tastes in gowns. Her ostrich-feather trimming was part of the secret financial burden of John Straker (*alias* William Derbyshire) (*Silver Blaze*).

DERBYSHIRE, WILLIAM, *Alias* of John Straker. He had a bill for an expensive hat from the milliner, Madame Lesurier, of Bond Street (*Silver Blaze*).

DE RESZKES. **H** and **W** were to celebrate by a box for "Les Huguenots" after a dinner at Marcini's. Presumably the De Reszkes were in the cast of "Les Huguenots" (*The Hound*).

DESBOROUGH. The second favorite for the Wessex Cup. In Lord Backwater's Mapleton Stable, near Tavistock (*Silver Blaze*).

DESMOND, JAMES. An elderly clergyman in Westmoreland. If anything happened to Sir Henry Baskerville, James would inherit the estate of about £1,000,000 (*The Hound*).

DETECTIVES. See Police Forces.

DEVIL'S FOOT, ADVENTURE OF THE. March, 1897. Action was in Cornwall and, with permission of **H, W** told the case thirteen years later. Dr. Sterndale's sample of *Radix pedis diaboli* killed or drove insane the four Tregennis siblings. **H** solved the case of "the Cornish horror" but did not intervene.

DEVINE. French sculptor who made a much-copied, and much-smashed bust of Napoleon (*Six Napoleons*).

DEVINE, MARIE. Maid of Lady Frances Carfax. Marie, engaged to one of the head waiters at the Hotel National in Lausanne, was given a wedding gift of £50 when she left Lady Frances. Marie went to 11 Rue de Trajan, Montpellier (*Lady Frances Carfax*).

*Devon County Chronicle*. Carried a

May 14, 1889, article on the death of Sir Charles Baskerville (*The Hound*).

DEVONSHIRE. Setting of *Silver Blaze.* Sir Charles Baskerville and the family had lived near Dartmoor (*The Hound*).

DEVOY, NANCY. She married James Barclay when he was a sergeant (*Crooked Man*).

DIAMOND-CUTTERS, HANDS OF. See Holmes.

DIAMOND HILL. Outside Pretoria, where, during Boer War, Godfrey Emsworth was shot (*Blanched Soldier*).

DIEPPE. **H** felt that he and **W** should go to this city from Newhaven (*Final Problem*).

DINGLE, THE. Home of Lord Harringby (*Wisteria Lodge*).

DIOGENES CLUB. Mycroft Holmes was a member (*Greek Interpreter* and *Bruce-Partington*).

DISGUISES, OF HOLMES. See Sherlock Holmes, methods.

DIXIE, STEVE. Negro bruiser, nicknamed Black Steve. Barney Stockdale sent him to warm **H** off the Three Gables case. **H** was not frightened, but Steve was (*Three Gables*).

DIXON, JEREMY. Owner of Pompey (*Three-Quarter*).

DIXON, MRS. Housekeeper for Mr. Carruthers (*Solitary Cyclist*).

DOBNEY, SUSAN. Retired in Camberwell. Old governess of Lady Frances Carfax. For four years Lady Frances had written Susan every fortnight. When she had not heard for five weeks, Susan consulted **H** (*Lady Frances Carfax*).

DOCTORS. See physicians.

DOCTORS' COMMONS. **H** expected to get helpful data here (*Speckled Band*).

DODD, JAMES M. Consulted **H** and was mystified by **H's** deductions. James was a friend of Godfrey Emsworth, had joined the Middlesex Corp in January, 1901, for the Boer War. After the war, James could not see his friend. **H** intervened, and Sir James Saunders found that Godfrey did not have leprosy (*Blanched Soldier*).

DOG. (1) **W** kept a bull pup before going with **H** to 221B Baker Street; **H** did not object, but no more was heard of this dog (*Study in Scarlet*).

(2) Of two pills collected by Lestrade in Stangerson's hotel room, **H** gave a half of each pill, dissolved in milk, one at a time, to a long-sick terrier that **H's** and **W's** landlady had asked **W** to "put out of its pain." The first was harmless, and the second was a deadly poison (*Study in Scarlet*).

(3) **H** asked **W** to borrow Toby from Sherman. Toby was half spaniel and half lurcher, and a good scent-trailer. Toby, after a false start, traced Jonathan Small and the Andaman Islander to

river's edge and was then returned to Sherman (*Sign of Four*).

(4) Carlo, a mastiff, guarded the grounds of the Copper Beeches at night. **W** shot it (*Copper Beeches*).

(5) Inspector Gregory asked **H** if there was any point he wished to emphasize. **H** replied that Gregory should direct his attention "to the curious incident of the dog in the night-time." Gregory replied, "The dog did nothing in the night-time." **H** responded, "That was the curious incident" (*Silver Blaze*).

(6) Victor Trevor's bull terrier bit **H** on the ankle (*Gloria Scott*).

(7) Cunningham had a dog, but it was chained (*Reigate Puzzle*).

(8) Milverton had a watchdog. Agatha locked the dog up at night when she became engaged (*Milverton*).

(9) Dr. Armstrong's coachman set a dog on **H** but was discouraged by **H's** stick (*Three-Quarter*).

(10) Pompey, with a draghound's passion for aniseed, led **H** and **W** to Godfrey Staunton (*Three-Quarter*).

(11) James Mortimer had a curly-haired spaniel. It disappeared, and later its skeleton was found on the island in the Grimpen Mire. The hound had probably devoured it (*The Hound*).

(12) The hound probably caused the death of Sir Charles and almost killed Sir Henry Baskerville. James Mortimer thought he had seen what looked like a black calf earlier, and then he found footprints a little way from Sir Charles's body—"Mr. Holmes, they were the footprints of a gigantic hound!" The prints belonged to Jack Stapleton's dog, which he painted with a phosphorescent compound. **H** shot the monster. (*The Hound*).

(13) Carlo, a spaniel, had been poisoned experimentally, and **H** and **W** found that he was partially paralysed (*Vampire*).

(14) **H** thought of writing a monograph on the uses of dogs in detective work (*Creeping Man*).

(15) Roy, Professor Presbury's devoted wolfhound, tried to kill his master and nearly did so. He was discovered, not to have broken his chain, but to have slipped his collar, which had been made originally for a thick-necked Newfoundland (*Creeping Man*).

(16) Ian Murdoch once threw Fitzroy McPherson's little dog through a plate-glass window (*Lion's Mane*).

(17) Fitzroy McPherson's

little dog, an Airedale, died "at the very place" his master had died. **H** was alerted and promptly solved the case (*Lion's Mane*).

(18) The Shoscombe spaniels were famous (*Shoscombe*).

(19) Sir Robert Norbertson gave away Lady Falder's favorite black spaniel, since, after her death, she could not be personated in the coach while her dog was about (*Shoscombe*).

DOLORES. Maid to Mrs. Robert Ferguson. Presumably Peruvian like her mistress (*Vampire*).

DOLSKY. In Odessa he was involved in the forcible administration of poison (*Study in Scarlet*).

DONCASTER. When the stand fell here, Mr. Harker fell with it (*Six Napoleons*).

DON JUAN. Brunton was said to be a bit like him (*Musgrave Ritual*).

DONNITHORPE. In Norfolk, where the Trevors lived (*Gloria Scott*).

DORAK, A. Bohemian who kept a large general store on Commercial Road. He corresponded with Professor Presbury, and sent special preparations to him (*Creeping Man*).

DORAN, ALOYSIUS. Wealthy American, living in San Francisco. His only daughter, Hatty, was to marry Lord St. Simon, and he took a house in London, at Lancaster Gate (*Noble Bachelor*).

DORAN, HATTY. Only daughter of Aloysius. Married to Francis Hay Moulton *and* Lord St. Simon. **H** rescued her from this predicament (*Noble Bachelor*).

DORKING, COLONEL. His engagement to the Honourable Miss Miles was broken two days before the wedding (*Milverton*).

DOUGLAS, IVY. Mrs. John Douglas. She tried to help her husband to represent the body of Ted Baldwin as that of John Douglas. **H** foiled the scheme. On the acquittal of her husband, Ivy and he sailed for South Africa on the "Palmyra," but, en route, her husband was "lost overboard." She cabled the bad news to Cecil Barker (*Valley of Fear*).

DOUGLAS, JOHN. Presumably "murdered" at his home, Birlstone Manor House in Sussex. Later **H** flushed John from a hiding place in the old house and identified the body as that of Ted Baldwin. On acquittal of John, **H** urged John and Ivy to leave England. When Cecil Barker had the news from Ivy that John was "lost overboard," **H** felt that it was the work of Professor Moriarty (*Valley of Fear*).

DOVERCOURT, EARL OF. The intolerant fiancé of Lady Eva Blackwell (*Milverton*).

DOWNING, CONSTABLE. Assisted in arrest of huge mulatto seen and chased earlier by Constable

Walters. Downing was bitten by the savage (*Wisteria Lodge*).

DOWNING STREET. Lord Holdhurst had chambers here (*Naval Treaty*).

DOWNS. As for Gravesend (*Sign of Four*). **H** retired to a farm near Eastbourne on Sussex Downs (Preface to *His Last Bow*).

*DOWSON, BARON. **H** was instrumental in his being hanged (*Mazarin Stone*).

DRAPER'S GARDEN. Firm of Coxon & Woodhouse here (*Stockbroker's Clerk*).

DREBBER, ENOCH J. From Cleveland, Ohio. He was dead at No. 3 Lauriston Gardens. In London he had stayed at Madame Charpentier's Boarding Establishment, Torquay Terrace, Camberwell (reported by the London *Standard*). He suggested that Alice, the landlady's daughter, "fly with him" and was attacked by her brother, Arthur. Drebber took a cab to escape Arthur Charpentier (*Study in Scarlet*).

DUBLIN. Browner's ship stopped at this port (*Cardboard Box*).

DUBUGUE, MONSIEUR. Of the Paris police. He was on the wrong track in the case of the *Second Stain, q.v.* (*Naval Treaty*).

DUNBAR, GRACE. Governess of the two J. Neil Gibson children. It looked as though she had murdered Mrs. Gibson, but **H** demonstrated that the latter had committed suicide and arranged the evidence because she was jealous of Grace (*Thor Bridge*).

DUNCAN STREET. London. Cf. Sawyer.

*DUNDAS SEPARATION CASE. **H** was engaged in clearing up some points in the matter (*Case of Identity*).

DUNDEE. Letter to Joseph Openshaw came from here January 4, 1885 (*Five Orange Pips*). The "Sea Unicorn," a sealer under command of Captain Cary, was from here (*Black Peter*).

DUNLOP. Bicycle tire identified by **H** from the tracks (*Priory School*).

DUPIN. **H** thought of him as a "very inferior fellow" (*Study in Scarlet*).

DURANDO, VICTOR. The San Pedro minister to London. He was murdered by the dictator, Don Juan Murillo, in San Pedro (*Wisteria Lodge*).

DYING DETECTIVE, ADVENTURE OF THE. 1889. Action takes place in second year of Watson's marriage. By malingering, **H** got **W** to persuade Culverton Smith to come and then kept **W** in the room as an unseen witness to Smith's confession of the murder of Victor Savage, his nephew. Inspector Morton makes the arrest.

*Dynamics of an Asteroid.* Abstruse mathematical paper written by Professor Moriarty (*Valley of Fear*).

# E

EAGLE COMMERCIAL HOTEL. Tunbridge Wells. A Mr. Hargrave, stopping here, owned a Rudge-Whitworth bicycle (*Valley of Fear*).

EAR. **H** has published two monographs on ears in the *Anthropological Journal.* Browner sent an ear of Mary Cushing and an ear of Alec Fairbairn to Sarah Cushing, but they went to Susan Cushing by mistake (*Cardboard Box*). **H** wired **W** for a description of the left ear of Dr. Shlessinger, a request which **W** saw fit to disregard (*Lady Frances Carfax*).

EAST ANGLIA. Scene of action of *Adventure of the Dancing Men.*

EAST END. London. Cf. Wilson, the canary-trainer (*Black Peter*).

EASTERN RAILWAY. South Africa, serving Pretoria. Its tracks were near Diamond Hill and Buffelsspruit (*Blanched Soldier*).

EAST HAM. Mr. Hargrave was reported from here, as well (*Valley of Fear*).

EAST RUSTON. Village in Norfolk (*Dancing Men*).

*Echo.* As for *Globe* (*Blue Carbuncle*).

ECKERMANN. Author of *Voodooism and the Negroid Religions* which **H** read with purpose (*Wisteria Lodge*).

EDGWARE ROAD. The Church of St. Monica was here (*Scandal in Bohemia*). Little Ryder Street was a small offshoot (*Garridebs*).

EDMONTON STREET. Mr. Henderson and his secretary, Mr. Lucas, escaped from a back entrance of a lodging-house here into Curzon Square (*Wisteria Lodge*).

EDMUNDS. A Berkshire constable who interviewed Mrs. Ronder and, still puzzled, consulted **H.** Later this officer was sent to Allahabad (*Veiled Lodger*).

EDWARDS, BIRDY. *Alias* John Douglas, *q.v.* (*Valley of Fear*).

EGRIA. A German-speaking section of Bohemia (*Scandal in Bohemia*).

EGYPT. Professor Coram's treatise dealt with its Coptic monasteries (*Pince-Nez*).

"1884." This date was on the visitor's stick, and **H** noted that it was five years ago (*The Hound*).

ELEY'S No. 2. **H** advised **W** to slip this

revolver in his pocket (*Speckled Band*).

ELISE. She saved Mr. Hatherley's life, and she called Colonel Lysander Stark "Fritz" (*Engineer's Thumb*).

ELMAN, J. C. Abused vicar at Little Purlington. He was angry when **W** and Josiah Amberley called to find out what he knew about Amberley's wife and the money (*Retired Colourman*).

ELRIGE'S. A lonely farm in the direction of East Ruston (*Dancing Men*).

EMBANKMENT, THE. John Openshaw must have been decoyed here and killed (*Five Orange Pips*).

EMPTY HOUSE, ADVENTURE OF THE. March 30, 1894. Honourable Ronald Adair murdered. **H** returned, and Colonel Moran and his air-gun were taken.

EMSWORTH, COLONEL. He was a Crimean V.C. His bad temper and worse manners did not prevent **H** from doing him a great favor (*Blanched Soldier*).

EMSWORTH, GODFREY. Only son of Colonel Emsworth. Lance-Corporal, B Squadron, Middlesex Corps. Shot by elephant gun in Boer War. On intervention first by his army friend, James M. Dodd, then **H**, and finally Sir James Saunders, it was demonstrated that Godfrey did not have leprosy (*Blanched Soldier*).

ENCYCLOPAEDIA BRITANNICA. Jabez Wilson's job at £4 a week was to copy this work each day between 10 A.M. and 2 P.M. (*Red-headed League*).

ENDELL STREET. **H** and **W** en route to enquire about the goose (*Blue Carbuncle*).

ENGINEER'S THUMB, ADVENTURE OF THE. Summer, 1889, not long after **W's** marriage, and **W** takes Victor Hatherley to consult **H.**

ENGLISCHER HOF. BADEN. Lady Frances stayed a fortnight, met the Shlessingers, and all three left for London. Her maid, Marie, had left Lady Frances' service here in "floods of tears" (*Lady Frances Carfax*).

ENGLISCHER HOF. Meiringen. Peter Steiler, the elder, was manager. **H** and **W** arrived here from London May 3, 1891 (*Final Problem*).

ENTERIC FEVER. **W** contracted this while recuperating from his shoulder wound and quite naturally considered it the "curse of our Indian possessions." Cf. Watson.

ERNEST, DR. RAY. He ran off with Mrs. Josiah Amberley and a good part of Josiah's savings, according to Josiah. When Dr. Ernest was missing, his family hired Mr. Barker to look into the matter for them. **H** and Barker cooperated. Dr. Ernest's body was found in a well on Josiah's property (*Retired Colourman*).

ESCOTT. Rising young plumber, engaged to Milverton's housemaid. This was an *alias* of **H** (*Milverton*).

ESHER. Wisteria Lodge was near this Surrey town (*Wisteria Lodge*).

"ESMERALDA." This ship was at Gravesend, to sail for the Brazils. Jonathan Small and Tonga hoped to board her from the "Aurora" (*Sign of Four*).

ESSEX. Little Purlington was here (*Retired Colourman*).

ETHEREGE, MRS. She told Mary Sutherland about **H's** finding her husband, and Mary consulted **H** forthwith (*Case of Identity*).

ETON. John Clay went to this school (*Red-Headed League*). So did Colonel Sebastian Moran (*Empty House*).

EUCLID, FIFTH PROPOSITION. Mentioned by **H** (*Sign of Four*).

EUSTON. London district in which were located the Euston Station and, in nearby Little George Street, Halliday's Private Hotel (*Study in Scarlet*).

EUSTON STATION. Drebber and Stangerson were seen on the platform, presumably waiting for the Liverpool Express—they had told their landlady, Madame Charpentier, that they were taking this train (*Study in Scarlet*). **H. W**, and Dr. Huxtable en route to Mackleton (*Priory School*). **H** and James M. Dodd were joined here by Sir James Saunders en route to Tuxbury Old Park (*Blanched Soldier*).

EVANS. *Alias* Beddoes. He was willing to join Armitage and Prendergast (*Gloria Scott*).

EVANS, CARRIE. Maid to Lady Beatrice Falder. According to John Mason, she was more devoted to Sir Robert Norbertson than to Lady Beatrice. Actually she was Mrs. Norlett, *née* Evans (*Shoscombe*).

EVANS, "KILLER." *Alias* James Winter, *alias* Morecroft, *alias* John Garrideb, *q.v.* Forty-four years old; native of Chicago; known to have killed three men in the United States; shot a man in Waterloo Road, who later was identified as Rodger Prescott, a forger and coiner from Chicago (*Garridebs*).

EVENING NEWS STANDARD. As for *Globe* (*Blue Carbuncle*). This paper carried the account of the capture of the false Hall Pycroft (*Stock-broker's Clerk*).

EYE COLOR. **H's** eyes were gray (*The Hound; Retired Colourman*).

EYFORD. Berkshire, where Colonel Stark asked Mr. Hatherley to come for a consultation (*Engineer's Thumb*).

# F

**Faber, Johann.** Manufacturer of pencils (*Three Students*).

**faint.** **H** pretends to faint in order that a valuable piece of information not be disclosed by a member of the party (*Reigate Puzzle*).

**Fairbairn, Alec.** Lover of Mrs. Jim Browner (*née* Mary Cushing). Jim killed Mary and Alec and sent an ear of each to Sarah Cushing, who had encouraged the *liaison* (*Cardboard Box*).

**Fairbank.** The residence of Alexander Holder (*Beryl Coronet*).

**Falder, Lady Beatrice.** Owner of Shoscombe Old Place. The Shoscombe spaniels were her special pride. Died of dropsy, and her brother, Sir Robert Norbertson, concealed her death until his horse, Shoscombe Prince, won the Derby and £80,000 (*Shoscombe*).

**Falder, Sir James.** After his death his wife, Lady Beatrice, maintained Shoscombe Old Place (*Shoscombe*).

**Falmouth.** The "Gloria Scott" sailed from this port (*Gloria Scott*).

**false fire alarms.** See Sherlock Holmes, methods and organization.

*Family Herald.* A current romantic periodical (*Thor Bridge*).

***Farintosh.** Mrs. Helen Stoner heard of her case, involving an opal tiara, and of **H**'s part in it. Since this case was before **W**'s advent, there may be trouble in getting the facts published (*Speckled Band*).

**Farquhar, Dr.** **W** bought his practise in the Paddington district soon after his marriage to Mary Morstan (*Stock-broker's Clerk*).

**Farnham.** On the borders of Surrey, where Violet Smith taught music (*Solitary Cyclist*).

**Farringdon Street.** **H** and **W** en route to capture John Clay (*Red-headed League*).

**Fenchurch Street.** Westhouse & Marbank had their claret importing firm here (*Case of Identity*).

**Ferguson, Captain.** Retired sea captain. He owned the Three Gables prior to Mary Maberley (*Three Gables*).

**Ferguson, Jack.** Crippled, elder son of Robert and stepson of the current Mrs. Ferguson. Jealous hatred of his younger half-brother led to the trouble. **H** solved the case and suggested that a year at sea for Jack might be the solution (*Vampire*).

FERGUSON, MR. Secretary and manager for Colonel Stark (*Engineer's Thumb*).

FERGUSON, MR. Secretary to J. Neil Gibson (*Thor Bridge*).

FERGUSON, MRS. Peruvian beauty. Second wife of Robert. **H** was able to establish her innocence and restore family unity (*Vampire*).

FERGUSON, ROBERT. Of Ferguson & Muirhead, Mincing Lane. He played as a three-quarter in rugby for Richmond. Called to consult **H** as to whether or not his wife was a vampire *sensu strictiore!* **H** established her innocence (*Vampire*).

FERGUSON & MUIRHEAD. Tea brokers in Mincing Lane (*Vampire*).

FERINGHEE. Jonathan Small was called this by Abdullah Khan (*Sign of Four*).

FERNWORTHY. Devonshire village near Grimpen, where Mr. Frankland was alternately in good and bad grace with the villagers (*The Hound*).

*FERRERS DOCUMENTS. **H** was retained in this case (*Priory School*).

FERRIER, DR. He took charge of Percy Phelps (*Naval Treaty*).

FERRIER, JOHN. He accompanied the Mormons to Utah. He adopted Lucy. Lucy was to marry Jefferson Hope, but she was forced to marry E. J. Drebber (*Study in Scarlet*).

FERRIER, LUCY. Adopted daughter of John (*Study in Scarlet*).

FFOLLIOTT, SIR GEORGE. Lived at Oxshott Towers, near Oxshott. It was a large house, but not the right one (*Wisteria Lodge*).

FIGHTING COCK INN. **H** sprained his ankle and talked with Reuben Hayes, the innkeeper. Later **H** looked in an inn window, and the £6000 was secure (*Priory School*).

FINAL PROBLEM, THE. Early May, 1891. **H** vs. Professor Moriarty. **W** probably wrote up the case *circa* 1893. **H** came to **W's** consulting room on April 24, 1891, to propose that they spend a week on the Continent. **H** and Moriarty fight on the brink of Reichenbach Falls, and **W** returned to London alone.

FINGER PRINTS. Mr. McFarlane's thumb print in blood was discovered by Lestrade (*Norwood Builder*).

FIRBANK VILLAS. Dr. Horsum resided at No. 13 (*Lady Frances Carfax*).

FISHER, PENROSE. As for Sir Jasper Meek.

FIVE ORANGE PIPS, THE. September, 1887? Mary Watson was visiting her mother. **W** with **H**. **H** unable to save his client from death and the criminals escaped but died at sea. Cf. John Openshaw; Watson.

FLAUBERT, GUSTAVE. Quoted by **H** (*Red-headed League*).

FLEET STREET. Duncan Ross had offices at 7, Pope's Court, in this street (*Red-headed League*). **H** and **W** took a walk here (*Resident Patient*).

FLORENCE. Italy. **H** took a week to slip from Reichenbach Falls to this city (*Empty House*).

FLORIDA. Elias Openshaw was a planter here (*Five Orange Pips*).

FLOWERS. **H** speaks of them as "Our highest assurance of the goodness of Providence" (*Naval Treaty*).

FLOWERS, LORD. Trelawney Hope had a note from him (*Second Stain*).

FLUSHING. Von Bork's family had left for this town the day before, with the less important papers (*Last Bow*).

*FOLKESTONE COURT. A cold-blooded murder case was tried here. There was no clue, but **H** felt that Jack Stapleton may have been the murderer (*The Hound*).

FOOTSTEPS (FOOTPRINTS). **H** had written a monograph on "the tracing of footsteps, with some remarks upon the uses of plaster of Paris as a preserver of impresses" (*Sign of Four*). Cf. dog (12).

FORBES, MR. Detective from Scotland Yard in charge of the case (*Naval Treaty*).

FORDHAM. Lawyer at Fordham, Sussex, was wanted by Elias Openshaw (*Five Orange Pips*).

FORDHAM, DR. He attended Trevor, Senior (*Gloria Scott*).

FORDINGBRIDGE. Letter from here to Trevor, Senior, caused the latter to suffer a stroke (*Gloria Scott*).

FORDINGHAM. Village in Hampshire (*Gloria Scott*).

FOREIGN OFFICE. Percy Phelps went into this branch of the government after he left Cambridge University (*Naval Treaty*). **H** communicated details of his visit to the Kalifa of Khartoum to this office (*Empty House*).

FOREST ROW. In Sussex. Captain Peter lived nearby (*Black Peter*).

FORMOSA CORRUPTION, BLACK. **W** had never heard of this affliction (*Dying Detective*).

FORRESTER, INSPECTOR. He asked **H** for help in Surrey (*Reigate Puzzle*).

*FORRESTER, MRS. CECIL. Employer of Miss Mary Morstan. She sent Mary to consult **H**, since he had once unraveled a small domestic complication for her (*Sign of Four*). This was probably one of the key decisions in the **H-W** association, because it provided **W** with a wife and affected numerous lesser circumstances in later cases. In addition, one would like to know about the problem that Mrs. Forrester brought to the attention of **H**, although **W** may not have been included in this.

FORT DODGE. Kansas. "A. H. Garrideb" bought land along the Arkansas River, west of this town (*Garridebs*).

FORTESCUE SCHOLARSHIP. Soames was worried about the safety of the examination questions (*Three Students*).

FORTON OLD HALL. Home of James Baker Williams (*Wisteria Lodge*).

FOULMIRE. A moorland farmhouse. **H** found it on his map (*The Hound*).

FOURNAYE, HENRI. Of Paris. *Alias* Eduardo Lucas, of London (*Second Stain*).

FOURNAYE, MME. HENRI. She was a Creole. Probably came from her Paris villa in Rue Austerlitz to spy on her husband. She killed him at his second establishment on Godolphin Street in London, where he was known as Eduardo Lucas (*Second Stain*).

FOWLER, MR. He wanted to marry Alice Rucastle, and so they eloped and went to Mauritius (*Copper Beeches*).

FRANCE. **H** visited this country (*Empty House*). Dutchess of Holdernesse had taken up residence in the south of the country (*Priory School*). Cf. Paris.

FRANCO-MIDLAND HARDWARE COMPANY, LIMITED. Mr. Pinner wanted Hall Pycroft to become the manager of this unlikely firm in Paris (*Stockbroker's Clerk*).

FRANK. Mrs. Moulton called her husband, Francis Hay, by this name (*Noble Bachelor*).

FRANKLAND, MR. Of Lafter Hall, Fernworthy. He was a friend of Sir Charles Baskerville. His daughter, Laura, married an artist who then deserted her. As Mrs. Laura Lyons, she met Jack Stapleton, who she thought was unmarried. **H** cleared the matter for all concerned (*The Hound*).

FRASER, MARY. Later, Lady Brackenstall (*Abbey Grange*).

FRASER, MR. A consumptive tutor hired by Mr. Vandeleur at St. Oliver's, a small school (*The Hound*).

FRASER. "Wife" of Holy Peters, *alias* Shlessinger (*Lady Frances Carfax*).

FRATTON WAY. Altamont's residence was toward Fratton (*Last Bow*).

FREEBODY, MAJOR. A friend of Joseph Openshaw at Portsdown Hill (*Five Orange Pips*).

FRESNO STREET. It branched out of Upper Swandam Lane (*Twisted Lip*).

*"FRIESLAND." A Dutch steamship. The case, **W** notes, nearly cost the lives of **H** and himself. No public report (*Norwood Builder*).

**FRITZ.** Elise (Stark?) called Colonel Lysander Stark by this name (*Engineer's Thumb*).

**FULHAM ROAD.** Ross and Mangles sold dogs here (*The Hound*).

**FULWORTH.** Small cove and village on the Channel Coast, not far from **H's** place in Sussex (*Lion's Mane*).

# G

G. See Lucca, Gennaro.

GABLES, THE. Well-known coaching school, under headship of Harold Stackhurst. It was a half-mile from **H**'s place in Sussex (*Lion's Mane*).

GABORIAU. **H** thought that Gaboriau's fictional detective, Lecoq, was "a miserable bungler" (*Study in Scarlet*).

GABRIEL. To Mrs. Ronder, at the time, Leonardo seemed like this angel (*Veiled Lodger*).

GANGES RIVER. A crocodile in this river bit off one of Jonathan Small's legs (*Sign of Four*).

GARCIA, ALOYSIUS. Of Wisteria Lodge, between Esher and Oxshott. He was found murdered a mile from his home on Oxshott Common (*Wisteria Lodge*).

GARCIA, BERYL. Of Costa Rica. She married Jack Baskerville, son of Rodger, in this country. Cf. Beryl Stapleton, and Vandeleur (*The Hound*).

"GARRIDEB, ALEXANDER HAMILTON." He was said to have made a fortune in real estate and wheat speculation. In his will it was said that he left all to three male Garridebs, if they could be found. This worked out at about $5,000,000 apiece (*Garridebs*).

"GARRIDEB, HOWARD." This was the third and last of the Garridebs needed to fulfil Alexander Hamilton's conditions. He was a manufacturer of agricultural machinery at Grosvenor Buildings, Aston, in or near Birmingham. Nathan protested that he seldom travelled, but John insisted that he was the one to go see Howard. As **H** suspected, "Howard Garrideb" was fictitious (*Garridebs*).

GARRIDEB, JOHN. Counsellor at Law, Moorville, Kansas. *Alias* "Killer" Evans, *q.v.* **H** saw through his plot (*Garridebs*).

GARRIDEB, NATHAN. He lived at 136 Little Ryder Street, W. He was a collector, interested in butterflies and moths, coins, flint instruments, fossil bones, and ancient man. When the $5,000,000 did not materialize, he broke down and had to enter a Brixton nursing-home (*Garridebs*).

GELDER & COMPANY. In Church Street, Stepney. They sold three plaster busts of Napoleon to Morse Hudson, and three of the same to Harding Brothers, for six shillings each. Beppo worked for them for a time (*Six Napoleons*).

GEMMI PASS. **H** and **W** en route from London to Meiringen (*Final Problem*).

GENEVA. **H** and **W** en route from Strasburg to their hide-out in Switzerland (*Final Problem*).

GEORGIA. Mr. Hebron and his only child were said to have died in Atlanta of yellow fever (*Yellow Face*).

GEORGIAN. Nathan Garrideb's house at 136 Little Ryder Street, W., was of this period (*Garridebs*).

GERMAN OCEAN. It could be seen over the green edge of the Norfolk Coast (*Dancing Men*).

GHAZIS. Indians fighting the British at battle of Maiwand, in which **W** was wounded. Cf. Watson.

GIBSON, MARIA. *Née* Pinto. Wife of J. Neil Gibson. She was so jealous of the governess, Grace Dunbar, that she committed suicide after arranging her death to look like murder by Grace (*Thor Bridge*).

GIBSON, J. NEIL. Gold-mining magnate and former Senator of a western state of the United States. Had estate in Hampshire for past five years. Formerly in love with his wife, Maria, now in love with the governess, Grace Dunbar. **H** proved that Maria died by suicide rather than by murder (*Thor Bridge*).

GILCHRIST. Scholar and athlete (Rugby, cricket, hurdles, and long jump). Son of Sir Jabez Gilchrist. He looked at the questions, hidden by Bannister, and confessed—but, he had previously decided to go to South Africa (*Three Students*).

GILCHRIST, SIR JABEZ. He ruined himself on the turf (*Three Students*).

GLASSHOUSE STREET. The two men that attacked **H** escaped through the Café Royal into this street (*Illustrious Client*).

*Globe*. **H** advertised finding of a hat and a goose (*Blue Carbuncle*). There was a rumor in this paper about the disappearance of the Duke of Holdernesse' son (*Priory School*).

GLORIA SCOTT, THE. This bark, by the name of which the case was designated, sailed from Falmouth October 8, 1855, bound for Australia. It was a prison ship and at sea was taken over by convicts. Ship exploded and sank. This was the first professional case for **H** and took place sometime between 1877 and 1880.

GLOUCESTER. Mr. Oldmore was once mayor here (*The Hound*).

GLOUCESTER ROAD. Kensington. Goldini's Restaurant was here (*Bruce-Partington*).

GLOUCESTER ROAD STATION. The Underground is clear of tunnels here, and Oberstein's windows at Caulfield Gardens were on the line (*Bruce-Partington*).

GODNO. In Little Russia. **H** recalled a case here in 1866 similar to the Baskerville case (*The Hound*).

GODOLPHIN STREET. Eduardo Lucas lived here (*Second Stain*).

GOETHE. Quoted and praised by **H** (*Sign of Four*).

GOLDINI'S RESTAURANT. Gloucester Road, Kensington. **H** asked **W** to meet him here for a meal and to bring a revolver and certain burglar tools (*Bruce-Partington*).

GOLD KING. **W**'s epithet for J. Neil Gibson, who had hunted gold in Brazil (*Thor Bridge*).

GOLDEN PINCE-NEZ, ADVENTURE OF THE. November, 1894. Willoughby Smith is dead, with a pair of broken spectacles clutched in his hand. The spectacles belong to Anna, Smith's killer and the Russian wife of Professor Coram of Yoxley Old Place.

GOODGE STREET. Peterson got a used hat and a Christmas goose here (*Blue Carbuncle*).

GOODWINS. The "Lone Star" must have passed them by evening, **H** thought (*Five Orange Pips*).

GORDON, GENERAL. **W** had a newly framed picture of him (*Resident Patient*).

GORDON SQUARE. Francis Hay Moulton lodged at No. 226 (*Noble Bachelor*).

GORGIANO, GIUSEPPE. Also known as Black Gorgiano and Gorgiano of the Red Circle, *q.v.* Gennaro Lucas killed him in a house in Howe Street (*Red Circle*).

GOROT, CHARLES. A clerk in the Foreign Office (*Naval Treaty*).

*GRAFENSTEIN, COUNT VON UND ZU. He was saved from murder at the hands of the Nihilist Klopman through the efforts of **H** (*Last Bow*).

GRAMOPHONE. **H** used a record on this machine, instead of playing his violin, and so was able to overhear the conversation between Sam Merton and Count Sylvius (*Mazarin Stone*).

GRAND HOTEL. **W** saw the bad news ("Murderous attack upon Sherlock Holmes") between here and Charing Cross Station (*Illustrious Client*).

GRAND NATIONAL. Sir Robert Norbertson's horse ran second in this race a few years back, according to **W** (*Shoscombe*).

GRAVESEND. Mordecai Smith often was on a job on the river as far as Gravesend. **H** thought that Jonathan Small might embark for America or the colonies on some ship, either here or in the Downs (*Sign of Four*). **H** wired here and learned that the "Lone Star" was homeward bound (*Five Orange Pips*). Mrs. St. Clair received a note from her husband postmarked here (*Twisted Lip*).

GRAY'S INN ROAD. **H** and **W** en route to King's Cross Station (*Three-Quarter*).

GREAT GEORGE STREET. Westminster. Adolph Meyer lived at No. 13 (*Bruce-Partington*).

GREATHED, COLONEL. Liberated the Agra area in the Indian Mutiny (*Sign of Four*).

GREAT MOGUL. A large diamond in the Agra Treasure (*Sign of Four*).

GREAT ORME STREET. Mr. and Mrs. Warren lived here (*Red Circle*).

GREAT PETER STREET POST-OFFICE. **H** wired from here for the Baker Street division of the detective police force (*Sign of Four*).

GREEK INTERPRETER, THE. Mycroft Holmes brought Sherlock a case. The murderers escaped and supposedly were killed by Sophy to avenge her presumed brother's murder. Cf. Paul Kratides.

GREEN, ADMIRAL. Commanded the Sea of Azov fleet in the Crimean War. Father of Philip Green (*Lady Frances Carfax*).

GREEN DRAGON. An inn at Crendall, and about three miles from Shoscombe Old Place (*Shoscombe*).

GREEN, HON. PHILIP. Son of Admiral Green. He went to South America, returned wealthy, and attempted to locate Lady Frances after many years. He followed Mrs. Shlessinger to Poultney Square, and **H** saved Lady Frances for him (*Lady Frances Carfax*).

GREENWICH. The "Aurora" could have touched either bank of the river between here and the end of Mordecai Smith's Broad Street wharf (*Sign of Four*). Venner & Matheson's engineering firm was here (*Engineer's Thumb*).

GREGORY, INSPECTOR. He asked for **H's** coöperation in solving the disappearance of the racehorse Silver Blaze (*Silver Blaze*).

GREGSON, TOBIAS. Scotland Yard Inspector. According to **H,** the "smartest of the Scotland Yarders." Jealous of Inspector Lestrade. A tall, white-faced, and flaxen-haired officer. He arrested Sub-Lieutenant Arthur Charpentier for the murder of E. J. Drebber. Later, he reported his failure in the case to **H** and **W** and asked for **H** to name the real murderer of E. J. Drebber and J. Stangerson (*Study in Scarlet*). **H** wanted him on the case of the *Greek Interpreter.* He was on the Aloysius Garcia-Scott Eccles case (*Wisteria Lodge*), also on the case of the *Red Circle.*

GRENOBLE. Home of Monsieur Oscar Meunier who made wax bust of **H** (*Empty House*).

GREUZE, JEAN BAPTISTE. Painted between 1750 and 1800. His work "La Jeune Fille a l'Agneau" was purchased by Professor Moriarty in 1865 for more than £40,000 (*Valley of Fear*).

*GRICE PATERSONS. W recorded this case in 1877, concerning adventures on the Island of Uffa, but has not given the account to the public (*Five Orange Pips*).

GRIGGS, JIMMY. Clown in the Ronder circus. He did what he could, but it was not enough (*Veiled Lodger*).

GRIMMS FAIRY TALE. On the occasion of the note from Morrison, Morrison, and Dodd "*Re* Vampires," **H** remarked on his sense of entering a similar atmosphere (*Vampire*).

GRIMPEN. James Mortimer lived in this village, near Dartmoor, in Devon (*The Hound*).

GRIMPEN MIRE. An impassable bog except to Jack Stapleton, his dog, and his servant, Anthony (*The Hound*).

GROSS & HANKEY'S. Regent Street. Probably sold wedding rings (*Scandal in Bohemia*).

GROSVENOR BUILDINGS. Aston, Birmingham. "Howard Garrideb" was reputed to have offices here (*Garridebs*).

GROSVENOR HOTEL. London. Peter Steiler was a waiter for three years here before becoming the manager of the Englischer Hof (*Final Problem*).

GROSVENOR MANSIONS. Lord St. Simon wrote to **H** from here (*Noble Bachelor*).

GROSVENOR SQUARE. Isadora Klein lived here (*Three Gables*).

*GROSVENOR SQUARE FURNITURE VAN. The case known by this name cleared up by **H** but is unpublished (*Noble Bachelor*).

GRUNER, BARON ADELBERT. **H** identifies him as "the Austrian murderer." Adelbert meant to marry Violet de Merville. He lived at Vernon Lodge, near Kingston. Kitty Winter threw vitriol in his face, **W** talked about Ming saucers, and **H** stole his diary for Violet to read (*Illustrious Client*).

GUILDFORD ASSIZES. Inspector Baynes thought that justice would be done here to the tenants of High Gable, but in this instance he was wrong (*Wisteria Lodge*).

GUILD OF ST. GEORGE. Met at Watt Street Chapel, Aldershot. Mrs. Barclay and Miss Morrison were in the Guild (*Crooked Man*).

GUION STEAMSHIP COMPANY. Letters for E. J. Drebber and Joseph Stangerson (*Study in Scarlet*).

# H

HAFIZ. **H** found him as instructive as Horace in dealing with clients like Miss Sutherland (*Case of Identity*).

HAGUE, THE. **H** notes that a case here was similar to that of Mary Sutherland (*Case of Identity*).

HAINES-JOHNSON. Auctioneer and valuer. **H** felt that if he were bona fide, he would have given Mary Maberley his business address (*Three Gables*).

HALES LODGE. Hampstead. Home of Cecil James Barker (*Valley of Fear*).

HALF MOON STREET. Dr. Hill Barton was supposed to live at No. 369 (*Illustrious Client*).

HALIFAX. Nova Scotia. Colonel Spence Munro moved here, and Violet Hunter wanted another position as governess (*Copper Beeches*).

HALLE'S CONCERT. This was where **H** wanted to hear Norman Neruda (*Study in Scarlet*).

HALLIDAY'S PRIVATE HOTEL. London. Joseph Stangerson's body was discovered in this Little George Street establishment (*Study in Scarlet*).

*HAMMERFORD WILL CASE. Sir James Damery arranged matters with Sir George Lewis. **H** appeared to have information in this matter, and it might be developed by **W** (*Illustrious Client*).

HAMMERSMITH. Mitton had an alibi—he had spent the critical period here with friends (*Second Stain*).

HAMMERSMITH BRIDGE. **H**, **W**, and Lestrade en route to Laburnum Villa (*Six Napoleons*).

HAMMERSMITH WONDER. See Vigor.

HAMPSHIRE. As for Berkshire (*Speckled Band*). Jephro Rucastle lived near Winchester in this county (*Copper Beeches*). Hudson went to see Mr. Beddoes in this county (*Gloria Scott*). Neil Gibson had an estate here for five years (*Thor Bridge*).

HAMPSTEAD. Hall Pycroft lived at No. 17 Potter's Terrace (*Stock-broker's Clerk*). **H** and **W** en route to an address in area (*Milverton*).

HAMPSTEAD HEATH. Two men rudely dumped poor Mr. Warren here (*Red Circle*).

HANDCUFFS. **H** suggested that Lestrade and Gregson should introduce a new type at Scotland Yard and illustrated his point with capture of Jefferson Hope (*Study in Scarlet*). Cf. Wiggins.

HANDS, EFFECTS OF TRADE UPON. See Sherlock Holmes, works.

HANOVER SQUARE. St. George's Church was here (*Noble Bachelor*).

*HARDEN, JOHN VINCENT. The well-known tobacco millionaire, whose peculiar persecution was occupying **H.** No public report as yet (*Solitary Cyclist*).

HARDING BROTHERS. High Street Station. They bought three cheap plaster busts of Napoleon from Gelder & Co. Sold one to Mr. Harker, one to Josiah Brown, and one to Mr. Sandeford (*Six Napoleons*).

HARDY, MR. Foreman in plumber's shop of Mr. Sutherland, in Tottenham Court Road (*Case of Identity*).

HARDY, SIR CHARLES. Trelawney Hope had his report (*Second Stain*).

HARDY, SIR JOHN. As for Mr. Murray (*Empty House*).

HARE, JOHN. **W** felt that **H** took on the disguise and the part of a Nonconformist clergyman with a flair that only Hare could have equalled (*Scandal in Bohemia*).

HARGRAVE. He owned a Rudge-Whitworth bicycle and put up at the Eagle Commercial Hotel in Tunbridge Wells (*Valley of Fear*).

HARGREAVE, WILSON. A friend of **H,** in the New York City Police Bureau. **H** cabled him about Abe Slaney (*Dancing Men*).

HARKER, HORACE. Lived at 131 Pitt Street. Bought a cheap bust of Napoleon from Harding Brothers. It was stolen, and a dead man was found on his very doorstep (*Six Napoleons*).

HARLEY STREET. **H** and **W** en route to inquire about the goose (*Blue Carbuncle*). **H** and **W** returning from Dr. Trevelyan (*Resident Patient*). **H** refers to this street (*Shoscombe*).

*HAROLD, MRS. **H** knew the real facts about her death. It will be remembered that she left Count Sylvius the Blymer Estate. **W** has not reported this case (*Mazarin Stone*).

HARRINGBY, LORD. He lived at The Dingle, near Oxshott. It was a large house but not the right one (*Wisteria Lodge*).

HARRIS, MR. Of Bermondsey. *Alias* of **H** when he was introduced to Mr. Pinner by Hall Pycroft (*Stock-broker's Clerk*).

HARRISON, ANNIE. She is to marry Percy Phelps. Her brother is Joseph (*Naval Treaty*).

HARRISON, JOSEPH. Brother of Annie. He did not hesitate to steal the papers from Percy Phelps (*Navy Treaty*).

HARROW. Miss Honoria Westphail lived near here (*Speckled Band*).

HARROW WAY. Barney Stockdale sent Steve Dixie to tell **H** that his life was not safe in this area (*Three Gables*).

HARROW WEALD CASE. The Spencer John gang wanted **H** to desist from looking into this affair for Mrs. Maberley (*Three Gables*).

HARVEY. One of John Mason's lads. He tended Lady Beatrice Falder's furnace and found therein what **W** identified readily as a part of a human femur (*Schoscombe*).

HARVEY'S. **W** said that such a house name would be found about Lamberley (*Vampire*).

HARWICH. The lights of the area could be seen from Von Bork's terrace (*Last Bow*).

HATHERLEY. A farm owned by John Turner and rented to Charles McCarthy (*Boscombe Valley Mystery*).

HATHERLEY, VICTOR. An engineer living on the third floor at 16A Victoria Street. When he lost his thumb, **W** treated him and then took him to consult with **H**. Victor was apprentice for seven years to Venner & Matheson (*Engineer's Thumb*).

HAVEN, THE. Home of Josiah Amberley, in Lewisham (*Retired Colourman*).

HAVEN, THE. Home of Tom Bellamy, in Fulworth (*Lion's Mane*).

HAYES, REUBEN. Surly innkeeper of the Fighting Cock Inn and murderer of the German master, Heidegger. **H** had him arrested at Chesterfield (*Priory School*).

HAYLING, JEREMIAH. Twenty-six-year-old hydraulic engineer. Disappeared, *circa* summer of 1888, and **H** thought that he had been murdered by Colonel Lysander Stark (*Engineer's Thumb*).

HAYMARKET THEATRE. Josiah Amberley had taken two upper circle seats, but he went alone, he said, since his wife had a headache (*Retired Colourman*).

HAYTER, COLONEL. A friend of **W**. He asked **W** and **H** to spend a week in the country in the spring of April, 1887, at his place near Reigate in Surrey (*Reigate Puzzle*).

HAYWARD. He was one of the Worthingdon bank gang (*Resident Patient*).

*Heavy Game of the Western Himalayas.* By Colonel Sebastian Moran. 1881 (*Empty House*).

HEBRON, EFFIE. Her first marriage. Cf. Effie Munro (*Yellow Face*).

HEBRON, JOHN. Atlanta lawyer and first husband of Effie. John and their only child were said by Effie to have died of yellow fever in Atlanta. John was a Negro (*Yellow Face*).

HEBRON, LUCY. The startling daughter of John and Effie (*Yellow Face*).

HEIDEGGER. German master at the Priory School. Both he and young Lord Saltire were missing. Heidegger was found dead, killed by a heavy blow on the head. **H** eventually caught the murderer (*Priory School*).

HELSTON. Presumably an insane asylum to which George and Owen Tregennis were taken (*Devil's Foot*).

HENDERSON, MR. Of High Gables, near Oxshott. It was a large house, and **H** therefore was interested in its occupants. Henderson was an *alias* of Don Murillo. He escaped in London and six months later, *alias* the Marquess of Montalva, was killed in Madrid (*Wisteria Lodge*).

HENRIETTA STREET. London. Constables Rance and Murcher talked here (*Study in Scarlet*).

HERCULES. Dr. Trevelyan said that one of his patients had a son that was of similar physical build (*Resident Patient*).

HEREFORD ARMS. **H** and **W** stayed here while involved in the *Boscombe Valley Mystery*.

HEREFORDSHIRE. The country district Boscombe Valley was near Ross in this county (*Boscombe Valley Mystery*).

HIGH GABLE. Near Oxshott. Home of Mr. Henderson (*Wisteria Lodge*).

HIGH STREET. Winchester. The Black Swan Hotel was here (*Copper Beeches*).

HIGH STREET STATION. London. Harding Brothers, near here, sold busts of Napoleon (*Six Napoleons*).

HIGH TOR. A moorland farmhouse. **H** found it on his map (*The Hound*).

HILL, INSPECTOR. He readily identified the dead man as Pietro Venucci, of Naples, connected with the Mafia (*Six Napoleons*).

HINDOO. A servant of Thaddeus Sholto, who ushered **H, W,** and Mary Morstan in to an audience with Thaddeus (*Sign of Four*).

HIS LAST BOW. August 2, 1914. **H,** in a last service to his country, came out of Sussex retirement and, as Altamont, Von Bork's top agent, captured Von Bork, chief German espionage agent in England. **W** appears briefly as Altamont's chauffeur.

HISTON. **H** searched here too (*Three-Quarter*).

*HOBBS, FAIRDALE. Mrs. Warren remembered that **H** had solved Mr. Hobbs's problem, when the latter was lodging with her. **W** may have the records of this unpublished case (*Red Circle*).

HOFFMAN'S "BARCAROLE." **H** said that he was going into his room and play this piece on his violin, but he played it on a gramophone instead (*Mazarin Stone*).

HOLBORN. London district. **H** and **W** en route to inquire about the goose (*Blue Carbuncle*).

HOLBORN BAR. Young Perkins was killed just outside (*Three Gables*).

HOLBORN, THE. Restaurant where **W** and young Stamford had lunch prior to Stamford's historic introduction of **W** to **H** (*Study in Scarlet*).

HOLDER, ALEXANDER. Of Holder & Stevenson, bankers. He consulted **H**, and then **H** and **W** came to his home, "Fairbank," in Streatham (*Beryl Coronet*).

HOLDER, ARTHUR. Son of Alexander. His father accused him of stealing public jewels. He was arrested. **H** intervenes to free Arthur and point out the real thief (*Beryl Coronet*).

HOLDER, MARY. Niece of Alexander (*Beryl Coronet*).

HOLDER, SERGEANT JOHN. Of the Third Buffs. He saved Jonathan Small when a crocodile in the Ganges bit off one of Jonathan's legs (*Sign of Four*).

HOLDER & STEVENSON. On Threadneedle Street. Second largest private banking firm in the City of London (*Beryl Coronet*).

HOLDERNESSE, DUKE OF. Once a cabinet minister. His son was abducted, and Dr. Huxtable came to town for **H**. The duke paid **H** £6000 when the latter solved the case (*Priory School*).

HOLDERNESSE HALL. **H** asked to see the horseshoes that made cow tracks. He found these the second most interesting thing he had seen in the case, the first being his reward cheque of £6000 (*Priory School*).

HOLDHURST, LORD. Uncle of Percy Phelps. His chambers were in Downing Street (*Naval Treaty*).

HOLLAND. Count Sylvius was all for getting the jewel to this country (*Mazarin Stone*).

*HOLLAND. **H** accomplishes a delicate and successful mission for the reigning family of this country (*Scandal in Bohemia*) and gets a fine ring for this service (*Case of Identity*).

HOLLAND GROVE. This was the beat of Constable Harry Murcher (*Study in Scarlet*).

HOLLIS. One of Von Bork's agents. According to Altamont, Hollis "went a bit woozy toward the end" (*Last Bow*).

HOLLOWAY & STEELE. Edgware Road house-agents for Nathan Garrideb (*Garridebs*).

HOLLY, SIR EDWARD. According to Trevor, Senior, Sir Edward had been attacked by a poaching gang (*Gloria Scott*).

HOLMES, MYCROFT. Seven years older than his brother, Sherlock. He belonged to the Diogenes Club. Brought a case to Sherlock's attention (*Greek Interpreter*). Later, when Professor Moriarty was hunting Sherlock, the latter spent the day in Mycroft's rooms in Pall Mall, and then Mycroft drove W to Victoria Station (*Final Problem*). While away, Sherlock confided his whereabouts only to Mycroft, since he had to obtain money for his travels (*Empty House*). Mycroft came a second time to Sherlock's chambers at 221B Baker Street on the matter of Cadogan West. According to Sherlock, Mycroft was paid only £450 a year, yet because of his peculiar gifts of memory and his syntheses of data, Mycroft could evaluate rapidly the impact of apparently unrelated matters on policy. For example, he could focus the interrelation of the Navy, India, Canada, and the bimetallic question in one complex opinion. At such times, according to Sherlock, Mycroft *was* the British Government.

Mycroft is a sedentary person of rather fixed habits and consequently a small orbit: his chambers in Pall Mall, the Diogenes Club, and his office in Whitehall. On his second visit to the rooms of Sherlock and W, Mycroft left happy that his brother would act in the case (*Bruce-Partington*).

HOLMES, SHERLOCK. *Pre-Watsonian:* Watson found it difficult to imagine Holmes as a member of a family, and perhaps that is why our meagerness of information about his background does not surprise us. We do know that the Holmes ancestors were typical English country squires. There was some French blood in the family, however, since Sherlock's grandmother was sister to the French artist, Vernet (*Greek Interpreter*). Finally, there were at least two children born to Mr. and Mrs. Holmes. These were both boys, Mycroft (*q.v.*) and Sherlock, seven years younger.

While Sherlock was at college, he apparently had few intimates. He was acquainted there with Reginald Musgrave (*Musgrave Ritual*), but his only friend during this period was Victor Trevor. The Trevor family must have had a large, if unconscious effect on the future shape of Sherlock's career. Thus, Victor's father, Trevor, Senior, praised young Sherlock highly on his ability to reason from data and detect the past course of events. This had been a hobby previously, but now Sherlock began to consider detection as a serious occupation by which one might earn a livelihood. Thus the "Gloria Scott" (*q.v.*) became his first case (*Gloria Scott*).

Once this decision was taken, all of Sherlock's activities became directed toward supremacy in the field of detection and later as a consulting expert. Even at this early period, he maintained an amateur status, helpful to, but independent of, the official police force in London.

While he was still unknown to the public, he had rooms in Montague Street, around the corner from the British Museum. Presumably while living here he became engaged in the curious affair at Hurlstone Manor House, in Sussex. He provided a brilliant solution of the case (*Musgrave Ritual*). One wonders if this early contact with this county in any way directed his thoughts in later years to retirement on the Sussex downs, near the Channel (*Last Bow; Lion's Mane*).

*The Historic Meeting:* John H. Watson, M. D., on pension from an early wound and secondary complications in the Second Afghan War, had returned to London. Cf. Watson. He had happened on young Stamford at the Criterion Bar, and the two had lunch at the Holborn. Watson was looking about for cheaper quarters. Stamford knew that Sherlock was interested in sharing the expenses of chambers, and upon this economic note Stamford took Watson to meet Holmes, forthwith. This historic meeting was in a chemical laboratory of a London hospital. Characteristically, at their first meeting Sherlock explained vividly his test for haemoglobin, while John listened in surprise.

It appeared that Sherlock had an eye on a set of rooms on Baker Street that he could not afford. John felt that if the chambers were suitable, they would have a good thing. At the time it appeared that neither had personal habits that would be objectionable to the other. On Sherlock's side, he confessed that he liked strong tobacco, often employed strong chemicals in experiments, was moody at times and would not speak for days, and that he played a violin well enough not to annoy a fellow lodger. John stated his shortcomings (*q.v.*), and the two agreed to meet the next day at noon and have a look together at the suite.

They liked the rooms and moved in. Early in the settling-in period John attempted to list Sherlock's general limits: he had no knowledge of literature, philosophy, astronomy; he was poor in politics, although he had a good, practical knowledge of British law; in botany, he knew nothing about gardening and much about poisons; he had a limited but practical knowledge of geology, especially the varieties of London soils; a profound knowledge of chemistry; an accurate but unsystematic fund of information on human anatomy; he played the violin well; he was expert in single stick, boxing, and swordplay (*Study in Scarlet*). Those familiar with the published data will realize that this listing by John was preliminary—to help him understand his fellow lodger—and that certain of the above views would not stand the test of long association and the information which accumulated.

*General Personality:* Holmes had a high regard for his own remarkable natural gifts, coupled with impatience and volatility. He was fair-minded and generous, though uneven in temperament, alternately depressed or exalted.

But while his attitude toward his achievements was not modest, neither was it self-deceptive. He loftily told Gibson the Gold King that his charges were fixed except when he remitted them entirely, and when Gibson offered the alternative lure of publicity, the cold answer was, "Thank you, Mr. Gibson, I do not think that I am in need of booming" (*Thor Bridge*). He was irritated when Mortimer said that Holmes was second to Bertillon among European experts of detection. But later he was amused and appreciative when the unknown passenger gave his name to the cabby as "Sherlock Holmes" (*The Hound*). He was flushed with success and dramatic in gesture when he plucked out the Black Pearl of the Borgias from its odd setting (*Six Napoleons*); yet in the event of his being incorrect, he was capable of humility. For example, he told Watson that if he ever became too confident of his opinion again, Watson had only to whisper "Norbury" as a reminder (*Yellow Face*).

All such change-abouts in behavior seemed characteristic of Holmes. He could spend days wordless, as he warned Watson earlier he might, scratching at his violin without producing what Watson thought of as "music." In contrast to these dull periods, he would sometimes enter into varied and sprightly conversation. Usually his choice of mood hung upon the degree to which his mind was occupied. Thus, on the eve of their pursuit of the "Aurora," Sherlock, John, and Inspector Jones were at dinner at 221B Baker, and Holmes discoursed on miracle plays, mediaeval pottery, Stradivarius violins, Buddhism of Ceylon, and warships of the future (*Sign of Four*).

Sherlock even had disparate hobbies. For example, he was interested in the Middle Ages and was working on a monograph of the *Polyphonic Motets of Lassus* (*Bruce-Partington*); yet, on the other hand, he made a minor specialty of opening safes (*Milverton*).

Certain aspects of his mercurial nature may have been a consequence of his drug-taking (cocaine and morphine). Watson made an early remonstrance against such bad habits and was bitterly offended when Holmes made a too deliberate injection of a seven-per-cent solution of cocaine. Eventually Watson was successful in helping to bring about Sherlock's victory over drug addiction (*Sign of Four*).

Despite his volatility, Holmes had a sense of fitness and a certain practicality about him. When Watson had been decoyed away, and Holmes and Moriarty were face to face at last, above the thundering Reichenbach Falls, Holmes left a note for Watson: (1) giving him full directions for finding and handing over to Inspector Patterson the details of the Moriarty gang stored at Baker Street against the day, and (2) telling Watson that the plans for the disposal of Sherlock's property were even now in brother Mycroft's hands (*Final Problem*). Further, when Sherlock did not go into the Falls, he had provident arrangements with Mycroft for funds to be sent to him while he was on his long journey (a stop in Florence, two years in Tibet, Persia, Khartoum, and France), part of the time at least disguised as Sigerson, a Norwegian explorer. In all this time only Mycroft knew that Sherlock was not dead (*Empty House*).

Such a long period of solitude and separation would not be a hardship for Sherlock. Apart from Watson, he did not seek out the company of men, and he consciously avoided that of women. His courtesy toward the latter was exemplary, but it was founded, according to Watson, upon a deep distrust and dislike (*Dying Detective*). At best, with one of the most admirable of the sex, Mary

Morstan, he displayed an indifference which Watson denounced as "inhuman" (*Sign of Four*). And yet, two women he honored with exceptional interest and approval. One was Maud Bellamy, whom Sherlock always remembered as "a most remarkable woman" (*Lion's Mane*). The second and the more extraordinary was Irene Adler, an American operatic *diva* retired in London. According to Watson, Irene was always *the* woman. Although duped at the time, Irene saw through Sherlock's stratagem which caused her to reveal the hiding-place of the letters, and she removed them. Later, Holmes asked the King of Bohemia for Irene's photograph in lieu of a reward (*Scandal in Bohemia*).

There were other hints, too, of humane feeling coexisting with detached intellect in the man. Holmes could be subtly both kind and generous. Though he repeatedly mocked Watson's slowness in matters of detection and once criticized him quite cruelly even as a doctor (*Dying Detective*), he was capable of kindness too in response to Watson's. When he felt Watson's pain in thinking his laborious reports had gone unread, Holmes was quick to assure him they were "very well thumbed" (*The Hound*). Then, too, he found the money for young Dr. Verner to purchase Watson's small Kensington practice, and it was long afterward before Watson understood why Dr. Verner had accepted his first price, the highest Watson had conceived possible (*Norwood Builder*).

Holmes was also liberal in his general philosophy. It is true that inactivity or monotony could impair this quality in him. "There is nothing new under the sun. It has all been done before" (*Study in Scarlet*). And on a foggy day of involuntary leisure, to Watson: "Crime is commonplace, existence is commonplace, and no qualities save those which are commonplace have any function upon earth" (*Sign of Four*). But activity stimulated a fresh excitement ("Now is the dramatic moment of fate, Watson, when you hear a step upon the stair which is walking into your life, and you know not whether for good or ill" [*The Hound*]), and eventually a benign optimism. Holmes termed the current board-schools the "light-houses of the future" (*Naval Treaty*). He expressed a high opinion of amateur athletics and thought that amateur sport was the best and soundest thing in England (*Three-Quarter*). A garden stroll with a client produced a singular effusion: "Our highest assurance of the goodness of Providence seems to me to rest in the flowers. . . . Our desires, our food, are all really necessary for our existence in the first instance. But this rose is an extra. Its smell and its colour are an embellishment of life, not a condition of it. It is only goodness which gives extras, and so I say again that we have much to hope from the flowers" (*Naval Treaty*). One far-reaching view indeed was his hope, expressed to an American, Francis Hay Moulton, that one day people would all be "citizens of the same world-wide country" (*Noble Bachelor*).

Ironically, it was while he was most deeply engaged in his precise, factual work that his mind took most pleasure in abstraction; moments were snatched for the contemplation of music and philosophy. Returning from a concert in the midst of the E. J. Drebber problem, Holmes remarked to Watson, "There are vague memories in our souls of those misty centuries when the world was in its childhood" (*Study in Scarlet*). And at another time, thinking over the bad ending of Colonel Moran, he theorized, "The person becomes, as it were, the epitome of the history of his own family" (*Empty House*).

*Methods and Organization:* Quite early in their association Holmes tried to explain to Watson just what he did for a living. He described himself as a "consulting detective" (*Study in Scarlet*) and on another occasion as "the only unofficial consulting detective. . . . I am the last and highest court of appeal in detection" (*Sign of Four*).

Yet Holmes was realistic about his role in the detection of crime. As an amateur he felt that it was necessary to stay in the good graces of the professionals, and over the years he slowly acquired their respect. At least when he felt that justice could best be served by recognizing their endeavors, he cooperated with the legal enforcers of the law. In this way they were encouraged to bring problems in detection to him for solution, and, in return, he assured them that the public acclaim would be theirs. In their first case together, he assured Watson, too, that Inspectors Gregson and Lestrade would pocket the glory (*Study in Scarlet*), and on numerous later occasions Holmes felt that it was necessary to reaffirm this article of faith, whether to the professionals of London or those in outlying counties and villages.

On the other hand, his anonymity gave him a latitude not available to the regular forces. He could, if he liked, collaborate with another, and gifted, amateur detective, Mr. Barker (*Retired Colourman*). He could refuse to act in a case (*Milverton*) if his sympathies were with the killer rather than the killed, and many of his investigations, with Watson as accomplice, were outside the law (*Scandal in Bohemia; Case of Identity; Twisted Lip; Noble Bachelor; Illustrious Client*). That is, they either did not involve police action, or Holmes' activities were those that could not be officially tolerated by the police.

Apparently the mystification of a policeman or of a client, and often of Watson, gave Holmes great satisfaction. He could note a small detail or series of details and, following a chain of unspoken inferences, arrive at a statement that sounded at first absurd or remarkable. Among his many such *tours de force* are the following typical examples: (1) In their first meeting Holmes remarks almost at once that Watson has been in Afghanistan (*Study in Scarlet*); (2) Holmes breaks in at the end of one of Watson's trains of thought about the folly of war (identical for paragraphs 3 to 19 for both *Resident Patient* and *Cardboard Box*); (3) Holmes amazes Mr. McFarlane by remarking on personal facts deduced from his appearance (*Norwood Builder*); (4) Holmes mystifies Watson by deductions regarding South African Securities (*Dancing Men*); (5) Holmes astonishes Stanley Hopkins by describing the wearer of the broken spectacles from the article in question (*Pince-Nez*); (6) Holmes mystifies James M. Dodd (*Blanched Soldier*); (7) Holmes deduces certain facts about the owner of a walking-stick from the article in question (*The Hound*).

For all his acumen, Holmes was frequently regarded with suspicion or contempt. Dr. Grimesby Roylott, to Holmes's indignation, called him "the Scotland Yard Jack-in-Office" (*Speckled Band*), which was surely an unconsciously wicked thrust, seeing that Holmes had reservations about the "Yarders." Lord

Cantlemere was at pains to show that he doubted Holmes's ability in detection (*Mazarin Stone*). And so it went.

At times, Sherlock received more than insults. When he came back from Farnham, in a jubilant mood, he had a lump on the head and a split lip (*Solitary Cyclist*), and a murderous attack was made on him near the Café Royal by two thugs in the pay of Baron Gruner (*Illustrious Client*).

On occasion he employed his hobby of opening safes in the pursuit of business. For example, he burgled Baron Gruner's study while Watson annoyed the Baron with a display of information about Ming saucers (*Illustrious Client*), and he burgled the home of Josiah Amberley while Watson and Josiah were having a frustrated and comical sojourn in the country (*Retired Colourman*). In another instance, Sherlock burgled the safe of a blackmailer and destroyed the contents (*Milverton*).

Such house-breaking and safe-cracking techniques were thought of by Holmes as necessary, although Watson frowned on such things, and the professional police were irritated, presumably by their own legal restrictions. On certain occasions, these illegal entrances were known to, and yet overlooked by, high administrative circles, as when Holmes and Watson burgled the home of Oberstein (*Bruce-Partington*).

Sherlock placed considerable value upon knowing, off-hand, integrated groups of data related to evaluation of a crime or tracing down a criminal. This ability undoubtedly saved him a good deal of time. For example, he could differentiate among 140 ashes of various tobaccos (*Sign of Four; Boscombe*); he knew 42 different tire impressions (*Priory School*); he was familiar with 75 perfumes (*The Hound*).

He also employed numerous devices in his investigations. Twice, at least, he employed a dummy in his image. Once it was used to assure watchers that he was in his Baker Street quarters and allow them to think that they could shoot him from the street (*Empty House*); but, in the *Mazarin Stone,* the dummy was exposed to the criminals, and then, later, Holmes took the place of the dummy, and was able to obtain the valuable jewel.

Nor was he averse to using ruses such as the false fire

alarm to smoke out a criminal in hiding (*Norwood Builder*) or to find out where valuable documents were hidden (*Scandal in Bohemia*); similarly, the early use of the gramophone, playing a violin recording instead of Holmes playing the instrument, betrayed criminals into revealing their stolen property (*Mazarin Stone*).

One of his most important adjuncts was disguise. He was a natural actor and brought to these varying appearances the essential perfection of behavior that renders disguise plausible. Among his many impersonations were the following: (1) an aged master mariner which was so deceptive that not only Watson but Inspector Athelney Jones were deceived (*Sign of Four*); (2) a drunken groom and, later in the same case, (3) an amiable Nonconformist clergyman (*Scandal in Bohemia*); (4) an old man (*Twisted Lip*); (5) a common loafer (*Beryl Coronet*); (6) a remarkably adept sham seizure, to prevent a vital piece of information from being given in the course of a conversation (*Reigate Puzzle*); (7) an Italian priest (*Final Problem*); (8) an elderly, deformed man presumably selling books (*Empty House*); (9) a rakish young workman, complete with clay pipe, goatee, and swagger (*Milverton*). In this last impersonation, as Escott, a plumber, he went so far as to become engaged to the housemaid, so that she would see that the dog was kept in nights. It says much for his art that the housemaid never appreciated the age of her fiancé. (10) A French workman (*Carfax*); (11) a workman, out of work (*Mazarin Stone*); (12) an old woman, a disguise which was so successful that it deceived the dangerous Count Sylvius (*Mazarin Stone*); (13) a dying man, with but a short time to live, a pose which was so realistic that Watson, a physician, was taken in when kept at arm's length (*Dying Detective*); (14) an Irish-American, anti-British espionage agent, very late in Sherlock's career and after his retirement (*Last Bow*).

Speed in obtaining the essential facts was uppermost. Holmes was constantly alive to the desirability of getting to the scene of a crime as soon as possible, before the footprints were obliterated and other delicate signs destroyed. Rapid communication was essential. He seldom wrote but often wired. When the telephone came into general service, he used this new device (*Retired Colourman*).

Although essentially an independent investigator, Sherlock had a small but efficient organization of his own. (1) In the first place, he had at least five small refuges in various parts of London, where he could hide or put on a disguise (*Black Peter*). (2) Then there was the "Baker Street Division of the detective police force," a group of six or more "street arabs." These city-wise urchins were swift, crafty, and inconspicuous and added many pairs of eyes and ears to an investigation (*Study in Scarlet; Sign of Four*). (3) Shinwell Johnson was Holmes's source of information about the London underworld (*Illustrious Client*); (4) an occasional pound or so to Fred Porlock brought tips from this stool-pigeon (*Valley of Fear*) presumably within the Moriarty organization; (5) for gossip in highly placed social circles, there was Langdale Pike. (6) After John Watson left the chambers in Baker Street, Holmes employed Mercer, who did routine business for Sherlock, becoming a "general utility man" (*Creeping Man*). This could have been about 1903 or a little earlier.

*Efficiency:* Before passing on to other things, something should be said here concerning the record of this consulting detective. Such an analysis is restricted largely to the sixty published cases. Unfortunately these represent not more than 43% of the cases in which Holmes is known to have participated (Cf. John H. Watson, Authorship). Nevertheless the published records form a fair sample of the range and type of cases in which he was involved and the efficiency with which he brought these to a conclusion.

It is difficult to assign some cases to a particular category. The following classification could have been modified in several ways. But for practical purposes, the sixty cases have been separated roughly into five groups: Murder; Robbery; Forgery; Disappearance; Alleviation.

*Murder* [23 cases (38%)]: Fourteen resulted in the murderer (s) being arrested, killed, or satisfactorily accounted for. These are: *Black Peter, Cardboard Box, Dancing Men, Dying Detective, Empty House, Final Problem, Lion's Mane, Pince-Nez, Reigate Puzzle, Retired Colourman, Sign of the Four, Silver Blaze, Speckled Band,* and *Study in Scarlet.*

Three of these involved non-human agents: *Lion's Mane,* in which the killer was a giant sea medusa; *Silver Blaze,* in which a horse was the killer; and *Speckled Band,* wherein a deadly snake was the killer. Of these three, the first was for a time thought to be murder but turned out to be purely accidental. The last two entailed well-deserved deaths—what may be regarded as poetic justice.

In all of these fourteen cases of outright murder, Holmes made a successful detection. Some of his most brilliant exploits are in this group.

Four additional cases were brought to a successful conclusion, but Holmes allowed the killer to go free. These are: *Abbey Grange, Boscombe, Devil's Foot, Veiled Lodger.* Holmes always felt that in his capacity of a private investigator he had the right to determine whether or not the "murderer" was ethically justified. If he decided an action was justified, he did not stand in the way of an official investigation, but neither did he make known to the police the identity of the person sought. This attitude is to be found often enough in these sixty cases to suggest that it was basic. The reader must read such cases and form an independent opinion as to the correctness of Holmes's attitude.

Five additional cases of murder, as such, were investigated, and in these Holmes reached a successful solution of the crime and identified the murderer or murderers, but the latter escaped the immediate justice of the law. These are: *Five Orange Pips, Greek Interpreter, Musgrave Ritual, Resident Patient,* and *Wisteria Lodge.* Again, poetically it seems, all but one of the killers were later involved in fatal accidents. For example, in the *Five Orange Pips* and the *Resident Patient* the murderers were presumably drowned at sea. In the adventure of *Wisteria Lodge* they were presumably hunted down and killed at a hotel in Madrid by avengers. The killers were themselves presumably killed later by Sophy after they had abducted her, in the case of the *Greek Interpreter.* Finally, in the *Musgrave Ritual* the murderess got away and was not heard from again.

*Robbery* [ (in the broad sense) 12 cases (20%) ]: Four cases involved the theft of gems. These are: *Mazarin Stone, Six Napoleons* (in both of which the thief was caught and jailed), *Beryl Coronet,* and *Blue Carbuncle* (in both of which the thief escaped justice, but for different reasons). In all four cases Holmes recovered the jewels.

Four cases were concerned with the theft of classified documents of, or relevant to, the British Government, and consequently in these affairs Holmes was acting in the interests of his country (as he was, of course, in the *Beryl Coronet*). These four are: *Bruce-Partington Plans, His Last Bow, Second Stain,* and *Naval Treaty*. In the last of these, the thief, for reasons of secrecy, was not jailed. In the other three the thieves were apprehended. In *His Last Bow,* which took place just before World War I, much of the data supplied was tampered with by Holmes himself, in the *alias* of Altamont, a supposedly bitter anti-English Irish-American espionage agent. In all four cases the missing documents were recovered before harm had been done.

Three cases dealt with the theft of money. These are the *Red-headed League, Stockbroker's Clerk,* and *Three Garridebs*. In all three the criminals were caught and the money recovered. In the last of these an important forgery plant was also confiscated.

Finally, one case had to do with the theft of a manuscript, *i.e., Three Gables,* in which Holmes allowed the principal to go free after making amends.

*Disappearances* [6 cases (10%)]: Three were cases of abduction: *Lady Frances Carfax, Priory School,* and *Solitary Cyclist*. In all three the abducted persons were recovered and Holmes demonstrated ability by providing correct solutions. In the first the abductors escaped, but in the other two they were punished for their crime, though in different ways.

Three were cases of voluntary disappearance: *Missing Three-Quarter, Noble Bachelor,* and *Valley of Fear*. Holmes provided a successful solution in all three, finding the missing persons involved. There was no crime committed in the first two. In the last, a villain was slain in self-defense, but Holmes thought that Professor Moriarty was behind the affair. In this case, *Valley of Fear,* the missing person was later lost overboard while at sea with his wife, and although it appeared to be an accident Holmes was not convinced.

*Forgery* [1 case (1.6%)]: This is the case of the *Engineer's*

*Thumb,* one of two cases brought to the attention of Holmes by Watson, and involving a murderous assault on an innocent person. Holmes provided the correct solution, but when the police went to arrest the forgers, they had fled.

*Alleviation* [18 cases (30%)]: In this rather loose category are placed quite a few cases which have in common some form of fear or persecution, and in which Holmes was very successful in alleviating the difficulty. The clients were in several types of predicaments.

One had to do with fear of disease, specifically leprosy. In the *Blanched Soldier* Holmes unraveled the peculiar circumstances and brought in a great dermatologist to relieve the family of their worry.

One had to do with large-scale blackmailing. In *Charles Augustus Milverton* Holmes and Watson burgled the blackmailer's safe, burned its contents, witnessed his death at the hands of one of his victims, and refused to assist the police in investigating the crime. The anxieties of many people were alleviated by the death of Milverton.

Eight adventures were concerned with the fear of either physical harm or public scandal. These are: *Copper Beeches, Creeping Man, Gloria Scott, Hound of the Baskervilles, Twisted Lip, Sussex Vampire,* and *Scandal in Bohemia.* Holmes provided successful solutions in all eight cases. In the *Scandal in Bohemia* he was foiled in his attempt to gain possession of what his employer regarded as incriminating evidence, but the case was correctly solved, and the King of Bohemia realized that he was no longer in danger of a scandal. In the famous *Hound,* the murderer, and would-be murderer for at least a second time, escaped but probably met his death in the Grimpen Mire.

Three cases dealt more or less with retribution: *Crooked Man,* in which a betrayal ended years later in shock followed by accidental death; *Illustrious Client,* in which Baron Gruner got full measure for his indiscretions; *Red Circle,* in which the villain died at the hands of a hero who was praised by the Pinkerton Agency.

One report, *A Case of Identity,* does not fall readily into ordinary types. It involved a particularly mean sort of misdeed, not easily prosecuted by law. Holmes provided the correct solution and alleviated the distressed Mary Sutherland as much as he could, but the future still seemed rather difficult for her.

One other case, *Yellow Face,* was unsatisfactory from the viewpoint of detection, but although Sherlock came to the wrong conclusion, his actions indirectly provided a happy ending.

One case, *Shoscombe Old Place,* involved fear of mounting debt. Holmes provided a correct solution of the problem, but the debt was paid off, not as a consequence of his intervention, but rather of his nonintervention and a winning horse.

Finally, there are two cases in which Holmes saves an innocent person from a deliberately planned false murder charge: *Thor Bridge* and *Norwood Builder.*

In summary, out of sixty cases in which there is a public record, Holmes provided the correct solutions for fifty-nine. In several, *e.g., Scandal in Bohemia, Case of Identity, Valley of Fear,* the case is not as neatly concluded as he would have liked, but for virtually unavoidable reasons.

This is a superb record of achievement. There are not too many investigators of crime who can show a 97% record of correct solution in a twenty-three-year (?) period. If the 67%, more or less, of Sherlock's cases that are as yet unpublished were available for study, the analysis would be more complete and consequently the statistics more reliable.

*Works: Published, in Progress, or Projected: The Book of Life.* A magazine article on the science of detection (*Study in Scarlet*). Published.

*Upon the Distinction between the Ashes of the Various Tobaccos* [*Sign of Four; Boscombe*]. Published.

*Monograph upon the tracing of footsteps, with some remarks upon the uses of plaster of Paris as a preserver of impresses* [*Sign of Four*]. Published.

*The influence of a trade upon the form of the hand, with lithotypes of the hands of slaters, sailors, cork-cutters, compositors, weavers, and diamond-polishers* [*Sign of Four*]. Published. The treatises, on tobacco ashes, footprints, and the effects of a trade upon hands, at least, are being translated into French for European use by the rising French detective, Francois le Villard (*Sign of Four*).

*Monograph on the typewriter and its relation to crime* [*Case of Identity*]. Projected.

*Monograph on cryptology* [*Dancing Men*]. Published.

*Art of Detection* [*Abbey Grange*]. Projected for a single volume.

*Age of Documents* [*The Hound*]. Published.

*Monographs on the human ear* [*Cardboard Box*]. Two separate monographs, published in the *Anthropological Journal.* For the importance Holmes placed on ears, see also *Lady Frances Carfax,* in which the turning point came in a description of Shlessinger's left ear.

*Monograph on the polyphonic motets of Lassus* [*Bruce-Partington*]. In progress. Music of the Middle Ages was a hobby of Holmes, and such a paper must have been a source of great satisfaction.

*Monograph on malingering* [*Dying Detective*]. Projected.

*On the Use of Dogs in Detective Work* [*Creeping Man*]. Projected.

*Practical Handbook of Bee Culture, with Some Observations upon the Segregation of the Queen* [*Last Bow*]. Published. Last work noted so far.

*Characteristic Views and Expressions:* These are legion. The following are selected as representative of Sherlock's volatile nature, his enthusiasms and prejudices. Many other typical examples appear elsewhere in the present paper.

The first day that Sherlock and John met, the former mentioned that he had a preference for strong tobacco. Tobacco seemed to be an important adjunct at 221B Baker, and it will be recalled that Holmes wrote a monograph upon the subject of tobacco ashes, in which 140 pipe, cigar, and cigarette ashes are discussed. It will not come as a surprise that Holmes had several pronounced views on tobacco, or that some tobacco was in the toe of a slipper, or that his pre-breakfast pipe was composed, according to Watson, of "all the plugs and dottles left from his smokes of the day before" (*Engineer's Thumb*). A few expressions follow on this general subject:

1. "It is quite a three pipe problem" (*Red-headed League*).

2. Holmes solved the case by "sitting on five pillows and consuming an ounce of shag" (*Twisted Lip*).

3. Holmes wanted Watson to close the window to prevent all

of the tobacco smoke from leaving, since he felt that a concentrated atmosphere aided in concentration of thought (*The Hound*).

Then there are a number of ideas on detection that should prove interesting and useful. A few of these follow:

4. "Nothing has more individuality [than pipes] save perhaps watches and bootlaces" (*Yellow Face*).

5. Holmes told Watson to look first at the hands, then the cuffs, trouser-knees, and boots for data on the individual (*Creeping Man*).

6. Holmes to Watson: "Here is my lens. You know my methods" (*Blue Carbuncle*).

7. Holmes told Watson to send for a hansom but to take neither the "first nor the second" (*Final Problem*).

8. Holmes warns Watson of the danger of too much reliance on circumstantial evidence (*Boscombe*).

9. Holmes fasted well (*Dying Detective* and *Mazarin Stone*), and in the latter case felt that starvation aided his thought, just as earlier he favored a concentrated atmosphere of tobacco. Hence, he generalized "Faculties become refined when you starve them" (*Mazarin Stone*).

10. When Dr. Sterndale noted that he saw no one following him, Holmes replied, "That is what you may expect to see when I follow you" (*Devil's Foot*). It will be remembered that Dr. Sterndale was an experienced African hunter and explorer, used to following big game, and wary of being followed in turn.

The three following views are among Sherlock's most trusted, and he repeats them in substance in different cases.

11. "It is of the highest importance in the art of detection to be able to recognize, out of a number of facts, which are incidental and which vital. Otherwise your energy and attention must be dissipated instead of being concentrated" (*Reigate Puzzle*).

12. "I have no data. It is a capital mistake to theorize before one has data" (*Scandal in Bohemia*). Variations on this point of view will be noted in *Second Stain, Valley of Fear,* and *Wisteria Lodge.*

13. To Watson: "How often have I said to you that when you have eliminated the impossible, whatever remains, *however improbable,* must be the truth?" (*Sign of Four*), and re-

phrased in *Bruce-Partington* and *Beryl Coronet.*

Holmes did not like to leave his quarters, especially between cases or during office hours, if there were any. He was not fond of leaving England in later years, after his reputation had become international. The two following instances bear this out.

14. Watson and Holmes took a walk in fine weather and missed a client. "So much for afternoon walks!" (*Yellow Face*).

15. Holmes felt that he could not leave London while Abrahams was in terror of his life. Moreover, Scotland Yard was lonely when he was away, and "it causes an unhealthy excitement among the criminal classes" (*Lady Frances Carfax*).

At times some of Holmes' views do not properly mesh:

16. "As a rule . . . , the more bizarre a thing is, the less mysterious it proves to be" (*Red-headed League*).

17. Yet, "The more outré and grotesque an incident is, the more carefully it deserves to be examined. . . ." (*The Hound*).

The sardonic remarks, however, are consistently pointed.

18. Holmes comments that "it is a remarkable cow which walks, canters, and gallops" (*Priory School*).

19. "Excellent!" cried Mr. Acton.

"But very superficial," said Holmes (*Reigate Puzzle*).

20. "Excellent!" I [Watson] cried.

"Elementary," said he (*Crooked Man*).

21. Mrs. Hudson: "When will you be pleased to dine, Mr. Holmes?"

"Seven-thirty, the day after to-morrow" (*Mazarin Stone*).

22. Lord St. Simon: "I am afraid it will take wiser heads than yours or mine. . . ."

Holmes: "It is very good of Lord St. Simon to honour my head by putting it on a level with his own . . ." (*Noble Bachelor*).

23. After the energetic capture of Colonel Sebastian Moran: " 'Ah, Colonel!' said Holmes, arranging his rumpled collar. ' "Journeys end in lovers' meetings," as the old play says. I don't think I have had the pleasure of seeing you since you favoured me with those attentions as I lay on the ledge above the Reichenbach Fall' " (*Empty House*).

Then there are the views of Holmes on people with whom he associated or upon whom he had accumulated information. Since he was an accurate judge of character, such commentaries are instructive.

24. Holmes said of Watson that he was "my Boswell" (*Scandal in Bohemia*).

25. He considered Charles Augustus Milverton "the worst man in London" (*Milverton*).

26. Of Professor Moriarty, he was "the Napoleon of crime" (*Final Problem*). Earlier, Holmes had been frustrated by Moriarty's machinations, but he had faith in his own powers and said, "I don't say that he can't be beat. But you must give me time . . ." (*Valley of Fear*).

27. In his index Holmes had marked Colonel Sebastian Moran as the second most dangerous man in London. After Moriarty's death, Moran advanced. Holmes then referred to him as "the most cunning and dangerous criminal in London" (*Empty House*).

28. Of John Clay, Holmes said that he was the fourth smartest man in London (*Red-headed League*).

29. He felt that Jack Stapleton, so-called, was also one of the most dangerous and cunning of criminals (*The Hound*).

30. Of Inspector Tobias Gregson, he was the "smartest of the Scotland Yarders" (*Study in Scarlet*).

31. Of Inspector G. Lestrade, he was the "best of the professionals" (*The Hound*). Holmes felt that although Lestrade was "devoid of reason," he had the tenacity of a bulldog, and this had brought him to the top at Scotland Yard (*Cardboard Box*). At their best, though, both officials were merely "the pick of a bad lot" (*Study in Scarlet*).

32. Holmes thought that the strangest case he had ever handled was the Cornish horror (*Devil's Foot*).

*Published Cases Noted:* Every now and then Holmes would hark back to a former case to illustrate a point or relive a memory. Since Watson was usually responsible for the recording of such matters, his published account must be followed:

(1) In *Copper Beeches: Scandal in Bohemia, A Case of Identity, Man with the Twisted Lip,* and *Noble Bachelor* were mentioned; (2) in

*Stock-broker's Clerk,* the *Sign of Four* is recalled; (3) in the early *Musgrave Ritual,* the still earlier *Gloria Scott* case is mentioned; (4) in the *Naval Treaty,* the case of the *Speckled Band* is noted; (5) in *Wisteria Lodge,* both the *Five Orange Pips* and the *Red-headed League* are recalled; (6) in the *Cardboard Box,* both the *Study in Scarlet* and the *Sign of Four* are cited; and (7) in the *Sussex Vampire,* the early *Gloria Scott* is thought of.

*Gifts and Honors from Admirers:* Sherlock received a gold snuffbox with an amethyst in the lid from the King of Bohemia, although he had asked only for the photograph of Irene Adler (*Scandal in Bohemia*), and he also was sent a fine ring for clearing up a matter for the ruling family in Holland (*Case of Identity*). Moreover, he received an emerald tie-pin from a friend at Windsor for his recovery of the stolen submarine plans by which the Navy set such store (*Bruce-Partington*). In addition, Holmes received a letter from the French President, as well as the Order of the Legion of Honour, for tracking down Huret the Boulevard assassin (*Pince-Nez*). Finally, Sherlock refused a knighthood in June, 1903 (*Garridebs*).

*Retirement:* Sherlock Holmes retired to a place on the southern slopes of the downs in Sussex. Although relatively isolated, his house was half a mile from the coaching school of which Harold Stackhurst was headmaster. It commanded a view of the Channel and was not too far from the small village of Fulworth, Sussex. Here he meditated and tended his bees (cf. Works), and it was from here that he consented to John Watson's reporting to the public the formerly guarded case of the *Second Stain.* And it was on the wave-swept Channel coast that the tragic case of the *Lion's Mane* was investigated by Holmes in July, 1907.

Well after becoming established here, Holmes was asked once more to take up an active role. He assented when both the Foreign Minister and the Premier asked him to penetrate and expose the espionage net that was being woven through the British defense perimeter. This would have been no small task for a young man, and for Holmes it must have presented a real hardship. First he had to be taken into the camp of the enemy. His start was far away, in the United States.

This initial effort was made some two years before actual

contact with German espionage. Holmes began in Chicago, then moved on to Buffalo, where he joined an Irish secret society. Later he gave the constabulary of Skibbareen serious trouble and so caught the glance of Von Bork, kingpin of German espionage in England. The case ended brilliantly. Holmes was joined by Watson, briefly, at the climax, and Von Bork was arrested in August, 1914, with his files. This final triumph is related in *His Last Bow, q.v.*

HOLY LAND. Dr. Shlessinger was preparing a map of the area (*Carfax*).

HOLY PETERS. Australian rascal. He and his "wife" made a business of preying on lonely ladies. *Alias* Dr. Shlessinger. His left ear was a distinguishing feature (*Lady Frances Carfax*).

*Holy War, The.* A book offered for sale by a disguised **H** to **W** (*Empty House*).

*Homer,* POPE'S. One odd volume of edition stolen from Acton's library in Surrey near Reigate (*Reigate Puzzle*).

HOOD, GENERAL. Elias Openshaw rose to the rank of colonel under him (*Five Orange Pips*).

HOOKAH. T. Sholto smoked this kind of pipe (*Sign of Four*).

HOPE, JEFFERSON. Murderer of Drebber and of Stangerson. He was handcuffed by **H** at the Baker Street chambers by a ruse (cf. Wiggins and handcuffs) and confessed to the murders. Drebber had forced a girl in America to marry him (cf. Watson, John H.) that Hope was to have married. Drebber and Stangerson had then murdered both this girl and her father and fled to Europe. Hope followed them (St. Petersburg, Paris, Copenhagen, London) seeking revenge. A poor man, Hope took up cab-driving in London, waylaid Drebber in an empty house at 3 Lauriston Gardens, and forced him to choose a pill from two in a box (cf. poison; York College). Drebber chose incorrectly and died of poisoning. Hope later climbed into the hotel window of Stangerson's room and offered him the same choice. Stangerson attacked Hope, and the latter killed him by knife. Hope died the night after his capture of a burst aortic aneurism (*Study in Scarlet*).

HOPE, LADY HILDA TRELAWNEY. She called on **H**, and later **H** returned the call. He prevailed, and all was well with her husband's political future (*Second Stain*).

HOPE, RIGHT HONOURABLE TRELAWNEY. Secretary for European Affairs. He came with Lord Bellinger for consultation (*Second Stain*).

HOPE TOWN. On the slope of Mount Harriet on Blair Island, the largest of the Andaman Islands, where Jonathan Small was imprisoned (*Sign of Four*).

HOPKINS, EZEKIAH. Supposititious American millionaire and founder of the *Red-headed League*.

HOPKINS, STANLEY. Thirty-year-old police inspector whom **H** regarded with high hopes. There was a professed mutual admiration. Stanley arrested J. H. Neligan. Later he came to breakfast with **H** and **W** and was able to arrest the man he should have been looking for, Patrick Cairns, who was supplied by **H** (*Black Peter*). Came to consult **H** on the affair at Yoxley Old Place, and after **H** investigated, Stanley could place a complete solution to his credit (*Pince-Nez*). Stanley advised Cyril Overton to consult **H** (*Three-Quarter*). Stanley asked for **H** (*Abbey Grange*).

HORACE. Mentioned with approval by **H** (*Case of Identity*). Cf. Huxtable (*Priory School*).

HORNER, JOHN. Plumber accused of taking the blue carbuncle from Countess of Morcar's rooms at Hotel Cosmopolitan. **H** cleared him (*Blue Carbuncle*).

HORSHAM. John Openshaw came from here to see **H** (*Five Orange Pips*). Town in Sussex, north of Lamberley (*Vampire*).

HORSOM, DR. No. 13 Firbank Villas. He certified the death of Rose Spender, ascribing it to senile decay (*Lady Frances Carfax*).

HOTEL. See inns and hotels.

HOTEL COSMOPOLITAN. Where the blue carbuncle was lost (*Blue Carbuncle*).

HOTEL DIRECTORY. **H** got a list of twenty-three hotels in the Charing Cross area for young Cartwright to visit (*The Hound*).

HOTEL DULONG. Lyons. **H** was ill here and wired for **W** (*Reigate Puzzle*).

HOTEL DU LOUVRE. Paris. Colonel Walter told **H** that he could reach Hugo Oberstein here—so **H** dictated a letter for him to sign (*Bruce-Partington*).

HOTEL ESCURIAL. Madrid. Marquess of Montalva and his secretary, Signor Rulli, were killed here (*Wisteria Lodge*).

HOTEL NATIONAL. Lausanne. M. Moser was the manager. Jules Vibart, one of the headwaiters, was engaged to Marie Devine, maid to *Lady Frances Carfax*.

HOTTENTOT. See Bushman.

"HOTSPUR." Brig that picked up Armitage and Evans and took them to Australia (*Gloria Scott*).

HOUND. See dog.

HOUND OF THE BASKERVILLES, THE. *Circa* 1889. (The year of the case tentatively is fixed at 1889 in October, since the visitor's stick was dated 1884, **H** said that this was five years ago, and **W**'s reports are dated October). A mythical beast with blazing eyes was said to be the cause of Hugo Baskerville's death. Jack Stapleton, *alias* Mr. Vandeleur, put a phosphorus preparation on the eye-margins and chops of a large hound which frightened Charles Baskerville and had a part in his death. When the trick was tried on Henry Baskerville, **H** intervened, and the criminal presumably dies in Grimpen Mire.

HOUNDSDITCH. The address here, No. 13 Duncan Street, was false (*Study in Scarlet*).

HOUSES OF PARLIAMENT. **H** and **W** passed en route to Shlessinger's house in Poultney Square (*Lady Frances Carfax*).

HOWELLS, RACHEL. Second housemaid at Hurlstone Manor House and engaged to Brunton. She had brain fever when he paid attentions to Janet Tregellis, then murdered Brunton and escaped (*Musgrave Ritual*).

HOWE STREET. The house here, as described in the *Daily Gazette,* was in sight of Mrs. Warren's house in Great Orme Street (*Red Circle*).

HUDSON. He visited Trevor, Senior, in Norfolk and Beddoes in Hampshire. Hudson was saved by Armitage and Evans but lived to blackmail them (*Gloria Scott*).

HUDSON, MORSE. A shop selling pictures and statues, in Kennington Road. Morse bought three cheap plaster busts of Napoleon from his supplier, Gelder & Company, Stepney. He sold two to Dr. Barnicot, and the third bust was smashed right on his counter (*Six Napoleons*).

HUDSON, MRS. Landlady of **H** and **W** at 221B Baker Street (rooms inspected in *Study in Scarlet,* and Mrs. Hudson is mentioned first in *Sign of Four;* nevertheless, see the inexplicable Mrs. Turner in *Scandal in Bohemia*). **H** facetiously noted that Mrs. Hudson should examine the crop of the woodcock that **H** and **W** were having for dinner (*Blue Carbuncle*). She wakened **H** early (*Speckled Band*). She served a Scotch breakfast (*Naval Treaty*). She became hysterical when **H** returned alive and well (*Empty House*). She brought in the cablegram (*Dancing Men*). **H, W,** and Stanley Hopkins were given breakfast by her (*Black Peter*). She ushered in Cecil Barker, with cable from Ivy Douglas (*Valley of Fear*). She ushered in Inspector Gregson and Inspector Baynes (*Wisteria Lodge*). She came to home of

W, in his second year of married life, to tell **W** that **H** was dying (*Dying Detective*). **H** wired her from the Continent (*Lady Frances Carfax*). **H** told Billy to tell Mrs. Hudson to send up dinner for **W** and himself (*Mazarin Stone*). She brought in John Garrideb's card (*Garridebs*).

HUDSON STREET. Aldershot. Mrs. James Barclay and Miss Morrison were coming from the Watt Street Chapel and saw Henry Wood after thirty years (*Crooked Man*).

HUGUENOT. Charles Gorot was of this extraction (*Naval Treaty*).

"HUGUENOTS, LES." **H** had a box for it, and **H** and **W** were to celebrate after the long Baskerville case (*The Hound*).

HUNGARY. Hungarian vampires were listed in **H's** index under "V" (*Vampire*). **H** and **W** received a newspaper from Buda-Pesth (*Greek Interpreter*).

HUNTER, NED. One of three boys working in King's Pyland training stable. Ned's curried mutton was drugged with opium (*Silver Blaze*).

HUNTER, VIOLET. Consulted **H** as to whether she should accept a position as governess. Later she became the head of a private school at Walsall (*Copper Beeches*).

*HURET, THE BOULEVARD ASSASSIN. His tracking down and arrest by **H** won **H** an autograph letter from the French President and the Order of the Legion of Honour (*Pince-Nez*). One is at a loss to understand why **W** has not given this case to the public.

HURLINGHAM. Baron Gruner played polo here (*Illustrious Client*).

HURLSTONE MANOR HOUSE. Oldest inhabited building in Sussex (*Musgrave Ritual*).

HUXTABLE'S *Sidelights on Horace*. The author was headmaster of the *Priory School*.

HUXTABLE, THORNEYCROFT, M. A., PH.D. Dr. Huxtable told **H** and **W** of the disappearance of the Duke of Holdernesse' son and of the Duke's offer of £6000 for data on his son's whereabouts and the person or persons responsible for his abduction. **H** saved his school from scandal and got the reward (*Priory School*).

HYAMS. He was tailor for Mr. Oldacre (*Norwood Builder*).

HYDE PARK. Lady St. Simon (*née* Doran) walked here with Flora Millar (*Noble Bachelor*).

HYNES, MR. HYNES. Of Purdey Place, near Oxshott. It was a large house but not the right one (*Wisteria Lodge*).

# I

ICHTHYOSIS. A pseudo-leprosy that Sir James Saunders told Colonel Emsworth that his son, Godfrey, had contracted. It was not leprosy (*Blanched Soldier*).

IDENTITY, CASE OF. Impersonation of a Mr. Hosmer Angel, a supposititious lover, by Mr. Windibank, stepfather of Mary Sutherland. Foiled by **H**.

ILLUSTRIOUS CLIENT, ADVENTURE OF THE. September 3, 1902. At request of Sir James Damery, **H** was able to prevent Violet de Merville from marrying Baron Gruner.

IMPERIAL YEOMANRY. James M. Dodd was a member in the Boer War (*Blanched Soldier*).

INDIA. Cf. Watson for his experiences here (*Study in Scarlet*). Cf. Jonathan Small for his experiences here (*Sign of Four*). The dread pips were mailed to Elias Openshaw from here (*Five Orange Pips*). Dr. Roylott practiced in Calcutta and owned a swamp adder, "the deadliest snake in India" (*Speckled Band*). Sergeant Barclay and Corporal Wood fought in the Mutiny and were in the old 117th (*Crooked Man*). **W** tried to interest Percy Phelps in this country (*Naval Treaty*).

*"INDIAN ARMY." This is painted on a box of notes, with **W's** name, in Cox & Co. bank. There are probably several cases here, stuffed away and forgotten (*Thor Bridge*).

INDIAN *lunkah*. Its ashes are reported upon in **H's** monograph. Cf. Holmes, Sherlock, under Works.

INNER TEMPLE. Godfrey Norton practiced law here (*Scandal in Bohemia*).

INNS, HOTELS, AND BOARDING-HOUSES (London area unless otherwise noted)

- Alpha Inn
- Anerly Arms (in Norwood)
- Bar of Gold (this was an opium dive, but it is probable that strong beverages were also for sale, as well as lodgings for rent).
- Bentley's Hotel
- Black Swan (in Winchester)
- Brambletye Hotel (in Sussex)
- Bull, The (in Surrey)

Charing Cross Hotel
Charpentier's, Madame, Boarding-house
Chequers, The (inn at Camford)
Chequers, The (inn at Lamberley)
Claridge's Hotel
Crown Inn
Dacre Hotel
Eagle Commercial Hotel (at Tunbridge Wells)
Englischer Hof (at Baden)
Englischer Hof (at Meiringen)
Fighting Cock, The (near Mackleton)
Grand Hotel
Green Dragon Inn (at Crendall)
Grosvenor Hotel
Halliday's Private Hotel
Hereford Arms (near Ross)
Hotel Cosmopolitan
Hotel Dulong (Lyons)
Hotel du Louvre (Paris)
Hotel Escurial (Madrid)
Hotel National (Lausanne)
Langham Hotel
Mexborough Private Hotel
Northumberland Hotel
Railway Arms (at Little Purlington)
Red Bull Inn (near Mackleton)
St. Pancras Hotel
Westville Arms (in Sussex)

INTERLAKEN. **H** and **W** en route from London to Meiringen (*Final Problem*).

IONIDES. He made special cigarettes for Professor Coram (*Pince-Nez*).

IRIS. Duke of Balmoral's horse, entered in the Wessex Cup race (*Silver Blaze*).

IRISH-AMERICAN. Altamont was one, and a bitter anti-English espionage agent, according to Von Bork. *Alias* for Sherlock Holmes (*Last Bow*).

IRISH CIVIL WAR. According to Von Herling, it was stirred up by German agents (*Last Bow*).

ISLE OF DOGS. As for pool.

ISLE OF WIGHT. As for Goodwins (*Five Orange Pips*).

ITALIAN QUARTER. London. Inspector Hill knew his way around here (*Six Napoleons*).

ITALY. In Posilippo, near Naples, Augusto Barelli and his daughter lived, as well as Gennaro Lucca, the future husband of Augusto's daughter (*Red Circle*). Douglas Maberley was here (*Three Gables*) and wrote in novel form of his relations with Isadora Klein. Holmes stopped in Florence (*Final Problem*).

"IT TOOK LONGER, BEING OUT OF THE ORDINARY." The coffin ordered by the Shlessingers was the item being discussed with the undertaker in Kennington Road. **H** solved the riddle just in time to save Lady Frances Carfax.

IVY LANE. The Commissionaire lived at No. 16 in the Brixton area (*Naval Treaty*).

"I WILL BE AT THOR BRIDGE AT NINE O'CLOCK." This was the note written by Grace Dunbar to Mrs. Gibson (*Thor Bridge*).

# J

J.A. These were the initials that Trevor, Senior, tried to forget. They stood for James Armitage, his real name (*Gloria Scott*).

JACK. The youngest son of Mr. & Mrs. Mordecai Smith. **H** gave Jack two shillings (*Sign of Four*).

JACK. Effie called her husband by this name, although he was Grant Munro (*Yellow Face*).

JACK. Edith Presbury called Trevor Bennett by this name when she rushed into **H's** chambers at 221B Baker Street (*Creeping Man*).

JACKSON, DR. He took over **W's** practice while **H** and **W** went to Aldershot (*Crooked Man*).

JACKSON, GENERAL. Elias Openshaw fought in his command (*Five Orange Pips*).

JACOBS. Butler to Trelawney Hope (*Second Stain*).

JACOBSON'S YARD. **H** directed the police launch to go to the Tower and stop opposite here, where the "Aurora" was waiting (*Sign of Four*).

JAMES. Son of Grimpen's postmaster. He was sent to deliver the wire to Barrymore. Instead, he gave it to Mrs. Barrymore, an error which, to **H**, was an unhappy circumstance (*The Hound*).

JAMES, JACK. One of Von Bork's espionage agents, but he was in jail in Portland (*Last Bow*).

JAPAN. Trevor, Senior, had been in this country (*Gloria Scott*).

JEM. Nickname for John Ryder (*Blue Carbuncle*).

JEWS, THE. Sir Robert Norbertson, heavily in debt to them, was holding off his creditors until after the Derby—his horse, Shoscombe Prince, had to win (*Shoscombe*).

JEZAIL BULLET. **W** received one in an Afghan campaign (*Study in Scarlet*). Much later, "a few weeks" before his marriage, **W** was in pain from this wound (*Noble Bachelor*).

J.H. These were the initials of Joseph Harrison (*Naval Treaty*).

"J.H. IS IN EUROPE." This telegram was found by Lestrade in the pocket of murdered Joseph Stangerson. Cf. Hope (*Study in Scarlet*).

J.H.N. 1883. John Hopley Neligan, Senior, banker, who started his flight in a boat bound for Norway (*Black Peter*).

JIM. Eldest son of the Mordecai Smiths; helped his father get the "Aurora" ready for her run down the Thames (*Sign of Four*).

JOHANNESBURG. South Africa. Jack Woodley was known here (*Solitary Cyclist*).

JOHN. Butler to Dr. Leslie Armstrong (*Three-Quarter*).

JOHN BULL, MR. Von Herling felt that this was the week of destiny for England: the English could fight now with allies, or later alone (*Last Bow*).

JOHN O'GROATS. **H** felt that a draghound would follow an aniseed trail from Cambridge to here (*Three-Quarter*).

JOHNSON. He was on the Oxford rugby team (*Three-Quarter*).

JOHNSON, SHINWELL. Formerly a dangerous villain. After two terms at Parkhurst, he reformed and became an ally of **H.** Porky was his nickname. He produced Kitty Winters at the critical moment (*Illustrious Client*).

JOHNSON, SIDNEY. Senior clerk at Woolwich Arsenal. He had one of the two keys to the safe where the submarine plans were kept. Sir James Walter had the other key (*Bruce-Partington*).

JOHNSON, THEOPHILUS. Coal operator from Newcastle and well known to the Northumberland Hotel (*The Hound*).

JOHN, SPENCER. See Spencer-John.

JONES, ATHELNEY. Detective mentioned in opening pages of the *Sign of Four,* along with Gregson and Lestrade. At the suggestion of **H,** he was called in by Thaddeus Sholto to investigate the murder of his twin-brother Bartholomew Sholto. He arrested Thaddeus, Mrs. Bernstone, McMurdo, and Lal Rao. Later he released Thaddeus and Mrs. Bernstone (as reported in the *Standard*), and he sought help from **H. H** enabled him to capture Jonathan Small (*Sign of Four*).

JONES, PETER. Official police agent of Scotland Yard. As a consequence of the work of **H,** he was able to capture John Clay and Duncan Ross (*Red-headed League*).

JOSEF, FRANZ. Altamont (*alias* for **H**) had been assured by Von Bork that the Tokay was from his [Franz Josef's] special cellar in the Schoenbrunn Palace (*Last Bow*).

*Journal de Genève.* Carried a short account of **H** vs. Moriarty on May 6, 1891 (*Final Problem*).

JUBILEE. In London. Mr. Cubitt attended the festivities (*Dancing Men*).

JUNKER. Von Bork felt that a bitter Irish-American, such as Altamont, was more anti-British than a pan-Germanic Junker (*Last Bow*).

JUPITER. Mycroft Holmes, in his descent upon 221B Baker Street, is so called by **H** (*Bruce-Partington*).

# K

KAISER, THE. He had a devoted espionage agent in Von Bork (*Last Bow*).

KANSAS. "John Garrideb" lived here, in Moorville (*Garridebs*).

KEMP, WILSON. An associate of Harold Latimer. Probably Sophy avenged her presumed brother, Paul Kratides (*Greek Interpreter*).

KENNINGTON LANE. H, W, and Toby on trail of the murderers of Bartholomew Sholto (*Sign of Four*).

KENNINGTON PARK GATE. See Rance (*Study in Scarlet*).

KENNINGTON ROAD. Morse Hudson's shop was here, and Dr. Barnicot lived here (*Six Napoleons*). Philip Green followed Mrs. Shlessinger to Stimson & Co., undertakers, here (*Lady Frances Carfax*).

KENSINGTON. The John Watsons lived here after their marriage (*Red-headed League*). Mr. Harold Latimer, who wanted Mr. Melas as an interpreter, said he lived here (*Greek Interpreter*). W sold his practice here to Dr. Verner (*Norwood Builder*). Mr. Harker lived at 131 Pitt Street in this area (*Six Napoleons*). Mr. Melville lived at Albemarle Mansion (*Wisteria Lodge*). Hugo Oberstein lived at 13 Caulfield Gardens (*Bruce-Partington*). Lower Burke Street was on the area's fringe (*Dying Detective*).

KENT. As for Surrey (*Sign of Four*). Neville St. Clair lived at the Cedars, near Lee (*Twisted Lip*). W watched his luggage disappear aboard the Continental Express (*Final Problem*). Yoxley Old Place was seven miles from Chatham (*Pince-Nez*). H and W came down for the investigation of the Brackenstall murder (*Abbey Grange*).

KENT, MR. Surgeon attending Godfrey Emsworth. He was glad of a consultation with Sir James Saunders (*Blanched Soldier*).

KESWICK. A London paperhanger whose address, 13 Duncan Street, Houndsditch, was falsely given to a four-wheeler to avoid pursuit by H (*Study in Scarlet*).

KHALIFA. **H** visited him at Khartoum (*Empty House*).

KHAN, ABDULLAH. One of the Four. He, with Mahomet Singh, was under orders of Jonathan Small at Agra Fort (*Sign of Four*).

KILBURN. Maudsley lived in area (*Blue Carbuncle*).

KIMBERLEY. South Africa. Roaring Jack Woodley was known here (*Solitary Cyclist*).

KING EDWARD STREET. William Morris, *alias* Duncan Ross, gave a fictitious address, No. 17, on this street near St. Paul's (*Red-headed League*).

KING, MRS. Cook for Hilton Cubitt, who, with the housemaid, Saunders, gave the alarm (*Dancing Men*).

KING OF BOHEMIA. See Ormstein.

KING'S COLLEGE HOSPITAL. Dr. Trevelyan occupied a minor position here for a while (*Resident Patient*).

KING'S CROSS. St. Saviour's Church was nearby (*Case of Identity*).

KING'S CROSS STATION. **H** and **W** had to go to Cambridge (*Three-Quarter*).

KING'S PYLAND. Colonel Ross had his training stable here (*Silver Blaze*).

KINGSTON. Baron Gruner lived here, at Vernon Lodge (*Illustrious Client*).

KIRWAN, WILLIAM. Coachman for Mrs. Cunningham. He was murdered by his employers in Surrey (*Reigate Puzzle*).

K. K. K. Ku Klux Klan sent five orange pips with its initials on the envelope to Elias Openshaw March 10, 1883, and after his death they sent the same with a message to Joseph Openshaw January 5, 1885, and after his death they sent the same to John Openshaw in September, 1887. John met his death at their hands as well. Cf. Captain James Calhoun (*Five Orange Pips*).

KLEIN. An aged German sugar king. He married Isadora of Pernambuco, Brazil (*Three Gables*).

KLEIN, ISADORA. Former Spanish beauty, married sugar-king Klein. As his widow, she had an affair with Douglas Maberley. On its termination, she had Barney Stockdale obtain the Maberley manuscript, for she was about to marry the Duke of Lomond, and the manuscript, in novel form, exposed her as a cruel despoiler. In the end, she gave **H** a check for £5000 to give to Mary Maberley, Douglas' mother (*Three Gables*).

*KLOPMAN. The Nihilist whose murderous designs upon Count von und zu Grafenstein were foiled by **H** (*Last Bow*).

KNELLER. He painted a portrait of one of the Baskervilles (*The Hound*).

KNIGHT'S PLACE. Miles Street turns in

here. **H, W,** and Toby on trail of murderers of Bartholomew Sholto. They followed a false trail from here to Broderick & Nelson's timber yard (*q.v.*); returned here and picked up the real trail. Cf. Broad Street (*Sign of Four*).

KRATIDES, PAUL. From Athens. Murdered by Harold Latimer and Wilson Kemp. See Sophy. (*Greek Interpreter*).

# L

Laburnum Lodge. Josiah Brown lived here (*Six Napoleons*).

Laburnum Vale. Laburnum Lodge was here (*Six Napoleons*).

Lachine. Villa of Colonel and Mrs. Barclay at Aldershot (*Crooked Man*).

Lady Day. Dr. Trevelyan moved into his Brook Street quarters on this day (*Resident Patient*).

LADY FRANCES CARFAX, DISAPPEARANCE OF. She fell into the hands of the Shlessingers, was nearly murdered, but was saved by **H.**

Lafter Hall. In Devon, near Baskerville Hall. Residence of Mr. Frankland (*The Hound*).

"La Jeune Fille À l'Agneau." See Greuze.

Lal Chowdar. Old servant, subsequently deceased, who admitted Captain Morstan to the home of Major John Sholto. The captain had come to claim his share of the Agra Treasure. Lal and the major disposed of the captain's body and the treasure (*Sign of Four*).

Lal Rao. Indian butler of Bartholomew Sholto. He was arrested by Athelney Jones as an accessory to the murder of Bartholomew (*Sign of Four*).

lama, head. **H** spent several days with him (*Empty House*).

Lamberley. In Sussex, south of Horsham (*Vampire*).

Lambeth. Sherman the taxidermist lived here at No. 3 Pinchin Lane (*Sign of Four*).

Lancaster Gate. Aloysius Doran took a furnished house here (*Noble Bachelor*).

Lancaster, James. **H** told him that the berth had been filled and gave him half a sovereign. He was too little a man (*Black Peter*).

*Lancet*. **H** thought that Mr. Kent might have been reading this journal rather than the *Spectator* (*Blanched Soldier*).

Langham Hotel. London. From this hotel, Captain Morstan telegraphed his daughter, Mary, to meet him December 3, 1878 (*Sign of Four*). Count Von Kramm, pseudonym of Ormstein, King of Bohemia, stayed here (*Scandal in Bohemia*). Philip Green stayed here (*Lady Frances Carfax*).

Langmere. In the Broads, Norfolk.

The Trevors lived nearby (*Gloria Scott*).

LANGUR. Largest and most human-like of the climbing monkeys. It was the best that Lowenstein could provide at the time (*Creeping Man*).

LANNER, INSPECTOR. In charge of the Blessington suicide, as he saw it. It was murder, as **H** demonstrated (*Resident Patient*).

LARK HALL LANE. Four-wheeler carrying **H**, **W**, and Mary Morstan en route to Thaddeus Sholto (*Sign of Four*).

LA ROTHIÈRE, LOUIS. One of three secret agents in London capable of such a large-scale and important transaction. The other two agents were Oberstein and Lucas (*Second Stain*). One of three secret agents in London capable of such a transaction. At *this* time the others were Oberstein and Meyer. La Rothière lived in Campden Mansions, Notting Hill (*Bruce-Partington*). Lucas, it will be remembered, was eliminated from the listing, and presumably Meyer was an earlier (or later?) espionage agent.

LASSUS. Cf. polyphonic motets of; also Holmes, Sherlock, under Works.

LATIMER, HAROLD. He wanted Mr. Melas as an interpreter. Probably Sophy avenged her presumed brother, Paul Kratides (*Greek Interpreter*).

LATIMER'S. On Oxford Street. **W** bought boots here (*Lady Frances Carfax*).

*LAUDER. **H** felt sure of his belief that Colonel Sebastian Moran had something to do with the death of Mrs. Stewart of this place in 1887. **W** did not remember the case (*Empty House*).

LAURISTON GARDENS. No. 3 was the scene of Drebber's murder (*Study in Scarlet*).

LAUSANNE. **W** carried on investigation at Hotel National here (*Lady Frances Carfax*).

LEADENHALL STREET. Hosmer Angel was supposed to be a cashier in an office here (*Case of Identity*).

LEATHERHEAD. Helen Stoner in a dog-cart from the Crown Inn to here, en route to consult **H**. Later, **H** and **W** from Waterloo Station to here, to help Helen. They succeeded (*Speckled Band*).

LEBANON. Town in Pennsylvania where Ezekiah Hopkins was said to have been at home (*Red-headed League*).

LE BRUN. French agent who was crippled in Montmartre district of Paris by Apaches. Baron Gruner recalled the incident to **H**. This was prior to **H's** severe beating by ruffians near the Café Royal (*Illustrious Client*).

LECOQ. **H** thought that he was a "miserable bungler." **W** felt that there was a touch of professional jealousy in **H** (*Study in Scarlet*).

LEE. Kent. Neville St. Clair lived near the town (*Twisted Lip*), and John Scott Eccles lived at Popham House (*Wisteria Lodge*).

LEE, GENERAL R. E. His surrender caused Elias Openshaw to return to his Florida plantation (*Five Orange Pips*).

*LEECH, RED. Its repulsive story is in one of **W's** manuscript volumes for 1894. Not yet published (*Pince-Nez*).

LEEDS *Mercury*. Once when he was young, **H** confessed that he had confused this paper's type with that of the *Western Morning News* (*The Hound*).

LEFEVRE OF MONTPELLIER. As for Von Bischoff, *q.v.*

LEGION OF HONOUR. To **H** in 1894 for arrest of Huret (*Pince-Nez*).

LEICESTER. Mr. Hargrave was reported from here (*Valley of Fear*).

LEONARDO. The strong man in the Ronder circus. He murdered his boss, Ronder, put the blame on Sahara King, and was shielded by Ronder's wife for some seven years, then drowned at Margate. Mrs. Ronder confessed their crime to **H** and **W** after Leonardo's death (*Veiled Lodger*).

LEPER HOSPITAL. A few miles from Buffelsspruit in South Africa. Godfrey Emsworth, wounded, spent the night here (*Blanched Soldier*).

LEPIDOPTERA. Jack Stapleton had a fine collection of moths and butterflies, and **H** was told at the British Museum (of Natural History) that a species of Yorkshire moth had been described by Stapleton (*The Hound*).

LEPROSY. Godfrey Emsworth was sequestered, but Sir James Saunders, on **H's** intervention, found that Godfrey was suffering from ichthyosis instead (*Blanched Soldier*).

LESTRADE, G. Scotland Yard inspector. Called at 221B Baker Street after **H** and **W** had been there for about a week. "Little, sallow, rat-faced, dark-eyed," as **W** describes him. Lestrade needed advice on a forgery case. He was jealous of Inspector Gregson. Lestrade reported the death of Joseph Stangerson and his own failure in the case to **H** and **W** and asked **H** for help (*Study in Scarlet*). Retained in the *Boscombe Valley Mystery,* and he asked **H** for help with the case. Retained in the *Noble Bachelor*. On instructions by **H,** he arrested Colonel Moran (*Empty House*). Arrested Mr. McFarlane for murder of Jonas Oldacre (*Norwood Builder*). **H** would not investigate the murder of *Charles Augustus Milverton,* although Lestrade asked him to do so. He consulted **H** on the breaking of plaster busts of Napoleon (*Six Napoleons*). He confided in **H** (*Second Stain*). He was on the way to Coombe Tracy with an unsigned warrant on the advice of **H** (*The Hound*). He wanted to see **H** (*Cardboard Box*). Lestrade and Mycroft Holmes came over to see **H** about Cadogan West (*Bruce-Partington*). He was sought for by **H** and, the warrant being late in arriving, the Shlessingers escaped (*Lady Frances Carfax*). He consulted **H** and found out that "John Garrideb" was "Killer" Evans (*Garridebs*).

LESURIER, MADAME. Bond Street milliner who did business with William Derbyshire (*Silver Blaze*).

LETURIER. In Montpellier. Cf. Dolsky for a similar reference.

LEUK. **H** and **W** left the Rhone Valley, and by way of the Gemmi Pass and Interlaken they came to Meiringen (*Final Problem*).

LEVERSTOKE, LORD. His son was at the *Priory School.*

LEVERTON, MR. A. American detective sent by Pinkerton Detective Agency. He was on the investigation of the case with Inspector Gregson. He was on the trail of Gorgiano and was pleased when Gennaro Lucca killed Gorgiano (*Red Circle*).

LE VILLARD, FRANCOIS. He was coming to the fore in French detective service. He consulted **H**, and the latter thought highly of him, although he was deficient in a wide range of exact knowledge. He was translating some works of **H** into the French (*Sign of Four*).

LEWES. Constable Anderson would hear from here, if he did not handle the McPherson death properly—so **H** told him how to start on the case (*Lion's Mane*).

LEWIS, SIR GEORGE. Sir James Damery arranged matters with him in the Hammerford Will Case (*Illustrious Client*).

LEWISHAM. Josiah Amberley retired at 61 from junior partnership of Brickfall & Amberley and bought a house here. At **H's** insistence, **W** went to investigate the Amberley-Ernest double disappearance (*Retired Colourman*).

LEWISHAM GANG. The Randalls, a father and two sons, composed this group. Inspector Hopkins thought that they had killed Sir Eustace (*Abbey Grange*).

LEXINGTON, MRS. Housekeeper of Mr. Oldacre. She had drawn the night constable's attention to McFarlane's thumb print. **H** thought that she was involved in Mr. Oldacre's disappearance (*Norwood Builder*).

LHASSA, TIBET. **H** was here for some days with the head lama (*Empty House*).

*Lieder*. See Mendelssohn.

LIME STREET. Van Seddar was here (*Mazarin Stone*).

LINCOLN, ABRAHAM. **W** likened J. Neil Gibson to an "Abraham Lincoln" keyed to base uses instead of high ones (*Thor Bridge*).

LION'S MANE. Before Fitzroy McPherson died, he cried what sounded to **H** like "the lion's mane." It turned out to be a reference to the nematocyst-studded tentacles of the medusa, *Cyanea capillata* (*Lion's Mane*).

LION'S MANE, ADVENTURE OF THE. **H** is the narrator. It was late July, 1907, and **H** had retired to his place on the Sussex downs. A giant medusa, *Cyanea capillata,* killed both McPherson and his Airedale.

LITHOTYPES OF HANDS. See Holmes, Sherlock, under Works.

LITTLE GEORGE STREET. Halliday's Hotel was here (*Study in Scarlet*).

LITTLE NEWSPAPER SHOP. Next to Mortimer's, the tobacconist, on the Strand (*Red-headed League*).

LITTLE PURLINGTON. Essex. Not far from Frinton. **W** spent a poor night here with Josiah Amberley, at the Railway Arms (*Retired Colourman*).

LITTLE RYDER STREET, W. N. Garrideb lived at No. 136 (*Garridebs*).

LIVERPOOL. Here was the Guion Steamship Company, with boats for New York (*Study in Scarlet*). False clue here as to Lord Saltire's whereabouts (*Priory School*). Mr. Hargrave was reported from here (*Valley of Fear*). Mary Cushman married Mr. Browner here (*Cardboard Box*). Count Sylvius was going to tell **H** that the jewel was here (*Mazarin Stone*).

LIVERPOOL, DUBLIN, & LONDON STEAM PACKET COMPANY. The "May Day" was one of their ships (*Cardboard Box*).

LIVERPOOL STATION. **W** found that he and Josiah Amberley could take a train from here to Little Purlington at 5:20 (*Retired Colourman*).

LIVERPOOL STREET. Mr. Cubitt was to reach here at 1:20 (*Dancing Men*).

L. L. These initials, in a woman's handwriting, were on a letter of assignation to Sir Charles Baskerville, asking him to be at "the gate by ten o'clock." Butler Barrymore related this to **W** and Sir Henry Baskerville. James Mortimer thought that the woman might be Laura Lyons (*The Hound*).

LLOYD'S. **H** spent a day over their files, tracing the "Lone Star" (*Five Orange Pips*).

LOMAX. A friend of **W**, sub-librarian of the London Library. He helped **W** select a volume on Chinese pottery (*Illustrious Client*).

Lombard Street. Mawson & Williams, stock-brokers, were here (*Stock-broker's Clerk*).

Lomond, Duke of. He was about to marry Isadora Klein (*Three Gables*).

London. ". . . That great cesspool into which all the loungers and idlers of the Empire are irresistibly drained" (*Study in Scarlet*).

Whether the case is solved in the Baker Street chambers or in metropolitan London, the London vicinity, or outlying districts, the record is full of references to this city. The comings and goings of Sherlock, John, their allies, and enemies are set down, often in detail. In the following list a certain amount of compression has been used, and the Greater London Area emphasized. Case references are not given after each street or place, for these are available in the regular alphabetical listings. Public buildings or places, as well as thoroughfares, are cited, and the number of times they are mentioned is noted following the reference. (Cf. inns and hotels; restaurants and bars; etc.)

Albert Dock 1
Aldersgate 1
Aldershot 1
Aldgate Station 1
Audley Court 1
Baker Street 22
Bank of England 1
Barking Level 1
Bayswater 1
Beckenham 1
Belmont Place 1
Bentinck Street 1
Berkeley Square 1
Big Ben 1
Blackheath 1
Blackwall 1
Blanford Street 1
Bloomsbury 1
Bond Street 2
Bow Street and Police Station 1
British Museum (of Natural History) 5
Brixton and Brixton Road 6
Broad Street 1
Brook Street 1
Camberwell and Camberwell Road 4
Campdenhouse Road 1
Cannon Street 1
Carlton Terrace 1
Cavendish Square 1
Charing Cross and Charing Cross Station 7
Charles Street 1
Chiswick 1
Church Row 1
Church Street 1
City, the 1
Clapham Junction 3
Coburg Square 1
Cold Harbour Lane 1
Commercial Road 1
Covent Garden 1
Craven Street 1
Curzon Square and Street 2
Deptford Reach 1
Doctor's Common 1

Downing Street 1
Duncan Street 1
East End 1
Edgware Road 2
Edmonton Street 1
Embankment, the 1
Endell Street 1
Euston Station 1
Farmingdon Street 1
Fenchurch Street 1
Fleet Street 2
Fresno Street 1
Fulham Road 1
Glasshouse Street 1
Gloucester Road & Street 1
Godolphin Street 1
Goodge Street 1
Gordon Square 1
Gravesend 2
Gray's Inn Road 1
Great George Street 1
Great Orme Street 1
Great Peter Street Post Office 1
Greenwich 2
Grosvenor Square 1
Half Moon Street 1
Hammersmith & Hammersmith Bridge 2
Hampstead & Hampstead Heath 3
Hanover Square 1
Harley Street 2
Henrietta Street 1
High Street Station 1
Holborn Street 2
Holland Grove 1
Houndsditch 1
Houses of Parliament 1
Howe Street 1
Hudson Street 1
Hyde Park 1
Inner Temple 1
Isle of Dogs 1
Italian Quarter 1
Ivy Lane 1
Kennington Land & Road 3
Kennington Park Gate 1
Kensington 5
Kilburn 1
King Edward Street 1
King's Cross 1
King's Cross Station 1
Kingston 1
Knight's Place 1
Laburnum Vale 1
Lambeth 1
Lancaster Gate 1
Lark Hall Lane 1
Leadenhall Street 1
Lime Street 1
Little George Street 1
Little Ryder Street 1
Liverpool Station 2
Lombard Street 1
London Bridge 3
London Bridge Station 2
London Library 1
London Road 1
Lower Brixton Road 1
Lower Burke Street 1
Lower Camberwell 1
Lower Grove Road 1
Lower Norwood 1
Lowther Arcade 1
Lyceum Theatre 1
Lyon Place 1
Manchester Street 1
Margate 1
Marylebone Lane 1
Mayfield Place 1
Metropolitan Station 1
Miles Street 1

Millbank Penitentiary 1
Mincing Lane 1
Minories 1
Montague Place 1
Montague Street 1
Mortimer Street 1
New Market Heath 1
Nine Elms Street 1
Norbury 1
Northumberland Avenue 3
Norwood 1
Notting Hill 2
Old Jewry 1
Oval, the 1
Oxford Street 11
Paddington & Paddington Station 4
Pall Mall 4
Park Lane 1
Park, the 1
Peckham 1
Pinchin Lane 1
Pitt Street 1
Plumstead Marshes 1
Pool, the 1
Pope's Court 1
Potter's Terrace 1
Poultney Square 1
Prince's Street 1
Priory Road 1
Queen Anne Street 1
Reading 1
Regent's Circus 2
Regent Street 3
Robert Street 1
Rochester Row 1
Rotherhithe 1
Russell Square 1
Saffron Hill 1
Saxe-Coburg Square 1
Scotland Yard 16
Serpentine Avenue 2
Shadwell Police Station 1
Shaftesbury Avenue 1
St. James's Hall 1
St. James and St. James's Square 3
St. John's Wood 1
St. Pancras 1
St. Paul's 1
Stepney 1
Stockwell Place 1
Strand 5
Streatham 2
Surrey-side 2
Thames River 2
Threadneedle Street 2
Throgmorton Street 1
Torquay Terrace 1
Tottenham Court Road 3
Tower 1
Trafalgar Square 2
Turpey Street 1
Underground, the 2
Upper Swandam Lane 1
Vauxhall Bridge Road 1
Vere Street 1
Victoria and Victoria Station 5
Vincent Square 1
Wandsworth Common 1
Waterloo Bridge 1
Waterloo Bridge Road 2
Waterloo Station 6
Welbeck Street 1
Wellington Station 1
West End 4
West India Docks 1
Westminster 4
Westminster Bridge 1
White Hall 1
Wigmore Street and Wigmore Street Post Office 2

Wimpole Street 1
Wordsworth Road 1
Zoo 1

It will be seen from this listing that Holmes and Watson covered a great deal of the metropolitan area of Greater London, much of it on foot and by cab. Of the entries listed 161 are cited once, 23 twice, 8 three times, 5 four times, 4 five times, 2 six times, 1 seven times, 1 eleven times, 1 sixteen times, and 1 twenty-two times. As would be expected, the Chambers at 221B Baker Street are often mentioned (22 times), and typically **H** and **W** strolled and did their shopping close by, *e.g.,* Oxford Street (cited eleven times). Holmes banked at the Oxford Street branch of the Capital & Counties Bank, and Watson bought boots at Latimer's in this street. Since many of their cases were in outlying areas of the city or in more remote counties, the Underground and railway stations were mentioned often, *e.g.,* Charing Cross seven times, and Waterloo and Brixton each six times. Scotland Yard would be a natural focus for many cases, and is noted sixteen times. The significance of these references is almost self-evident: Watson knew London quite well, though he claimed only a "limited knowledge," while Holmes knew it extraordinarily well. Witness his calling out of each name during the swift ride through the foggy night (*Sign of Four*).

LONDON BRIDGE. Upper Swandam Lane was on the north bank (*Twisted Lip*). **H** *et al* were here at 9:45 P.M. (*Greek Interpreter*). **W** caught sight of his shadow again (*Retired Colourman*).

LONDON BRIDGE STATION. McFarlane was followed from here to 221B Baker (*Norwood Builder*). If Cadogan West were returning, this would have been his station, but his body was at Aldgate (*Bruce-Partington*).

LONDON LIBRARY. In St. James's Square. **W**'s friend, Lomax, was the sub-librarian (*Illustrious Client*).

LONDON ROAD. **H** and **W** en route from the Cedars to London (*Twisted Lip*).

LONDON *Times*. See *Times*.

LONDON UNIVERSITY. **W** took his degree here in 1878 (?) (*Study in Scarlet*). Dr. Trevelyan also had his degree here (*Resident Patient*).

"LONE STAR." Bark out of Savannah, Georgia, Captain James Calhoun in command. Sailed from London for Savannah and presumed lost at sea (*Five Orange Pips*).

LONG DOWN. James Mortimer excavated here and found a prehistoric skull (*The Hound*).

LONG ISLAND CAVE MYSTERY. **H** recognized this case as a triumph for Mr. Leverton (*Red Circle*).

LOPEZ. Secretary to Mr. Henderson. *Alias* Lucas, *alias* Rulli. Escaped from London and six months later was killed in Madrid (*Wisteria Lodge*).

LOWENSTEIN, H. Prague correspondent of Professor Presbury. According to **W**, Lowenstein was an obscure scientist striving for a technique of rejuvenescence via monkey redactions. At the time, he could supply Presbury only with Langur serum but thought that anthropoid sera would be better. **H** was annoyed with Lowenstein (*Creeping Man*).

LOWER BRIXTON. Mycroft Holmes said that J. Davenport had written his reply from here (*Greek Interpreter*).

LOWER BRIXTON ROAD. Dr. Barnicot had an ancillary surgery and dispensary here (*Six Napoleons*).

LOWER BURKE STREET. Culbertson Smith, the Sumatra planter, lived at No. 13 (*Dying Detective*).

LOWER CAMBERWELL. See Camberwell.

LOWER GILL MOOR. Near Priory School.

LOWER GROVE ROAD. Mr. Sandeford lived here (*Six Napoleons*).

LOWER NORWOOD. Jonas Oldacre lived here (*Norwood Builder*).

LUCAS. See Lopez.

LUCAS, EDUARDO. With quarters on Godolphin Street, one of three secret agents in London capable of large transactions—the others, at the time, were Oberstein and La Rothière. He held an indiscreet letter of Lady Hilda Trelawney Hope and was blackmailing her. *Alias* for Henri Fournaye, *q.v.* (*Second Stain*).

LUCCA, EMILIA. Wife of Gennaro. After Gennaro killed Gorgiano, **H** used their cipher to bring her from Great Orme Street to Howe Street. *Née* Emilia Barelli (*Red Circle*).

LUCCA, GENNARO. New York Italian. Killed Gorgiano in a vacant apartment in Howe Street. Mr. Leverton of Pinkerton's was pleased (*Red Circle*).

LUCERNE. One of the labels on Douglas Maberley's luggage (*Three Gables*). The fictitious consumptive that needed **W's** professional service at the Englischer Hof was said to be on her way to join friends here (*Final Problem*).

LUCKNOW. Indian city invaded in the Great Mutiny (*Sign of Four*).

*lunkah*. See Indian *lunkah*.

LUXEMBOURG. **H** felt that he and **W** should go to Switzerland via this country (*Final Problem*).

LYCEUM THEATRE. Mary Morstan was asked to come to this theatre at 7:00 P.M., about July 7, 1888, with two friends if she wished. She was to be at the "third pillar from the left outside the Lyceum." No police were to be brought, and her anonymous "unknown friend" said that she was a "wronged woman and shall have justice." Mary turned the note over to **H**. **H**, **W**, and Mary kept the assignation and went in Williams' cab to Pondicherry Lodge to meet Bartholomew Sholto, after first picking up Thaddeus Sholto. (*Sign of Four*).

LYNCH, VICTOR. Forger. In **H**'s index under "**V**" (*Vampire*).

LYON PLACE, CAMBERWELL. The Windibanks and Mary Sutherland lived at No. 31 (*Case of Identity*).

LYONS. France. **H** was ill in the Hotel Dulong and wired **W** to come; **W** was there in twenty-four hours (*Reigate Puzzle*).

LYONS, LAURA. *Née* Laura Frankland. She married an artist, who deserted her. She lived in Coombe Tracey, and James Mortimer told **W** that she might be the mysterious "L. L." When **H** demonstrated to her that Jack Stapelton's "sister," Beryl, was his wife, Laura promised to tell **H** all (*The Hound*).

# M

MABERLEY, DOUGLAS. Son of Mary. When Isadora Klein refused him marriage, he wrote up their affair, disguised as a novel. Isadora obtained and burned the manuscript but had to give **H** a check for £5000 for Mary (*Three Gables*).

MABERLEY, MARY. Mother of Douglas. She was unconscious of the course of events, but in the end **H** gave her £5000 that came from Isadora Klein, who owed her "a little change of air" (*Three Gables*).

*MABERLEY, MORTIMER. Deceased husband of Mary and early client of **H**. Case not recorded (*Three Gables*).

MACDONALD, INSPECTOR ALEC. **H** called him "Mr. Mac." Told **H** that Mr. Douglas of Birlstone Manor was "murdered." He was surprised to see Fred Porlock's cipher on the matter at 221B Baker. **H** solved the case of Ted Baldwin's body being represented for that of John Douglas and convinced the inspector that Moriarty was behind the scenes (*Valley of Fear*).

MACKINNON, INSPECTOR. He was mollified when **H** assured him that **H** and Barker would not rob him of the credit in the Josiah Amberley case (*Retired Colourman*).

MACKLETON. In northern England. Dr. Huxtable's school was nearby (*Priory School*).

MACKLETON STATION. This was where **H** could send telegrams (*Priory School*).

MACPHAIL. Coachman for Professor Presbury (*Creeping Man*).

MACPHERSON, CONSTABLE. He did not tell all to Inspector Lestrade, but **H** got on the trail at last (*Second Stain*).

MADEIRA. **H** asked Mary Maberley if she would like to go there (*Three Gables*).

MADRAS. Jonathan Small imprisoned here (*Sign of Four*).

MADRID. Trelawney Hope had a note from here (*Second Stain*). Don Murillo was traced here from Barcelona (*Wisteria Lodge*), and he and his secretary, under the *alias* of Marquess of Montalva and of Signor Rulli, respectively, were killed in the Hotel Escurial in this city.

MAGGIE. Sister of James Ryder (*Blue Carbuncle*).

MAIWAND, BATTLE OF. See Watson.

MALINGERING. **H** was thinking about writing a monograph on this subject (*Dying Detective*).

MALPLAQUET DATE. It was on the door lintel of old Mr. Cunningham's fine Queen Anne home, near Reigate (*Reigate Puzzle*).

MALTHUS, PRINCIPLES OF. The *Daily Telegraph* managed to find connection between these and the murder of E. J. Drebber (*Study in Scarlet*).

MAN WITH THE TWISTED LIP, THE. June, 1889. Kate Whitney asked the Watsons for help. **W** found Kate's husband, Isa, and sent him home in a cab and in doing so met **H** in the Bar of Gold. The twisted lip belonged to Hugh Boone.

MANAOS. Brazil. J. Neil Gibson married Maria Pinto of this city (*Thor Bridge*).

MANCHESTER STREET. **H** and **W** en route to Camden House (*Empty House*).

*MANOR HOUSE CASE. Mycroft Holmes thought that Sherlock would find this case too difficult, but Sherlock replied that he had solved it (*Greek Interpreter*). So far no account is available.

MANSON OF BRADFORD. As for Von Bischoff, *q.v.*

MAPLETON. Training stable of Lord Backwater, near Tavistock. Under the management of Silas Brown. Desborough, the second favorite, was stabled here (*Silver Blaze*).

MAPS. (1) Priory School area (*Priory School*). (2) Professor Coram's house, by Stanley Hopkins (*Pince-Nez*). (3) Dr. Shlessinger was making a map of the Holy Land (*Lady Frances Carfax*). (4) Percy Phelps showed **H** a chart of the Foreign Office (*Naval Treaty*). (5) **H** consulted a map of London (*Bruce-Partington*).

MARCINI'S. Restaurant where **H** and **W** were to have dinner and then go on to a box for "Les Huguenots." This was in celebration of the long and difficult Baskerville case (*The Hound*).

MARENGO. **H** thought of this case that it was their Marengo, not their Waterloo, since it began in defeat and ended in victory (*Abbey Grange*).

MARGATE. The woman was suspect because she did not have powder on her nose (*Second Stain*). Leonardo drowned here (*Veiled Lodger*).

MARINES, ROYAL, LIGHT INFANTRY, RETIRED SERGEANT IN. **H** mystified **W** by deducing this much after a glance at their caller (*Study in Scarlet*).

MARKER, MRS. Elderly housekeeper for Professor Coram (*Pince-Nez*).

MARSEILLES. France. **H** refers to a case here (*Case of Identity*).

MARSHAM. In Kent. Stanley Hopkins wired for **H** (*Abbey Grange*).

MARTHA. Von Bork's housekeeper. She was actually an agent of Altamont, *alias* for Sherlock Holmes, and was to report to **H** later at Claridge's Hotel (*Last Bow*).

MARTIN, INSPECTOR. Of Norwich. Called in to investigate the death of Hilton Cubitt. He arrested Abe Slaney with the help of **H** (*Dancing Men*).

MARTIN, LIEUTENANT. In charge of eighteen soldiers on the "Gloria Scott."

MARTINI BULLET. Mentioned by **H** (*Sign of Four*).

*Martyrdom of Man, The.* **W** could not concentrate on Winwoode Reade's book for thoughts of Mary Morstan (*Study in Scarlet*).

MARX & CO. High Holborn. Supplied clothing to Aloysius Garcia but knew nothing about him except that he was a good spender (*Wisteria Lodge*).

MARY. Servant of Elias Openshaw (*Five Orange Pips*).

MARY. Maid to Mary Maberley (*Three Gables*).

MARY JANE. Maid to whom Mary Morstan Watson gave notice (*Scandal in Bohemia*).

MARYLEBONE LANE. The van that almost ran down **H** was gone in an instant (*Final Problem*).

MASON. Plate-layer employed by the Underground. He discovered the body of Cadogan West just outside the Aldgate Station (*Bruce-Partington*).

MASON, JOHN. Head trainer of the Shoscombe stud and training stables. He wrote to **H**, and **H** exposed the concealment of Lady Falder's death (*Shoscombe*).

MASON, MRS. Nurse at Robert Ferguson's home in Sussex (*Vampire*).

MASON, WHITE. Local police officer at Birlstone, Sussex. He wired Inspector MacDonald to come from London, with **H** if possible, to investigate the death of "John Douglas." **H** solved the substitution of Ted Baldwin's body for that of Douglas and told them that Professor Moriarty was involved in the case (*Valley of Fear*).

*MATHEWS. He knocked out **H's** left canine in the Charing Cross waiting room (*Empty House*). This might seem small beer, but a case may be involved worthy of **W's** attention.

*"MATILDA BRIGGS." This ship was associated with the giant rat of Sumatra in a case not yet disclosed to the public (*Vampire*).

MAUDIE. She had written "I will be there, you may be sure," and the message was in Fitzroy McPherson's pocket, in his card-case. She was Maud Bellamy of Fulworth (*Lion's Mane*).

MAUDSLEY. He was an evil influence on James Ryder (*Blue Carbuncle*).

*MAUPERTIUS, BARON. He had colossal schemes (*Reigate Puzzle*).

MAURITIUS. Mr. Fowler took a government appointment here (*Copper Beeches*).

MAWSON & WILLIAMS. Stock-brokers in Lombard Street (*Stock-broker's Clerk*).

"MAY DAY." Jim Browner, steward of this ship, was married to Mary (*née* Cushing). He was arrested by Lestrade in London, on **H**'s information, for the murders of Mary and Alec Fairbairn (*Cardboard Box*).

MAYFIELD PLACE, PECKHAM, LONDON. No. 3 was the dubious address of the dubious Sally Dennis (*Study in Scarlet*).

MAYNOOTH, EARL OF. Governor of an Australian colony. His wife, Lady Maynooth, and his son and daughter, Ronald and Hilda Adair, were in London for his wife's cataract operation (*Empty House*).

MAYNOOTH, LADY. Wife of the earl, in town for an operation, and living with Ronald and Hilda Adair at 427 Park Lane (*Empty House*).

MAZARIN STONE. Yellow, worth at least 100,000 quid. **H** snatched it from Count Sylvius and, later, put it in the pocket of Lord Cantlemere (*Mazarin Stone*).

MAZARIN STONE, ADVENTURE OF THE. Prior to February 13, 1892. Lord Cantlemere came to sneer but remained to praise as **H** foiled Count Sylvius and recaptured the jewel.

MCCARTHY, CHARLES. Of Australia. He "rented" the Hatherley Farm from John Turner (*Boscombe*).

MCCARTHY, JAMES. Son of Charles. He was seen in an altercation with his father by Patience Moran, near Boscombe Pool. He was tried for murder but acquitted, with information supplied by **H** (*Boscombe*).

MCFARLANE, JOHN HECTOR. **H** saves him from a murder conviction (*Norwood Builder*).

MCFARLANE'S CARRIAGE-BUILDING DEPOT. Next to the Vegetarian Restaurant on the Strand (*Red-headed League*).

MCGINTY, "BODYMASTER." Mrs. John Douglas associated this man's name with the *Valley of Fear.*

MCLAREN, MILES. Brilliant student; wayward, unprincipled, and innocent in the case (*Three Students*).

MCMURDO. Servant of Bartholomew Sholto. He allowed Thaddeus Sholto, **H**, **W**, and Mary Morstan to enter Pondicherry

Lodge. Later he was arrested by Athelney Jones as an accessory to the murder of his employer, Bartholomew (*Sign of Four*).

MCPHERSON, FITZROY. Science master at The Gables. He died exclaiming "the lion's mane" to **H** and Harold Stackhurst, or so **H** thought. Later, his Airedale was killed near the same spot, and still later Murdoch was attacked there. **H** led the survivors to the culprit (*Lion's Mane*).

MCQUIRE'S CAMP. Near the Rocky Mountains, where Francis Moulton became engaged to Hatty Doran in 1884 (*Noble Bachelor*).

MECCA. Visited by **H** (*Empty House*).

MEDIEVAL POTTERY. As for miracle plays.

MEEK, SIR JASPER. Distinguished physician that **W** wanted to bring in to examine **H** (*Dying Detective*).

MEIRINGEN, SWITZERLAND. On May 3, 1891, **H** and **W** arrived and put up at the Englischer Hof (*Final Problem*).

MELAS, MR. Of Greek extraction, and a remarkable linguist. **W** and **H** saved his life (*Greek Interpreter*).

MELBOURNE. Australia. A gold convoy on its way here was attacked by the Ballarat gang (*Boscombe*).

MELVILLE. Retired brewer living at Albemarle Mansion, Kensington. He was a friend of John Scott Eccles (*Wisteria Lodge*).

MENDELSSOHN'S *Lieder*. **H** played some for **W** on his violin (*Study in Scarlet*).

MERCER. He became a general utility man for **H** after **W** stopped living at 221B Baker, *circa* 1903 or a little earlier (*Creeping Man*).

MEREDITH, GEORGE. **H** wanted to talk to **W** about him (*Boscombe*).

MEREER. Second Mate on the "Gloria Scott."

*MERIVALE, INSPECTOR. Friend of **H** at Scotland Yard who asked **H** to look into the St. Pancras case. This was not one of **H's** cases, as such, but he obviously contributed to its solution. Probably there are no notes of the affair (*Shoscombe*).

*MERRIDEW. He was in **H's** index of biographies and was of "abominable memory" (*Empty House*).

MERRILOW, MRS. South Brixton landlady. She asked **H** to come and talk to her lodger whose face she had seen only once in seven years (*Veiled Lodger*).

MERRIPIT HOUSE. Home of Stapleton, the local naturalist (*The Hound*).

MERROW, LORD. Trelawney Hope had his letter (*Second Stain*).

MERRYWEATHER, MR. A director of the Coburg branch of the City & Suburban Bank. He led **H's** party to the bank to capture John Clay and his accomplice (*Red-headed League*).

MERTON, SAM. A boxer. He was to take the Mazarin stone to Van Seddar, but **H** gave it to Lord Cantlemere, and Sam was arrested with Count Sylvius (*Mazarin Stone*).

METROPOLITAN. Some of the Underground trains passing the Aldgate Station were of this sort (*Bruce-Partington*).

METROPOLITAN STATION. Near 221B Baker Street, on the Underground (*Beryl Coronet*).

MEUNIER, MONSIEUR OSCAR. Of Grenoble. He made a wax bust of **H** with which to decoy Colonel Moran. Mrs. Hudson moved the bust every quarter-hour (*Empty House*).

MEXBOROUGH PRIVATE HOTEL. On Craven Street. Jack and Beryl Stapleton stayed here (*The Hound*).

MEYER, ADOLPH. An important spy, living at 13 Great George Street. He was one of three agents capable of handling large affairs—the others at the time were Oberstein and La Rothière (*Bruce-Partington*).

MEYERS. Boot-maker in Toronto, Canada. Henry Baskerville bought a pair of boots here, and after one boot disappeared at the Northumberland Hotel, **H** recovered it later in the Grimpen Mire at Dartmoor (*The Hound*).

MICHAEL. Stable-hand at the Ferguson estate in Sussex (*Vampire*).

MIDDLESEX. **H** and **W** en route to the Cedars, in Kent (*Twisted Lip*). Miss Pinner lived here (*Yellow Face*).

MIDDLETON. Mr. Frankland won the case which established a right-of-way through the center of the magnate's park (*The Hound*).

MIDIANITES. Dr. Shlessinger was writing a monograph on their kingdom—or so it was said (*Lady Frances Carfax*).

MIDLAND ELECTRICAL COMPANY. Cyril Morton worked here (*Solitary Cyclist*).

MIDLANDS. Hall Pycroft was foolish enough to go to Birmingham (*Stockbroker's Clerk*).

MILANO. One of the labels on Douglas Maberley's luggage which was sent from Italy to his mother, Mary (*Three Gables*).

MILES, HONOURABLE MISS. Her marriage to Colonel Dorking was off when she could not provide £1,200 to retrieve imprudent documents from Milverton the blackmailer (*Milverton*).

MILES STREET. **H**, **W**, and Toby on trail of murderers of Bartholomew Sholto (*Sign of Four*).

MILLAR, MISS FLORA. A *danseuse* at the Allegro, arrested by Lestrade. She was friendly with Lord St. Simon (*Noble Bachelor*).

MILLBANK PENITENTIARY. **H** and **W** landed near here, after missing the "Aurora" (*Sign of Four*).

MILNER, GODFREY. He and his partner, Lord Balmoral, lost £420 to Ronald Adair and Colonel Moran at one sitting (*Empty House*).

MILVERTON, CHARLES AUGUSTUS. "The worst man in London," according to **H**. He was an unscrupulous rascal, a king of blackmailers. He wanted £7000 from Lady Eva Blackwell as his price not to reveal indiscreet letters to her fiancé, the Earl of Dovercourt. **H**, disguised as a young plumber, Escott, became engaged to Milverton's housemaid, so that the watchdog would be locked up nights. **H** and **W** burgled Milverton's safe, destroyed the contents, and Milverton was killed by a lady in disguise. **H** refused to investigate the death of Milverton (*Milverton*).

MINCING LANE. Firm of Ferguson & Muirhead was here (*Vampire*).

MING DYNASTY. The blue saucer was of this period. Sir James Damery had borrowed it for **H**, to loan to **W**, to discuss its possible sale with Baron Gruner (*Illustrious Client*).

MINORIES. Old Straubenzee had his gunsmith shop here (*Mazarin Stone*).

MIRACLE PLAYS. This was one of a number of topics discoursed upon by **H** when he, **W**, and Inspector Athelney Jones were at dinner at 221B Baker, on the eve of the chase of the "Aurora" (*Sign of Four*).

MISSING THREE-QUARTER, ADVENTURE OF THE. February. Cyril Overton consulted **H**; his rugger ace has vanished, and Cambridge was to meet Oxford the next day. Oxford won by a goal and two tries. Missing Godfrey Staunton was at his secret wife's bedside. She died despite Dr. Armstrong's efforts, and **H** and **W** said nothing about it to Lord Mount-James.

MITTON, JOHN. Valet to Eduardo Lucas. He was arrested but released in connection with his master's murder (*Second Stain*).

MOFFAT. One of the Worthingdon bank gang (*Resident Patient*).

MOLESEY MYSTERY. This was a case that **H** felt that Lestrade handled with less than his customary obtuseness while **H** was away (*Empty House*).

MONGOOSE. "Teddy" was poor Henry Wood's mongoose (*Crooked Man*).

MONOGRAPHS OF **H**. See Holmes, Sherlock, under Works.

MONTAGUE PLACE. Address of Violet Hunter (*Copper Beeches*).

MONTAGUE STREET. **H** had his first London rooms here as a professional student of crime. His chambers were "just around the corner from the British Museum" (*Musgrave Ritual*).

MONTALVA, MARQUESS OF. *Alias* Mr.

Henderson of High Gable, Surrey. *Alias* for Don Juan Murillo, San Pedro dictator. He was killed, with his secretary, Signor Rulli, at the Hotel Escurial in Madrid, six months after the escape from London (*Wisteria Lodge*).

Montana. Francis Moulton prospected here (*Noble Bachelor*).

Montgomery, Inspector. Took Jim Browner's statement at the Shadwell Police Station, and Lestrade sent a copy to **H** (*Cardboard Box*).

Montmartre district of Paris. Le Brun was crippled here in an assault by Apaches. Baron Gruner recalled the incident to **H**, and later **H** was assaulted in London, near the Café Royal (*Illustrious Client*).

Montpellier. France. The Crédit Lyonnais at which Marie Devine's check was cashed was here (*Lady Frances Carfax*). Miss Devine lived here, at 11 Rue de Trajan.

Montpellier Laboratory. In southern France. **H** visited here long enough for some research on coal-tar derivatives (*Empty House*).

*Montpensier, Mme. See Carère, Mlle.

Montrachet. **H** and **W** had a bottle with a cold partridge before interviewing Mrs. Ronder (*Veiled Lodger*).

Moorhouse. He was on the Cambridge rugger team (*Three-Quarter*).

Moorside Gardens, N.W. Count Sylvius lived at No. 136 (*Mazarin Stone*).

Moorville, Kansas. "John Garrideb" was said to have lived here (*Garridebs*).

Moran, Colonel Sebastian. He was Professor Moriarty's chief of staff, and his salary ran to £6000 a year (*Valley of Fear*). **H** considered him the second most dangerous man in London (he moved into first place after Professor Moriarty's death). He played cards often with Ronald Adair. See Mr. Murray, for a particular game. The Colonel and Ronald, as partners, once won £420 from Godfrey Milner and Lord Balmoral at a sitting. He murdered Ronald Adair and, later, shot a dummy of **H** at 221B Baker from Camden House—where he was captured by **H** and **W** and turned over to Lestrade. He was once in Her Majesty's Indian Army, and the best heavy-game shot in the Eastern Empire. Author of *Heavy Game of the Western Himalayas* (1881) and *Three Months in the Jungle* (1884) (*Empty House*). **H** recalls him in *His Last Bow*.

Moran, Patience. Fourteen-year-old daughter of John Turner's lodgekeeper. She saw James and Charles McCarthy quarreling at Boscombe Pool (*Boscombe*).

MORCAR, COUNTESS OF. Her blue carbuncle finally was found in the crop of a Christmas goose (*Blue Carbuncle*).

*MORGAN. He was a poisoner listed in **H's** index of biographies (*Empty House*). There may be notes of a case here, although the suggestion is not as strong as in the instance of Merridew.

MORECROFT. *Alias* "Killer" Evans, *q.v.*

MORIARTY, COLONEL. He defended the memory of his brother, Professor Moriarty (*Final Problem*).

MORIARTY, PROFESSOR. One of the world's great criminals, with an intricate and far-flung organization. He was responsible for much of the major crime in London, yet was cloaked in an air of respectability. His professorship was a chair of only £700 a year, yet he paid his chief of staff, Colonel Moran, £6000 a year (*q.v.*) and could purchase very expensive paintings (cf. Greuze). He was a brilliant man, author of the abstruse *The Dynamics of an Asteroid.* As usual, there were some weak spots in his organization, and Porlock (*q.v.*) was one that **H** had contacted. Moriarty apparently had at least two brothers. His younger brother was a West England station master (*Valley of Fear*), and the other one was Colonel Moriarty (*q.v.*).

When John Douglas was lost overboard, **H** felt that Moriarty was at the bottom of the whole case and that he was the author of the odd note that was sent to **H** (*Valley of Fear*).

**H** described him as a great mathematician and king of the criminals, a "Napoleon of crime." After presumably a long contest between Moriarty and **H**, Moriarty escaped **H's** net, along with Colonel Moran, although most of the gang was captured. When **H** and **W** left England secretly, to escape retaliation while the gang was being rounded up, Moriarty must have deduced their plan and followed them to Switzerland. He sent a bogus message that separated **W** from **H** and then trailed **H**, and the two fought on a ledge overlooking the Reichenbach Falls. Moriarty fell into the chasm (*Final Problem*).

Several years later, when **H** made a dramatic reappearance in London to secure the arrest of Colonel Sebastian Moran, he recalled Moriarty as "one of the great brains of the century" (*Empty House*).

**H** felt that Dr. Leslie Armstrong could fill Professor Moriarty's place, were he to turn his great talents from good to evil (*Three-Quarter*).

**H** recalled Professor Moriarty in *His Last Bow.*

MORLAND, SIR JOHN. It cost Mr. Frankland £200 to get a verdict against Sir John for shooting in his own warren (*The Hound*).

MORMONS. See Country of the Saints (*Study in Scarlet*).

*Morning Chronicle, The.* London newspaper that carried the advertisement of the *Red-headed League* on April 27, 1890. Carried the advertisement of the wanted whereabouts of Hosmer Angel (*Case of Identity*). Gave an account of John Straker's murder and the disappearance of the race favorite, *Silver Blaze.*

*Morning Post.* London newspaper that carried the news that Lord St. Simon was to marry Miss Hatty Doran (*Noble Bachelor*). Contained a paragraph stating that the Miles-Dorking wedding was off (*Milverton*). Also a paragraph to the effect that the Gruner-de Merville nuptials were off (*Illustrious Client*).

MORPHINE. **H** took this drug on occasion, instead of cocaine (*Sign of Four*).

MORPHY, ALICE. Daughter of Professor Morphy and engaged to Professor Presbury (*Creeping Man*).

MORPHY, PROFESSOR. Father of Alice and Colleague of Professor Presbury in chair of comparative anatomy at Camford University (*Creeping Man*).

MORRIS, WILLIAM. *Alias* of John Clay, when he posed as a lawyer who wished to rent the office of the fictitious *Red-headed League* at 7 Pope's Court. Cf. John Clay.

MORRISON, ANNIE. **H** did not know just what her relations were with Alec Cunningham and William Kirwan (*Reigate Puzzle*).

MORRISON, MISS. She went with Mrs. Barclay to a meeting at the Guild of St. George. She saw Henry Wood and later told **H** what she knew. This information was crucial in the case (*Crooked Man*).

MORRISON, MORRISON & DODD. Old Jewry machinery assessors (*Vampire*).

MORSTAN, CAPTAIN ARTHUR. In the 34th Bombay Infantry. He was second-in-command, under Major Sholto, in the Andaman Islands. He obtained a year's leave and returned to England, where he took a room at the Langham Hotel. He wired his daughter, Mary, to meet him at the hotel. Mary came in to find his luggage in his room, but he had disappeared. This was on December 3, 1878.

Nearly ten years later Thaddeus Sholto, son of the major,

related what his father had told him. Namely, that the captain had come to Pondicherry Lodge, where Major Sholto then lived in retirement, on his arrival in England on his year's leave. Captain Morstan had disagreed with Major Sholto on the division of the Agra Treasure. In the course of this argument, Captain Morstan had had a heart attack, fallen, hit his head on the Agra treasure-chest, and died. Major Sholto and Lal Chowdar had then disposed of the captain's body (*Sign of Four*).

MORSTAN, MISS MARY. Daughter of Captain Morstan. Blond, dainty, petite, and well-gloved, according to **W**, yet apparently in reduced circumstances. She called on **H**, on the advice of Mrs. Cecil Forrester (*q.v.*). **W** started to leave, but with her blue eyes upon him, Mary asked him to stay. The conquest of **W** had begun.

Having lost his wife when Mary was a small child, and not having any living kin, Captain Morstan placed Mary in an Edinburgh boarding school until she was seventeen. Later, Mary got her father's wire and came to the Langham Hotel to meet him after so long a time, only to find her father gone (*vide supra*). With her father disappeared, she notified the police and also contacted his former superior officer, Major Sholto. The major told Mary that he did not even know that her father was in England.

Some six years before the call on Holmes, on May 4, 1882, an advertisement had appeared in the London *Times* requesting the address of Mary Morstan. At the time she was governess for Mrs. Cecil Forrester, and acting on the latter's advice, Mary gave her address in a *Times* advertisement. On the same day Mary received a large pearl in the post. Since then, a large pearl had been sent to her each year on the same date in early May. There had been six such pearls. An expert had pronounced them to be of a rare variety, and very valuable. Mary had not parted with them as yet.

On July 7 (probably 1888), Mary received a letter asking for a meeting. This is the reason Mary called on **H**. **H**, **W**, and Mary kept the appointment. For subsequent events in the case, see Thaddeus Sholto.

Mary and **W** held hands on the grounds of Pondicherry Lodge. This became the residence of Bartholomew Sholto. Later on in the case **W** called on Mary and Mrs. Forrester to give them news of the hunt after the murderers of Bartholomew Sholto. Still later, **W** brought the Agra treasure-chest to Mrs. Forrester's house. When they forced the lid of the chest, they found that it was empty. Apparently both Mary and **W** were relieved by this lack of wealth, and **W** promptly proposed marriage to Mary. She accepted happily (*Sign of Four*).

See Mary Watson for subsequent events in her life.

MORTIMER. Gardener to Professor Coram, he was an "old Crimean man" (*Pince-Nez*).

MORTIMER, JAMES. Grimpen, Dartmoor, Devon. As **H** thought, he did have a curly-haired spaniel. Although he had no wish to be fulsome, he did covet **H's** skull. Nonetheless, he irritated **H** by saying **H** was the second greatest detective in Europe (after Bertillon, *q.v.*). He returned with **W** and Henry Baskerville, after consultation with **H**, to Baskerville Hall. After the case was over, he had to go with Sir Henry for a year's voyage around the world. His spaniel was eaten by the black dog of Jack Stapleton in the Grimpen Mire (*The Hound*).

MORTIMER STREET. **H** took **W** via an alley that led to this street (*Final Problem*).

MORTIMER'S. A tobacconist's shop on the Strand (*Red-headed League*).

MORTON. He was on the Oxford rugger team (*Three-Quarter*).

MORTON, CYRIL. He was in love with Violet Smith. Eventually he married Violet and with her fortune became senior partner of a Westminster electricians' firm (*Solitary Cyclist*).

MORTON, INSPECTOR. He was an old acquaintance from Scotland Yard. He told **W** that he had heard of **H's** illness. Later he arrested Culverton Smith on **H's** evidence (*Dying Detective*).

MORTON & KENNEDY. Famous Westminster electricians (*Solitary Cyclist*).

MORTON & WAYLIGHT'S. In Tottenham Court Road. Mr. Warren was their timekeeper. When two men seized Mr. Warren and later dumped him out on Hampstead Heath, Mrs. Warren felt that it was the fault of her unknown lodger (*Red Circle*).

MOSER, M. Manager of the Hotel National in Lausanne (*Lady Frances Carfax*).

MOSSMOOR CUM LITTLE PURLINGTON. The living of the Vicar, J. C. Elman (*Retired Colourman*).

MOULTON, FRANCIS HAY. He married Hatty Doran (*Noble Bachelor*).

MOULTON, MRS. FRANCIS HAY. *Née* Hatty Doran (*Noble Bachelor*).

MOUNT HARRIET. See Hope Town.

MOUNT-JAMES, LORD. Uncle of Godfrey Staunton. He never learned of his nephew's marriage (*Three-Quarter*).

MOUNTS BAY. **H's** and **W's** quarters on the Cornish peninsula looked out over this area (*Devil's Foot*).

M.R.C.S. Mr. James Mortimer (not Dr.) was a member (*The Hound*).

MULLER, THE NOTORIOUS. As for Von BISCHOFF, *q.v.*

MUNICH. Germany. There was a case here, the year after the Franco-Prussian War, that **H** felt was similar to the affair of the *Noble Bachelor.*

MUNRO, COLONEL SPENCE. He moved to Halifax, Nova Scotia (*Copper Beeches*).

MUNRO, EFFIE. She went to America when young and married Mr. Hebron of Atlanta, Georgia. She returned to live with her aunt at Pinner in Middlesex, and in due course she was married a second time, to Grant Munro. Her first husband and child were said to have died of yellow fever (*Yellow Face*).

MUNRO, GRANT. Husband of Effie. He was a hop merchant. He consulted **H** (*Yellow Face*).

MURCHER, HARRY. London constable and an acquaintance of Constable John Rance (*Study in Scarlet*).

MURDOCH, IAN. Mathematics coach at The Gables. He went for the police at Fulworth. He, too, was almost killed in the lagoon. When **H** exposed *Cyanea* as the killer, Ian and Harold Stackhurst composed their differences (*Lion's Mane*).

MURGER, HENRI. Author of *Vie de Boheme,* which was read by **W** (*Study in Scarlet*).

*MURILLO. An ex-President. His papers, according to **W**, led to a case that, presumably, was investigated some months after the capture of Colonel Moran, but there has been no further word (*Norwood Builder*).

MURILLO, DON JUAN. Tiger of San Pedro. *Alias* Mr. Henderson, of High Gable, near Oxshott, in Surrey. *Alias* Marquess of Montalva. The dictator escaped from the palace with his secretary and daughters and came to England finally, via Paris, Rome, Madrid, and Barcelona (*Wisteria Lodge*).

MURPHY. An intoxicated gipsy horse-dealer who heard cries in the night (*The Hound*).

MURPHY, MAJOR. Under the command of Colonel James Barclay. He told **H** what he knew, but it was not enough (*Crooked Man*).

MURRAY. Watson's orderly, who saved him from Ghazis at the battle of Maiwand when **W** was wounded (*Study in Scarlet*). Cf. Watson, John.

MURRAY. He played a rubber of whist at the Bagatelle card club on the afternoon of March 30, 1894, with Ronald Adair, Sir John Hardy, and Colonel Moran (*Empty House*).

MUSEUM. The Alpha Inn was nearby (*Blue Carbuncle*). Cf. British Museum; Scotland Yard Museum (*Empty House*). James Mortimer spent an afternoon at the Museum of the College of Surgeons (*The Hound*). **H** inquired of Jack Stapleton at the British Museum (*The Hound*). **H** spent a morning at the British Museum (*Wisteria Lodge*). The Warrens lived near the British Museum, on Great Orme Street (*Red Circle*). **H's** first chambers were near the British Museum (*Musgrave Ritual*).

MUSGRAVE, REGINALD. He had a slight acquaintance with **H.** He dismissed Brunton, his butler, and **H** solved this early case (*Musgrave Ritual*).

MUSGRAVE RITUAL, THE. This case was before the collaboration of **W** with **H** and early in **H's** career as a professional, not long after the *Gloria Scott* case. Laid in Sussex, at Hurlstone Manor House. **H** solved the problem. Possibly sometime between 1877 and 1880.

MUSGRAVE, SIR RALPH. This devoted follower of Charles the Second was an ancestor of Reginald Musgrave. The latter did not appreciate his ancestor's position (*Musgrave Ritual*).

MUTINY. Great Indian Mutiny is implied. **W** was wounded in this struggle (*Study in Scarlet*). Jonathan Small and his three companions obtained the Agra Treasure (*Sign of Four*). The Royal Munsters served (*Crooked Man*).

MYRTLES, THE. Beckenham. Sophy was staying here. Cf. Paul Kratides (*Greek Interpreter*).

# N

NANA SAHIB. Escaped over the frontier on the collapse of the Indian Mutiny (*Sign of Four*).

NAPLES. Italy. Pietro Venucci came from this city and met his death in London (*Six Napoleons*). Nearby was the village of Posilippo (*Red Circle*).

NAPOLEON. Busts of him were being stolen and then smashed. Lestrade was mystified, and **H** was elated (*Six Napoleons*). "Napoleon of crime," **H** said of Professor Moriarty (*Final Problem*).

NARBONNE. France. **W** had a note from **H** from here in the spring of 1891 (*Final Problem*).

NAVAL TREATY, THE. July after the marriage of **W.** Percy Phelps needed **H** to save his reputation, for papers had been stolen. **H** intervened.

"NEAL, OUTFITTER, VERMISSA, U. S. A." This was the tab on the neck of the yellow overcoat. It had a long pocket that could have held the sawed-off shotgun. The coat belonged to Mr. Hargrave (*Valley of Fear*).

NEAPOLITAN SOCIETY, A. The Red Circle was such and was allied to the Carbonari (*Red Circle*).

NED, UNCLE. He left his niece, Mary Sutherland, an income of £100 a year from New Zealand stock (*Case of Identity*).

NEGRO, THE. This was Mr. Heath Newton's horse in the Wessex Cup race (*Silver Blaze*).

NEILL, GENERAL. His column relieved Bhurtee, India, the day after Corporal Henry Wood was betrayed and captured by rebels in the Mutiny (*Crooked Man*).

NELIGAN, JOHN HOPLEY. Son of Neligan, the junior partner of Dawson & Neligan. His father fled to Norway with securities. Later some of these appeared on the London market, sold by Captain Peter Carey. John was arrested by Inspector Stanley Hopkins but released when **H** supplied the killer (*Black Peter*).

NEPAUL [NEPAL]. Tortured Henry Wood was taken here by rebels during the Indian Mutiny (*Crooked Man*).

NERUDA, NORMAN. "Her attack and

her bowing are splendid," according to **H**, who felt that she played Chopin "magnificently" (*Study in Scarlet*).

NETHER WALSLING. Home of Rev. Joshua Stone (*Wisteria Lodge*).

*NETHERLAND-SUMATRA COMPANY. **H** exerted himself in this case in the spring of 1887 (*Reigate Puzzle*).

NETLEY. This is where **W** took the prescribed course for army surgeons (*Study in Scarlet*).

NEW BRIGHTON. Alec Fairbairn and Mrs. Jim Browner took tickets for this place (*Cardboard Box*).

NEW FOREST. **W** yearned for it sometimes (*Resident Patient* and *Cardboard Box*).

NEWGATE CALENDAR. **H** did not expect **W** to carry all of it in his mind (*Garridebs*).

NEWHAVEN. **H** and **W** got off the train at Canterbury and went cross-country to this town (*Final Problem*).

NEW JERSEY. Irene Adler was born here in 1858 (*Scandal in Bohemia*).

NEWMARKET HEATH. Sir Robert Norbertson horsewhipped Sam Brewer here (*Shoscombe*).

NEW MEXICO. Francis Hay Moulton prospected here (*Noble Bachelor*).

NEW STREET. Birmingham. Hall Pycroft put up at a hotel here (*Stock-broker's Clerk*).

NEW STREET. Wallington. Sarah Cushing lived here (*Cardboard Box*).

NEWTON, HEATH. His horse, Negro, ran in the Wessex Cup race (*Silver Blaze*).

NEW YORK. The Guion Steamship Company boats plied between this city and Liverpool (*Study in Scarlet*). The Randall gang was arrested here and so could not be involved in the murder of Sir Eustace Brackenstall (*Abbey Grange*). Mlle. Carere was located here, well and married (*The Hound*). Mr. Leverton traced Gorgiano from here to London (*Red Circle*).

NEW ZEALAND. Uncle Ned, of Aukland, left income to Mary Sutherland (*Case of Identity*). Trevor, Senior, made his money in gold fields here (*Gloria Scott*).

NEW ZEALAND CONSOLIDATED. The stock was 104, according to Hall Pycroft (*Stock-broker's Clerk*).

NIAGARA. All of the Falls' noise was in Jim Browner's ears, or so it seemed, when he saw his wife off with Alec Fairbairn (*Cardboard Box*).

NIHILISM. The murders of the Marquess of Montalva and his secretary, Signor Rulli, in the Hotel Escurial, Madrid, were ascribed to adherents of this doctrine (*Wisteria Lodge*).

NÎMES. France. **W** had a note from here from **H** in the spring of 1891 (*Final Problem*).

NINE ELMS STREET. **H**, **W**, and Toby on a false trail (*Sign of Four*). Cf. Knight's Place.

NOBLE BACHELOR, ADVENTURE OF THE. Action was a few weeks prior to marriage of John Watson and Mary Morstan, which puts it in 1888 after July. Lord St. Simon was maritally involved with Hatty Doran of San Francisco. **H** looked up the birth of St. Simon, 1846, and noted that he was 41; but if this were so, it would place the case in 1887, which is hardly feasible.

"NORAH CREINA." Steamer that was lost with all hands on the Portuguese coast some leagues north of Oporto. Scotland Yard thought that the rest of the Worthingdon bank gang were aboard (*Resident Patient*).

NORBERTSON, SIR ROBERT. Daredevil rider, boxer, gambler, beau. He lived with his widowed sister, Lady Beatrice Falder, owner of Shoscombe Old Place. His horse, Shoscombe Prince, won the Derby and made £80,000 for his debt-ridden master (*Shoscombe*).

NORBURY. The Grant Munros had a villa here (*Yellow Face*).

NORFOLK. The Trevors lived here (*Gloria Scott*); also the Cubitts (*Dancing Men*).

NORFOLK CONSTABULARY. They supplied Inspector Martin of Norwich for the case (*Dancing Men*).

NORLETT, MR. Husband of Carrie Evans Norlett, maid to Lady Beatrice Falder (*Shoscombe*).

NORLETT, MRS. *Née* Carrie Evans, under which name Sir Robert Norbertson installed her as maid to his widowed sister, Lady Beatrice Falder (*Shoscombe*).

NORTH CAROLINA. The Anderson murders occurred here (*The Hound*).

NORTH DEVON RAILWAY. Jack Stapleton brought the dog via this line to the Dartmoor area (*The Hound*).

*North Surrey Observer*. Biweekly that carried the story that Inspector MacKinnon had found the missing Dr. Ernest and Mrs. Josiah Amberley in a well. **H** was not mentioned, as was to be expected (*Retired Colourman*).

NORTHUMBERLAND. Annie and Joseph Harrison came from here (*Naval Treaty*).

NORTHUMBERLAND AVENUE. Francis Hay Moulton stayed briefly in a select hotel on this street (*Noble Bachelor*). **H** and **W** patronized a Turkish bath here (*Illustrious Client*).

NORTHUMBERLAND AVENUE HOTELS. Mr. Melas acted as a guide to the Orientals at these hotels (*Greek Interpreter*). Francis Hay Moulton stayed in one of them (*Noble Bachelor*). Sir

Henry Baskerville stayed at one (*The Hound*).

NORTHUMBERLAND HOTEL, THE. Sir Henry Baskerville stayed here and got a warning message here (cf. "As you value your life . . ."). Later he lost a new brown boot, then an old black boot here. The old black one was recovered later by **H** in the Grimpen Mire in Dartmoor (*The Hound*).

NORTH WALSHAM. **H** and **W** en route to Riding Thorpe Manor (*Dancing Men*).

NORTHWEST PROVINCES. Abel White's plantation at Muttra was near the border (*Sign of Four*).

NORTON, GODFREY. Lawyer, married Irene Adler (*Scandal in Bohemia*).

NORWAY. After his bank failed, J. H. Neligan's father started to flee to this country with securities; he never arrived. **H** and **W** were off to this country after the case was settled (*Black Peter*).

NORWICH. Inspector Martin was from here (*Dancing Men*).

NORWOOD. Brother Bartholomew lived here, in "Upper Norwood." Cf. Lower Norwood (*Sign of Four*).

NORWOOD BUILDER, ADVENTURE OF THE. Disappearance of Jonas Oldacre meant possible murder conviction for McFarlane. **H** saved him with a false fire alarm.

NOTTINGHAM. Mr. Hargrave was reported from here (*Valley of Fear*).

NOTTING HILL. Louis La Rothière lived in Campden Mansions (*Bruce-Partington*). Selden was the neighborhood murderer (*Hound*). Lower Burke Street was on the fringe of this area (*Dying Detective*).

"NOTTING HILL HOOLIGAN." Inspector Gregson's behavior toward one of these and toward Emilia Lucca was similar, but **H** intervened (*Red Circle*).

"NOTTING HILL MURDERER." This was Selden, who escaped from the Princetown convict prison about the time **W** and Sir Henry arrived at the Hall (*The Hound*).

NOVA SCOTIA. Colonel Spence Munro had moved to Halifax, and Violet Hunter wanted another position as governess (*Copper Beeches*).

# O

OAKINGTON. **H** searched here also (*Three-Quarter*).

OAKSHOTT, MRS. She was at No. 117 Brixton Road and sold some geese to Mr. Breckinridge of the Covent Garden Market (*Blue Carbuncle*).

OAKSHOTT, SIR LESLIE. A famous surgeon who attended **H** after the murderous attack was made in Regent Street (*Illustrious Client*).

OBERSTEIN, HUGO. He was one of three secret agents in London capable of handling such a transaction at the time; the others were La Rothière and Lucas (*Second Stain*). Oberstein was similarly important on another occasion, but the others were La Rothière and Meyer (*Bruce-Partington*). Since the submarine patents were tampered with in 1895, in the *Bruce-Partington* case, and since Lucas was killed in the *Second Stain* case, the suggestion arises that Meyer replaced Lucas in this ring of dishonor, and therefore the *Second Stain* adventure may be said to have been the earlier of the two exploits. **H** triumphed in both to save England from a dangerous position.

In the *Bruce-Partington* adventure, Hugo Oberstein, living at No. 13 Caulfield Gardens, Kensington, was selected by **H** because of the relation of the back of his house to the Underground.

*ODESSA. **H** was called to this place to investigate the Trepoff murder (*Scandal in Bohemia*). **W** was married at the time and merely heard of this by vague report—thus the case history may never be available to us. **H** was reminded of Dolsky and the forcible administration of poison (*Study in Scarlet*).

ODLEY'S. **W** said that such a house name would be found about Lamberley (*Vampire*).

OHIO. See Cleveland (*Study in Scarlet*).

OLDACRE, JONAS. A builder who lived at Deep Dene House in Lower Norwood. His disappearance almost resulted in McFarlane's conviction for his murder. **H** smoked Jonas out by a false fire alarm (*Norwood Builder*).

Old Deer Park. This was where Robert Ferguson threw **W** into the crowd, presumably in a rugby match (*Vampire*).

Old Jewry. Morrison, Morrison & Dodd had their office here (*Vampire*).

Oldmore, Mrs. Of High Lodge, Alton. Her husband was once mayor of Gloucester. She and her maid were at the Northumberland Hotel (*The Hound*).

One Hundred and Seventeenth, The Old. This was now the First Battalion of the Royal Munsters at Aldershot (*Crooked Man*).

Openshaw, Elias. Uncle of John. He had emigrated to America, became a Florida planter, fought under Jackson and later rose to a colonelcy under Hood. He returned to Sussex, near Horsham, in 1869 or 1870. He received five orange pips from Pondicherry, India on March 10, 1883. Died May 2, 1883, and left his estate to his brother Joseph (*Five Orange Pips*).

Openshaw, John. Son of Joseph and nephew of Elias. He received five orange pips and a cryptogram. He then consulted **H.** On his way back to Waterloo Station he died, apparently accidentally. **H** thought otherwise (*Five Orange Pips*).

Openshaw, Joseph. Father of John and brother of Elias. Elias left him his estate. Joseph received five orange pips on January 4, 1885, and was told to leave "the papers" on the sundial. He died January 9 (?), 1885 (*Five Orange Pips*).

opera. On at least one occasion **H** and **W** went to an opera. This was at the close of the long Baskerville case. **H** had a box for "Les Huguenots" (*The Hound*).

Oporto. The steamer Norah Creina was lost north of here (*Resident Patient*).

Order, the. Or the Brotherhood. It was after Sergius, *alias* Professor Coram (*Pince-Nez*).

*Origin of Tree Worship, The.* **H**, disguised, was at the crowd's fringe at the Ronald Adair home at 427 Park Lane and carried this book. **W** knocked the volume from **H's** hands, accidentally it seemed, and without recognizing his old companion (*Empty House*).

"Orontes." The troopship that carried **W** from India to Portsmouth (*Study in Scarlet*). Cf. Watson, John.

"Our own colours, green and white. Green open, white shut. Main stair, first corridor, seventh right, green baize. Godspeed. D." This message was recovered by Inspector Baynes from a grate of Wisteria Lodge. Later the inspector pointed out that they were the colors of San Pedro (*Wisteria Lodge*).

OVAL, THE. **H**, **W**, and Toby, trailing the murderers of Bartholomew Sholto, pass to the east of here, in Kennington Lane (*Sign of Four*).

OVERTON, CYRIL. Of Trinity College, Cambridge University, and skipper of the Varsity rugger team. His star, Godfrey Staunton, disappeared before the game with Oxford, and Oxford won (*Three-Quarter*).

OXFORDSHIRE. Eyford, in Berkshire, was near the border of this county (*Engineer's Thumb*).

OXFORD STREET. **W** on his way to Baker Street to meet **H** (*Red-headed League*). **H**, **W** en route to inquire about the goose (*Blue Carbuncle*). **H** and **W** returning from Dr. Trevelyan's (*Resident Patient*). Mr. Melas and Mr. Latimer en route presumably to Kensington (*Greek Interpreter*). **H** had business here (*Final Problem*). **W** strolled, puzzling the murder of Ronald Adair (*Empty House*). **H** banked the Duke of Holdernesse' check for £6000 at the branch of the Capital & Counties Bank (*Priory School*). **H** and **W** got a cab here (*Milverton*). Rain, wind, and splashing cabs (*Pince-Nez*). **H** and **W** following Sir Henry Baskerville and James Mortimer (*The Hound*). **W** bought boots at Latimer's here (*Lady Frances Carfax*).

OXFORD UNIVERSITY. John Clay was at school here (*Red-headed League*). So was Colonel Sebastian Moran (*Empty House*). Oxford's Morton and Johnson could romp around Cambridge's Moorhouse (in rugger) (*Three-Quarter*).

OXSHOTT. Wisteria Lodge was near this town (*Wisteria Lodge*).

OXSHOTT COMMON. Aloysius Garcia was murdered here (*Wisteria Lodge*).

OXSHOTT TOWERS. Home of Sir George Ffolliott (*Wisteria Lodge*).

# P

PADDINGTON DISTRICT. **W** bought Mr. Farquhar's practice here shortly after his marriage to Mary Morstan (*Stock-broker's Clerk*).

PADDINGTON STATION. **H** wired **W** to meet him here to catch the 11:15 (*Boscombe*). **W** lived near this station. Victor Hatherley came into London by this station (*Engineer's Thumb*). **H** and **W** just had time to catch the train for Exeter (*Silver Blaze*). **H** and **W** were to meet Sir Henry Baskerville and James Mortimer here (*The Hound*).

PAGANINI. **H** talked to **W** about him, about violins in general, and about his own Stradivarius in particular (*Cardboard Box*).

PALACE CLOCK. It struck 3:00 A.M. when **W** returned with Toby to Pondicherry Lodge (*Sign of Four*).

PALLADIO. Abbey Grange was pillared in front like one of his buildings (*Abbey Grange*).

*Pall Mall.* As for the *Globe* and the *Star* (*Blue Carbuncle*).

PALL MALL. Mycroft Holmes had chambers here (*Greek Interpreter; Bruce-Partington;* and *Final Problem*). In Farnham, where **W** inquired about Charlington Hall, they told him to ask a well known Pall Mall firm (*Solitary Cyclist*). The Adelaide-Southampton Line had a shipping office here (*Abbey Grange*).

PALMER. A make of bicycle tire used by Heidegger (*Priory School*).

PALMER, DR. He turned to crime (*Speckled Band*).

"PALMYRA." John and Ivy Douglas sailed on this ship bound for South Africa. John was lost overboard off St. Helena, and **H** felt that Moriarty was back of his death (*Valley of Fear*).

PARADE, THE. At New Brighton, where Alec Fairbairn and Mrs. Jim Browner walked and then took a boat. Jim took a boat after them (*Cardboard Box*).

*PARADOL CHAMBER. **W** recorded this case in 1887, but as yet he has not seen fit to publish it (*Five Orange Pips*).

PARIS. The Francis Hay Moultons probably would have gone on

to this city had not **H** explained (*Noble Bachelor*). Don Murillo was traced from this city to Rome (*Wisteria Lodge*). Mr. Pinner told Hall Pycroft that he would manage a depot in Paris that handled English pottery for the Franco-Midland Company (*Stock-broker's Clerk*). **H** felt that Moriarty would go to this city (*Final Problem*). Lucas did not take Mitton here. Mme. Fournaye left her villa on the Rue Austerlitz here to spy on her husband in London (*Second Stain*).

PARK, THE. **W** walked from his Kensington home across here to meet **H** at Baker Street (*Red-headed League*). Hattie Doran was last seen entering Hyde Park (*Noble Bachelor*). **H** and **W** took a walk here and missed a client, to **H's** annoyance (*Yellow Face*).

PARKER. Manager of Coxon & Woodhouse. Mr. Pinner said that Mr. Parker had spoken highly of Hall Pycroft (*Stock-broker's Clerk*).

PARKER. "A garroter by trade," in the Moriarty-Moran gang (*Empty House*).

PARKHURST. Shinwell Johnson served two terms here for villainy (*Illustrious Client*).

PARK LANE. The Adairs lived at No. 427 (*Empty House*).

"PARK LANE MYSTERY." The murder of Ronald Adair (*Empty House*).

PARLIAMENT. It had risen (*Resident Patient*).

PARR, LUCY. Second waiting-maid in home of Mr. Holder (*Beryl Coronet*).

PATRICK, ELSIE. An American lady who married Hilton Cubitt. Although badly wounded, she recovered to care for the poor and administer her late husband's estate (*Dancing Men*).

PATTERSON, INSPECTOR. In charge of convicting the Moriarty gang. **H** wrote **W** from Reichenbach Falls to give the inspector the papers that were in a blue envelope inscribed "Moriarty" in pigeon-hole "M" (*Final Problem*).

PATTINS, HUGH. He was a "long, dried-up creature" who received the same treatment from **H** as did James Lancaster (*Black Peter*).

PAUL, JEAN. See Richter.

PAUL'S WHARF. At the back of the Bar of Gold there was a trapdoor near this pier (*Twisted Lip*).

PAWN SHOPS. Jabez Wilson had such a shop in Coburg Square (*Red-headed League*). Bevington's shop was in Westminster Road (*Lady Frances Carfax*). Probably one in Tottenham Court Road (cf. Stradivarius).

PEACE, CHARLIE. A great criminal who was also a violin virtuoso (*Illustrious Client*).

PEAK COUNTRY. Dr. Huxtable's famous school was located here (*Priory School*).

PEARL. Mary Morstan received a fine one each year for six years (*Sign of Four*). Cf. Black Pearl of the Borgias (*Six Napoleons*).

PECKHAM. London district. See Dennis.

"PENANG LAWYER." **W** thought that the unknown visitor's stick was of this type (*The Hound*).

PENGE. Susan Cushing had lived here (*Cardboard Box*).

PENNSYLVANIA. Ezekiah Hopkins reportedly made his home in Lebanon, in this state (*Red-headed League*).

PENNSYLVANIA SMALL ARMS COMPANY. They made the shotgun that murdered John Douglas, or so everyone thought at first (*Valley of Fear*).

PENTONVILLE PRISON. Maudsley was serving time here (*Blue Carbuncle*).

PERFUMES. See Holmes, Sherlock, under Methods and Organization.

PERKINS. Groom and coachman to Sir Charles Baskerville. He was sent to fetch James Mortimer on Charles's death, and later he met Sir Henry, Mortimer, and **W** and took them from the London train to the Hall (*The Hound*).

PERKINS, YOUNG. He was killed outside the Holborn Bar (*Three Gables*).

PERNAMBUCO. Brazil. Isadora Klein's family had been leaders here for generations (*Three Gables*).

*PERSANO, ISADORA. Well-known journalist and duelist. He was found insane with a remarkable worm (said to be unknown to science) in a matchbox before him (*Thor Bridge*). No published account extant.

PERSHORE. In Worcestershire, where Jonathan Small once lived (*Sign of Four*).

PERSIA. Visited by **H** (*Empty House*).

PERSIAN SLIPPER. **H** kept tobacco in it (*Empty House*).

PESHAWUR. **W** recuperated in a base hospital here. See Watson, John.

PETER. Groom hired to drive the dog-cart with Violet Smith from Mr. Carruthers' to Farnham Station. He was knocked on the head by Violet's abductors (*Solitary Cyclist*).

PETERS, HENRY. Of Adelaide, Australia. Nicknamed Holy Peters. *Alias* Rev. Dr. Shlessinger of Baden and South America. **H** and **W** called at his house in Poultney Square (*Lady Frances Carfax*).

PETERSFIELD. Lord Backwater had a place near here (*Noble Bachelor*).

PETERSON. The commissionaire who obtained a hat and a goose and took both to **H**. Later **H** offered him a goose (*Blue Carbuncle*).

PETRARCH. **H** read a pocket edition on the train en route (*Boscombe*).

PHELPS, PERCY. Brilliant student and school-days friend of **W.** He obtained a scholarship to Cambridge University and then went into the Foreign Office. His nickname was "Tadpole." Percy was to marry Annie Harrison, and then the treaty was stolen. Joseph Harrison did not hesitate (*Naval Treaty*).

PHILADELPHIA, PENNSYLVANIA. Mr. Rucastle's daughter by his first wife was said to be in this city (*Copper Beeches*).

*PHILLIMORE, JAMES. The case data are in Cox & Co. bank. The case is unfinished. James stepped back into his home to get an umbrella, and "was never more seen in this world" (*Thor Bridge*).

PHOENICIAN TIN TRADERS. **H** thought that they had contributed to the Cornish language (*Devil's Foot*).

PHYSICIANS (These are all "doctors" in the sense that they have an M.D. degree, with the exception of Mr. Kent and Mr. Mortimer.)

Agar, Moore
Ainstree
Anstruther
Armstrong, Leslie
Barnicot
Barton, Hill (*alias* of John H. Watson)
Becher
Bennett, Trevor
Farquhar
Ferrier
Fordham
Horsom
Jackson
Kent
Meek, Sir Jasper
Mortimer, James
Oakshott, Sir Leslie
Palmer
Pritchard
Richards (in Cornwall)
Roylott (in Surrey)
Saunders, Sir James
Somerton (In Hope Town)
Sterndale
Trevelyan, Percy
Verner
Watson, John H.
Willows
Wood

PICKWICK, MR. **W** felt that Charles Augustus Milverton, the blackmailer, had Pickwick's benevolent manner except for his insincere smile and hard eyes (*Milverton*).

PIERROT. The name Hugo Oberstein chose to transact the sale of the stolen submarine plans in the agony column of the *Daily Telegraph.* **H** joined in this correspondence and caught Colonel Valentine Walter (*Bruce-Partington*).

PIKE, LANGDALE. A human reference work on social scandal, especially of the London scene. He contributed bits of gossip to the "garbage papers" that catered to an inquisitive public. His working hours were spent in a club on St. James Street. **H** on occasion consulted him (*Three Gables*).

PINCHIN LANE, No. 3. In Lambeth, where Sherman, the taxidermist and owner of Toby lived. Cf. dog (*Sign of Four*).

PINKERTON AMERICAN AGENCY. Mr. Leverton, disguised as a Cabman, was on the case with Inspector Gregson. He was a Pinkerton operative pursuing Gorgiano (*Red Circle*).

PINKERTON PRIZE. See Bruce Pinkerton Prize.

PINNER, ARTHUR. *Alias* of Beddington No. 1. Posed as financial agent who wanted Hall Pycroft to work for him. He tried to commit suicide (*Stock-broker's Clerk*).

PINNER, HARRY. The second *alias* of the first Beddington. Hall Pycroft was supposed to think that Harry and Arthur were brothers (*Stock-broker's Clerk*).

PINNER. Effie Munro, then Mrs. Hebron, lived in this Middlesex town with a maiden aunt for about seven months (*Yellow Face*).

PINTO, MARIA. Daughter of a Brazilian government official at Manaos. She married J. Neil Gibson (*Thor Bridge*).

PIPES. Brier root pipe (*Sign of Four*); black clay pipe (*The Hound* and *Case of Identity*). Then there was the long cherry-wood pipe (a "Churchwarden?") which replaced the "clay" (*Copper Beeches*), but one feels that the clay was the favorite, as it is noted in several case histories in addition to *The Hound*.

PITT. Sir William Baskerville served under him in the House of Commons (*The Hound*).

PITT STREET. **H** listened to the owner of No. 131, where murder was suggested as a corollary of the breaking of Napoleon busts (*Six Napoleons*).

PLASTER OF PARIS. See footsteps; also Holmes, Sherlock, under Works.

PLUMSTEAD MARSHES. As for pool.

PLYMOUTH. **H** pretended to think that he had met Mrs. Straker at a garden party here (*Silver Blaze*). Dr. Sterndale was about to leave from here for Africa (*Devil's Foot*).

POE, EDGAR ALLAN. **H** thought that Poe's detective, Dupin, was "a very inferior fellow." **W** felt that there might be a touch of jealousy (*Study in Scarlet*). Later, **H** read Poe to **W** (*Resident Patient*).

POISON. **H** said that E. J. Drebber was poisoned. Lestrade found two pills in Stangerson's room at Halliday's Private Hotel. **H** used a long-sick terrier, which his landlady wanted put away, to demonstrate that one pill was harmless and one was poison. Cf. dog; also Dolsky (*Study in Scarlet*). Bartholomew Sholto was killed by a poisoned dart shot by Tonga at Pondicherry Lodge, and later a police inspector was similarly dealt with on the Thames (*Sign of Four*). Anna took poison when she was about to be arrested for the murder of Willoughby Smith (*Pince-Nez*). Carlo, a spaniel, was experimentally poisoned (*Vampire*).

POLDHU BAY. Off the Cornish Peninsula, where **H** and **W** were staying in a cottage overlooking this body of water. **H** was fretting out a rest cure (*Devil's Foot*).

POLICE FORCES. As in the category of criminals, there is a certain difficulty in fixing limits. The primary consideration here is that this is the group that is preventing crime. Within this group there are the amateurs and the professionals. Among the latter, it is difficult at times to determine which police organization an individual belongs to: C.I.D., Scotland Yard, the Greater London Police Force, or some County Police Force. Where no parenthetical notation states otherwise, it is assumed that the person is operating in the London area.

Amateur

Baker Street Division of the detective police force
Barker
Holmes, Sherlock
Leverton (Pinkerton American Detective Agency)

Professional

Anderson, Constable (Fulworth)
Bardle, Inspector (Sussex)
Barton
Baynes, Inspector (Surrey)
Blondin, Constable
Bradstreet, Inspector
Brown, Sam
Cook, Constable
Downing, Constable
Dubugue (Paris)
Edmunds, Constable (Berkshire)
Forbes, Detective
Forrester, Inspector (Surrey)
Gregory, Inspector (Devonshire?)
Gregson, Inspector Tobias
Hargreave, Wilson (New York City)
Hill, Inspector
Hopkins, Inspector Stanley
Jones, Athelney
Jones, Peter
Lanner, Inspector
Le Brun (Paris)
Lestrade, Inspector G.
le Villard (Paris)
Lewes (Fulworth)
MacDonald, Inspector Alec
MacKinnon, Inspector
MacPherson, Constable
Martin, Inspector (Norfolk)
Mason, White (Sussex)

Merivale, Inspector
Montgomery, Inspector
Morton, Inspector
Murcher, Constable Harry
Patterson, Inspector
Pollock, Constable
Rance, Constable
Tuson, Sergeant
von Waldbaum, Fritz (Danzig)
Walters, Constable
Wilson, Constable
Wilson, Sergeant (Sussex)
Youghal

"POLICE NEWS OF THE PAST." Stamford suggested **H** might start a paper with this name (*Study in Scarlet*).

*"POLITICIAN, THE LIGHTHOUSE, AND THE TRAINED CORMORANT." Both **W** and **H** have been incensed, justifiably, by recent outrageous attempts to get at earlier case histories filed away in their possession. **H** has granted **W** permission to give the quoted case to the public if these efforts do not cease forthwith (*Veiled Lodger*).

POLLOCK, CONSTABLE. He assisted Sergeant Tuson to capture Beddington (*Stock-broker's Clerk*).

*Polyphonic Motets of Lassus.* **H** was working on this monograph (*Bruce-Partington*). Cf. Holmes, Sherlock, under Works.

POMPEY. Locally famous dog—a drag-hound. He followed **H's** aniseed trail for **H** and **W**, and they found Godfrey Staunton (*Three-Quarter*). Cf. dog.

PONDICHERRY. India. Elias Openshaw received a letter from here (*Five Orange Pips*).

PONDICHERRY LODGE. In Upper Norwood. Major Sholto retired here, and after his death one of his sons, Bartholomew, lived here. Scene of the crime. (*Sign of Four*).

POOL. Section of the Thames River, noted in the chase of the "Aurora" (*Sign of Four*).

*POPE, THE. **H** was anxious to oblige him (*The Hound*). Cf. Cardinal Tosca (*Black Peter*). Are all the data available, and could they be published?

POPE'S COURT. Duncan Ross had an office at No. 7 (*Red-headed League*).

POPE'S *Homer*. An odd volume of it was stolen from Acton's library, near Reigate in Surrey (*Reigate Puzzle*).

POPHAM HOUSE. Home of John Scott Eccles, in Lee (*Wisteria Lodge*).

POPLAR. Athelney Jones received a wire from **H**, dated from Poplar at twelve o'clock, asking him to wait at 221B Baker (*Sign of Four*).

PORKY. Nickname for Shinwell Johnson (*Illustrious Client*).

PORLOCK, FRED. He was a weak link in Professor Moriarty's criminal organization. He sent a message in cipher and a note that the Professor suspected him. **H** and **W** solved the cipher, which told them that Douglas, of Birlstone Manor, was in danger (*Valley of Fear*).

PORT. **H**, **W**, and Athelney Jones finished dinner with a glass at 221B Baker (*Sign of Four*). **H** said that the Chequers in Camford served some that was above mediocrity (*Creeping Man*).

PORTER, MRS. Old cook and housekeeper for the Tregennis family at Tredannick Wartha. She had heard nothing but the next morning she sent a boy for Dr. Richards (*Devil's Foot*).

PORTLAND. Jack James, an agent for Von Bork, was in jail here (*Last Bow*).

PORTSDOWN HILL. Major Freebody lived here (*Five Orange Pips*).

PORTSMOUTH. **W** landed here from India (*Study in Scarlet*). **H** and **W** took a Portsmouth train from Woking to London (*Naval Treaty*). Altamont, an *alias* for **H**, wired Von Bork from here; Steiner, another espionage agent of Von Bork, was in jail here (*Last Bow*).

PORTUGUESE COAST. The ship "Norah Creina" was lost off this coast (*Resident Patient*).

POSILIPPO. Italy, near Naples. Augusto Barelli lived here, and his daughter, Emilia, married Gennaro Lucca here (*Red Circle*).

POTTER'S TERRACE. Hall Pycroft lived at No. 17 (*Stock-broker's Clerk*).

POULTNEY SQUARE. Brixton. The Shlessingers had Lady Frances at No. 36, and nothing could be done until the warrant arrived (*Lady Frances Carfax*).

*Practical Handbook of Bee Culture with Some Observations upon the Segregation of the Queen.* Von Bork was expecting the Navy Signals but this is what Altamont, *alias* of **H**, gave him for £500 (*Last Bow*). This was **H's** last work apparently. See Holmes, Sherlock, under Works.

PRAGUE. King of Bohemia came incognito from here to consult **H** (*Scandal in Bohemia*). **H** felt that Baron Gruner had contrived a murder here (*Illustrious Client*). A fellow-student of Trevor Bennett wrote Trevor that he had seen Professor Presbury here (*Creeping Man*).

PRENDERGAST, JACK. He was a leader in the convicts' taking over of the "Gloria Scott" but died when the first mate blew up the ship (*Gloria Scott*).

*PRENDERGAST, MAJOR. See Tankerville Club Scandal (*Five Orange Pips*).

PRESBURY, EDITH. Fiancée of Trevor Bennett (*Creeping Man*).

PRESBURY, PROFESSOR. Chair of Physiology at Camford University. He was sixty-one years old when the case opened and at this time became engaged to Alice Morphy. Subsequently, as a consequence of certain anthropoid preparations, he began to behave like an ape, and his devoted wolfhound, Roy, almost killed him. **H** intervened (*Creeping Man*).

PRESCOTT, RODGER. Chicago forger and coiner. He was slain by "Killer" Evans in 1895 in Waterloo Road. *Alias* Waldron, he lived at 136 Little Ryder Street prior to his death. The forging machinery was still there, unsuspected by the new tenant, unworldly Nathan Garrideb (*Garridebs*).

PRETORIA. South Africa. Godfrey Emsworth was shot here, at Diamond Hill in the Boer War (*Blanched Soldier*).

PRICE, MR. Of Birmingham. This was an *alias* of **W** when he was introduced to Mr. Pinner by Hall Pycroft (*Stock-broker's Clerk*).

PRINCE OF COLONNA. See Colonna, Prince of.

PRINCE'S STREET. **H**, **W**, and Toby on the trail of the murderers of Bartholomew Sholto (*Sign of Four*).

PRINCESS OF COLONNA. See Colonna, Princess of.

PRINCETOWN CONVICT PRISON. **H** found it on his ordnance map of the Dartmoor area. Selden, the Notting Hill murderer, had escaped from here when **W** and Sir Henry Baskerville arrived at the Hall (*The Hound*).

PRIORY ROAD. A four-wheeler carried **H**, **W**, and Mary Morstan en route to confer with Thaddeus Sholto (*Sign of Four*).

PRIORY SCHOOL. Near Mackleton. A famous school, with Dr. Huxtable in charge. Young Lord Saltire had disappeared from here (*Priory School*).

PRIORY SCHOOL, ADVENTURE OF THE. **H** and **W** solved the disappearance of Lord Saltire, and **H** got a tidy check for £6000.

PRITCHARD, DR. He turned to crime (*Speckled Band*).

PROSPER, FRANCIS. He was greengrocer to the Holders and attentive to Lucy Parr, according to Mary Holder. Francis had a wooden leg (*Beryl Coronet*).

P.T. These were the initials on the note to **H**: "For God's sake come at once." They stood for Dr. Percy Trevelyan (*Resident Patient*).

PUGILIST. Colonel Wardlaw's horse in the Wessex Cup race (*Silver Blaze*).

PULLMAN CAR. **H**, **W**, and Colonel Ross returned in one to London, after the running of the Wessex Cup (*Silver Blaze*).

PUNJAB. India. Henry Wood finally got back and went to Aldershot (*Crooked Man*).

PURDEY PLACE. Home of Mr. Hynes

Hynes, J.P. (*Wisteria Lodge*).

"Put the papers on the sundial." Message which twice accompanied the pips (*Five Orange Pips*).

Pycroft, Hall. He was turned adrift because of the Venezuelan Loan failure. Lived at No. 17 Potter's Terrace, Hampstead. Mr. Pinner wanted him to become the Manager of the Franco-Midland offices in Paris. One of the troubles was that there was no such company (*Stock-broker's Clerk*).

# Q

Queen Anne period. Old Cunningham's estate, near Reigate in Surrey, was of this vintage (*Reigate Puzzle*). Nathan Garrideb's house was not (*Garridebs*).

Queen Anne Street. In September, 1902, **W** was in his own quarters, apart from 221B Baker, in this street (*Illustrious Client*).

"Queen's shilling, taking the." An expression used by Jonathan Small when he referred to joining the Third Buffs (*Sign of Four*).

"Queer Street." According to Lestrade, Constable MacPherson would land in this predicament if it happened again (*Second Stain*). According to **W**, Sir Robert Norbertson was far down this precarious way (*Shoscombe*).

# R

RABBI, HEBREW. His biography is next to Irene Adler's in **H's** index (*Scandal in Bohemia*).

"RACHE." This was scrawled, presumably in blood, on the wall of the room where E. J. Drebber was found. Lestrade discovered the word and thought that it was a start at spelling Rachel. Gregson was unimpressed. **H** noted that it was a German word for revenge. This word was written in blood above the body of Drebber's secretary at Halliday's Private Hotel (*Study in Scarlet*).

*Radix pedis diaboli.* "Devil's foot root." Unknown to **W.** There were two European samples—one in a Buda laboratory, and one with Dr. Leon Sterndale. The powder, on ignition, either killed or drove insane the three Tregennis men and their sister. The root came from the Ubanghi area of West Africa (*Devil's Foot*).

RAGGED SHAW. A grove of trees behind the Priory School.

RAILWAY ARMS. In Little Purlington. **W** telephoned **H** at Baker Street from here. He was as surprised as **W** and Josiah Amberley that the Reverend Vicar Elman knew nothing, or so it seemed (*Retired Colourman*).

RAJPOOTANA. This was traversed by Achmet (*Sign of Four*).

RALPH, OLD. Butler to Colonel Emsworth, at Tuxbury Old Park (*Blanched Soldier*).

RANCE, JOHN. Constable that discovered the body of E. J. Drebber at No. 3 Lauriston Gardens. Lestrade gave **H** the address of Rance as 46 Audley Court, Kennington Park Gate (*Study in Scarlet*).

RANDALLS, THE. A father and two sons, known as the "Lewisham gang." Hopkins felt that they had killed Sir Eustace (*Abbey Grange*).

RAS, DAULAT. He came to ask some questions about the Greek examination for the Fortesque Scholarship. He was innocent (*Three Students*).

RASPER. Lord Singleford's horse in the Wessex Cup race (*Silver Blaze*).

RAT, GIANT, OF SUMATRA. See Sumatra.

RATCLIFF HIGHWAY MURDERS. The *Daily Telegraph* referred to these in reporting E. J. Drebber's murder (*Study in Scarlet*).

READE, WINWOOD. Author of *The Martyrdom of Man,* which **H** suggested that **W** should read. **H** spoke of Reade approvingly during conversation with **W** and Athelney Jones while they were waiting for the "Aurora" to show (*Sign of Four*).

READING. **H** and **W** en route to scene of action from Paddington Station (*Boscombe*). The Armitages lived at Crane Water near Reading (*Speckled Band*). Eyford was seven miles from Reading (*Engineer's Thumb*). Some counterfeit had been traced as far as here (*Engineer's Thumb*). **H** and **W** en route for Exeter (*Silver Blaze*). Mr. Sandeford lived on Lower Grove Road (*Six Napoleons*).

RED BULL INN. Near the Priory School.

RED CIRCLE, ADVENTURE OF THE. Gennaro Lucca wins Mr. Leverton's vote of thanks for killing Gorgiano.

RED-HEADED LEAGUE, THE. June, 1890. Jabez Wilson consulted **H,** and this led to capture of John Clay and accomplice.

RED KING. He granted the Birlstone estate to Hugo de Capus (*Valley of Fear*).

REDRUTH. The Tregennis family were once tin-miners here (*Devil's Foot*).

REGENCY, THE. Sir Robert Norbertson should have been a "buck" in this period, according to **W** (*Shoscombe*).

REGENT'S CIRCUS. **H** and **W** identified the murderer of Milverton from a photograph in a shop window here (*Milverton*). **H** and **W** en route to the Diogenes Club (*Greek Interpreter*).

REGENT STREET. Gross & Hankey's was here (*Scandal in Bohemia*). **H** and **W,** following Sir Henry Baskerville and James Mortimer, noted that there was a follower in a hansom cab also (*The Hound*). The murderous attack on **H** was here, near the Café Royal (*Illustrious Client*).

REICHENBACH FALLS. In Switzerland, near Meiringen. **W** left for the Englischer Hof, and **H** was left by the roaring waters to await Professor Moriarty (*Final Problem*).

REIGATE PUZZLE, THE. April 25, 1887. In Surrey **H** triumphed over the Cunninghams.

REIGATE. Surrey. Colonel Hayter lived nearby (*Reigate Puzzle*).

RESIDENT PATIENT, THE. Dr. Percy Trevelyan consulted **H**

on why Mr. Blessington wanted to help. His benefactor was murdered, although Inspector Lanner thought it was suicide. Blessington was an *alias* for Sutton. Cf. *Cardboard Box.*

RESTAURANTS AND BARS.
- Bar of Gold (see note under inns)
- Blue Anchor
- Café Royal
- Criterion Bar
- Goldini's Restaurant
- Holborn Bar
- Holborn Restaurant, The
- Marcini's Restaurant
- Simpson's Restaurant
- Vegetarian Restaurant
- White Eagle Tavern
- White Hart

RETIRED COLOURMAN, ADVENTURE OF THE. *Circa* 1899. **H** and Barker cooperated on the case. Josiah Amberley murdered his wife and Dr. Ernest and threw the bodies in a well. **W** had a difficult time keeping Josiah in the country while **H** investigated.

REUTER'S. They had a dispatch in the English papers on May 7, 1891, on the struggle between **H** and Moriarty (*Final Problem*).

REYNOLDS. He painted a portrait of one of the Baskervilles (*The Hound*).

RHODESIAN POLICE. Gilchrist had decided to accept a commission with this force and go to South Africa (*Three Students*).

RHONE VALLEY. **H** and **W** wandered about here for a week (*Final Problem*).

"RIBSTON PIPPIN." **W** said James Lancaster looked like one (*Black Peter*).

RICHARDS, DR. Cornwall physician who was partially overcome, apparently by the sight of dead Brenda and insane George and Owen Tregennis. It could have been the atmosphere (*Devil's Foot*).

RICHMOND. In the hunt for the "Aurora" a search party was sent upriver as far as this city (*Sign of Four*). Mr. Hargrave was reported from here (*Valley of Fear*). Robert Ferguson played three-quarter in rugby for this city (*Vampire*).

RICHTER, JOHANN PAUL FRIEDRICH. Also called Jean Paul. A German novelist mentioned by **H** (*Sign of Four*).

*RICOLETTI, of the club-foot, and his abominable wife. **H** referred to a former, and unpublished case (*Musgrave Ritual*).

RIDING THORPE MANOR. Mr. Cubitt lived here, in Norfolk (*Dancing Men*).

RIGA, 1857. **H** referred Francois le Villard to this case (*Sign of Four*).

RIPLEY. A little village in Surrey where **H** had tea (*Naval Treaty*).

RIVIERA. **H** thought that Count Sylvius had contrived a robbery here on February 13, 1892, but the Count said that he was innocent (*Mazarin Stone*). **H** asked Mary Maberley if she would like to go here for a vacation (*Three Gables*).

ROARING JACK WOODLEY. See Jack Woodley.

ROBERTS, LORD. Noted in passing (*Blanched Soldier*). This could be Earl Frederick Sleigh Roberts (1832–1914), a British field marshal. (Personal communication from Mr. Vincent Starrett.)

ROBERT STREET. A four-wheeler was taking **H**, **W**, and Mary Morstan en route to confer with Thaddeus Sholto (*Sign of Four*).

ROBINSON, JOHN. *Alias* for James Ryder, *q.v.*

ROCHESTER ROW. A four-wheeler was taking **H**, **W**, and Mary Morstan en route to confer with Thaddeus Sholto (*Sign of Four*).

"ROCK OF GIBRALTAR." Ship of the Adelaide-Southampton Line (*Abbey Grange*).

RODNEY. Rear-Admiral Baskerville served under him in the West Indies (*The Hound*).

ROMAN CATHOLIC CHURCH. Mrs. Barclay was a member and much interested in the Guild of St. George, which gathered at the Watt Street Chapel (*Crooked Man*).

ROME. Don Murillo was traced by Inspector Baynes here from Paris (*Wisteria Lodge*). Douglas Maberley was attaché here at time of his death (*Three Gables*).

RONDER, EUGENIA. She plotted successfully with Leonardo to murder her husband and put the blame on Sahara King. Mauled by the lion, she lived for seven years in Mrs. Merrilow's house, and her landlady saw her face only once in this period. Finally she confessed to **H**, with **W** as witness (*Veiled Lodger*).

RONDER, MR. Rival of both Wombwell and Sanger, he stopped his circus caravan at Abbas Parva en route to Wimbledon. His wife and the strongman, Leonardo, successfully murdered him and blamed it on his lion, Sahara King (*Veiled Lodger*).

ROSA, SALVATOR. A painting at the home of Thaddeus Sholto's home by him (*Sign of Four*).

ROSENLAUI. **H** and **W** intended to spend a night (May 4, 1891) at this hamlet (*Final Problem*).

ROSS. A town in Herefordshire, near Boscombe Valley (*Boscombe*).

ROSS, COLONEL. Owner of Silver Blaze, the favorite. When his horse vanished, he wanted to consult **H** (*Silver Blaze*).

ROSS, DUNCAN. A red-headed official of the Red-headed League, with office at 7 Pope's Court, Fleet Street. He hired Jabez

Wilson. Ross was called "Archie" by John Clay and was caught with Clay by **H** and Peter Jones while breaking into a bank vault (*Red-headed League*).

ROSS & MANGLES. In Fulham Road. Jack Stapleton bought a large, fierce, black dog from them and brought it circuitously via the North Devon Railway into the Baskerville area (*The Hound*).

*ROTHERHITHE. **H** was said to be working on a case here, in an alley near the river. As far as Mrs. Hudson and **W** could judge, **H's** health did not prosper here (*Dying Detective*).

ROTHIÈRE. See La Rothière.

ROTTERDAM. **H** recognized from the stump that the cigar was Indian but rolled in this city (*Boscombe*).

ROUNDHAY, MR. Vicar of the Cornwall parish that included Tredannick Wollas (*Devil's Foot*).

ROY. Professor Presbury's devoted wolfhound, but on certain occasions he tried to bite his master and finally slipped his collar and almost killed him (*Creeping Man*). Cf. dog.

ROYAL MUNSTERS. A famous Irish regiment of the British Army, based at Aldershot. Colonel Barclay was in command (*Crooked Man*).

ROYLOTT, DR. GRIMESBY. Of Stoke Moran, Surrey. It was one of the oldest Saxon families to which he belonged. Among other things, he had the bad luck to confuse **H** with the official police force. He was so strong of hand that he bent **H's** and **W's** poker at 221B Baker Street. They were not frightened off, and in the end he was killed by a swamp adder (*Speckled Band*).

ROYLOTT, MRS. By her first marriage with Major-General Stoner, she had two daughters, Julia and Helen. She later married Dr. Roylott. Eventually she died (*Speckled Band*).

RUCASTLE, ALICE. Daughter of Mr. Rucastle. She was said to have gone to Philadelphia. She was rescued by Mr. Fowler, whom she married (*Copper Beeches*).

RUCASTLE, EDWARD. The cruel child of the Rucastles (*Copper Beeches*).

RUCASTLE, JEPHRO. Resident of the Copper Beeches, near Winchester. He wanted Violet Hunter to cut her hair very short if she came to work for him (*Copper Beeches*).

RUCASTLE, MRS. The pallid but devoted second wife of Jephro (*Copper Beeches*).

RUDGE-WHITWORTH. Make of bicycle supposedly belonging to the murderer of John Douglas (*Valley of Fear*).

RUE AUSTERLITZ, PARIS. Henri Fournaye and his wife lived here

(*Second Stain*). Cf. Fournaye; also Lucas, Eduardo.

RUE DE TRAJAN. Montpellier. Marie Devine lived at No. 11 (*Lady Frances Carfax*).

RUFTON, EARL OF. Lady Frances Carfax was the only direct survivor of his estate (*Lady Frances Carfax*).

RULLI, SIGNOR. *Alias* Mr. Lucas, *alias* of Lopez. He was killed at the Hotel Escurial in Madrid six months after he and Don Murillo escaped from London (*Wisteria Lodge*).

"RURITANIA." Of the Cunard Line. It was leaving from Liverpool Friday, with Baron Gruner aboard, for the United States. The time was short (*Illustrious Client*).

RUSSELL, CLARK. W read one of his sea-stories (*Five Orange Pips*).

RUSSELL SQUARE. Mr. Cubitt stayed at a boarding house here (*Dancing Men*).

RUSSIA. Sergius betrayed Anna, his wife, and Alexis, his wife's true love, and came to Yoxley Old Place under the *alias* Professor Coram (*Pince-Nez*). See also Godno (*The Hound*).

RUSSIAN EMBASSY, IN LONDON. H and W took Anna's letters and diary here to save Alexis (*Pince-Nez*).

*RUSSIAN WOMAN, THE OLD. This adventure was in the pre-Watsonian period, but records exist, for they were shown to W (*Musgrave Ritual*).

RUSSO-GERMAN GRAIN TAXES. Trelawney Hope had a note on this subject too (*Second Stain*).

RYDER, JAMES. *Alias* John Ryder. An upper-attendant at the Hotel Cosmopolitan (*Blue Carbuncle*).

# S

SAFFRON HILL. Inspector Hill knew this area well (*Six Napoleons*).

SAHARA KING. North African lion in the Ronder circus. The animal was blamed for the murder of Ronder but was innocent (*Veiled Lodger*).

SAILORS, HANDS OF. See Holmes, Sherlock, under Works.

SAINT CLAIR, NEVILLE (ST. CLAIR, NEVILLE). He lived at the Decars, near Lee in Kent, and worked in London. Mrs. St. Clair saw her husband in the window of the Bar of Gold, an opium den in Upper Swandam Lane. When the police aided her in trying to extricate her husband, he had disappeared from the room, and the cripple, Hugh Boone, was there instead. Subsequently she heard from Neville by letter that he was unharmed. Later, **H** exposed Hugh Boone in the Bow Street Police Station as Neville in disguise (*Twisted Lip*).

ST. GEORGE'S CHURCH. In Hanover Square. The St. Simon-Doran wedding was here (*Noble Bachelor*).

ST. GEORGE, GUILD OF. See Guild.

ST. GEORGE'S, THEOLOGICAL COLLEGE OF. Elias Whitney was the Principal here (*Twisted Lip*).

ST. HELENA. John Douglas was lost overboard the "Palmyra" in a gale near here. Ivy Douglas cabled the news to Cecil Barker. **H** felt that it was not accidental but that Moriarty was involved (*Valley of Fear*).

ST. IVES. Mrs. Porter's family lived here (*Devil's Foot*).

*St. James's*. As for the *Globe* (*Blue Carbuncle*).

ST. JAMES'S END OF PALL MALL. **H** and **W** en route to the Diogenes Club (*Greek Interpreter*).

ST. JAMES'S HALL. Sarasate played here (*Red-headed League*).

ST. JAMES'S SQUARE. London Library was here (*Illustrious Client*).

ST. JAMES'S STREET. Langdale Pike spent his waking hours in a club on this street, listening to and transmitting or publishing London gossip (*Three Gables*).

St. John's Wood. Irene Adler lived in this section of London (*Scandal in Bohemia*).

St. Louis, Missouri. **H** refers Francois le Villard to the case here of 1871 (*Sign of Four*).

St. Luke's. See College of St. Luke's.

St. Oliver's. A private school kept by the Vandeleurs (*The Hound*).

St. Pancras case. See Merivale, Inspector.

St. Pancras Hotel. The Hosmer Angels were to have a wedding breakfast here (*Case of Identity*).

St. Paul's. Near here, at 17 King Edward Street, Mr. William Morris was supposed to have law offices (*Red-headed League*).

St. Saviour's. Near King's Cross, where Mary Sutherland was to marry Hosmer Angel (*Case of Identity*).

St. Simon, Lady Clara. Sister of Lord St. Simon (*Noble Bachelor*).

St. Simon, Lord Robert. When his fiancée, Hatty Doran, disappeared, he consulted **H.** He was at one time undersecretary for the colonies. Second son of the Duke of Balmoral and owner of a small estate, Birchmoor (*Noble Bachelor*).

St. Simon, Lord Eustace. Younger brother of Lord Robert St. Simon and so the third son of the Duke of Balmoral (*Noble Bachelor*).

Saltire, Lord. Ten-year-old son of the Duke of Holdernesse. He vanished from Priory School. The young pupil, Arthur, had his sympathies with his mother, who was living abroad, and was in danger from James Wilder. **H** solved the disappearance of Arthur and the murder of the German master, then lectured the Duke and got £6000 (*Priory School*).

Samson of New Orleans. As for Von Bischoff, *q.v.*

Samuel, 1st or 2d chapter. According to **H**, it was one of these chapters which explained why Mrs. Barclay called her husband "David," since he had betrayed Henry Wood in India (*Crooked Man*). (Samuel II:11 is the correct reference.)

Sand, George. **H** quotes from a letter from Flaubert to her (*Red-headed League*).

Sandeford, Mr. He bought a cheap bust of Napoleon from Harding Brothers for 15 shillings and sold it to **H** for £10 (*Six Napoleons*).

Sanders, Ikey. He refused to cut up the stolen jewel for Count Sylvius (*Mazarin Stone*).

San Francisco, California. Home of Aloysius Doran (*Noble Bachelor*).

Sanger. His circus was in competition with those of Wombwell and Ronder (*Veiled Lodger*).

San Paulo (São Paulo), Brazil. An entry in J. H. Neligan's notebook (*Black Peter*).

SAN PEDRO. Where Don Murillo, the dictator, and Lopez, his secretary, ruled until it was expedient to flee to Barcelona in 1886 (*Wisteria Lodge*).

SARASATE. Played at St James's Hall. A violinist (*Red-headed League*).

SAUNDERS. Housemaid to Hilton Cubitt. She sent for the physician (*Dancing Men*).

SAUNDERS, MRS. Caretaker of house in which Nathan Garrideb lived (*Garridebs*).

SAUNDERS, SIR JAMES. A distinguished dermatologist. At **H**'s request, he examined Godfrey Emsworth. It was not leprosy. (*Blanched Soldier*). ***H** said he had rendered Saunders a professional service. There might be a good case hidden here.

SAVAGE, VICTOR. Nephew of Culverton Smith. Uncle Culverton killed Victor in four days by means of a microbial infection of Asiatic strain. **H** avenged Victor by seeing to it that the uncle was charged with the murder (*Dying Detective*).

"SAWYER, MRS." She came for the ring that was advertised by **H** in **W**'s name. The false address given was 13 Duncan Street, Houndsditch (*Study in Scarlet*).

SAXE-COBURG SQUARE. As for Coburg Square.

SAXE-MENINGEN, CLOTILDE. See von Saxe-Meningen.

SAXON FAMILIES. One of the oldest was the Roylotts, of Stoke Moran, in western Surrey (*Speckled Band*).

SCANDAL IN BOHEMIA, A. Irene Adler was always *the* woman to **H** and was prominent in this early case (March, 1888). The Watsons were married and well settled, and **H** was alone (and so faintly susceptible?) at 221B Baker.

SCENE OF ACTION. Of the sixty published cases, a large majority take place in southwest England, especially in the London area and adjacent counties. Although certain cases had their origins elsewhere, the scene of action in which Sherlock Holmes participated usually was located not far from the epicenter at 221B Baker Street. Put another way, a circle of a radius of fifty miles, centered in London, would enclose most of the adventures.

Two cases were placed much farther away but were exceptions in that **H** had not been called in to consult. One of these, *The Adventure of the Devil's Foot,* was placed in his all too willing hands while he was fretting out a rest cure in Cornwall. The other was *The Final Problem,* in Switzerland, where he was followed by Professor Moriarty.

The distribution is as follows:

27 London (Three cases have

been rather difficult to assign, but probably fall within the London district: *Last Bow; Veiled Lodger; Norwood Builder*).

1 Bedfordshire (*Blanched Soldier*).

2 Berkshire (*Engineer's Thumb; Shoscombe*).

1 Cambridgeshire (*Missing Three-Quarter*).

2 Either Cambridgeshire or Oxfordshire (*Creeping Man; Three Students*).

1 Cornwall (*Devil's Foot*).

2 Devonshire (*The Hound; Silver Blaze*).

1 Hallamshire (*Priory School*).

2 Hampshire (*Copper Beeches; Thor Bridge*).

1 Herefordshire (*Boscombe Valley*).

3 Kent (*Abbey Grange; Pince-Nez; ? Greek Interpreter*).

2 Norfolk (*Dancing Men; Gloria Scott*).

1 Southampton (*Crooked Man*).

5 Surrey (*Cardboard Box; Reigate Puzzle; Solitary Cyclist; Speckled Band; Wisteria Lodge*).

6 Sussex (*Five Orange Pips; Lion's Mane; Musgrave Ritual; Vampire; Valley of Fear; Black Peter*).

2 ? Middlesex (*Three Gables; Yellow Face*).

1 Bern Canton, Switzerland (*Final Problem*).

SCHOENBRUNN PALACE. Of Franz Josef. Von Bork's Tokay came from here (*Last Bow*).

SCHOOLS.

Abbey School
College of St. Luke's
Cambridge University (Trinity College is mentioned)
Camford University
Eton
Gables, The (Sussex)
London University
Oxford University
Priory School (Hallamshire)
St. Oliver's (Yorkshire)
Theological College of St. George's
Uppingham
York College (America, probably United States of America)

SCOTLAND. This was referred to as a possible site of John Clay's work (*Red-headed League*). Mrs. Hudson believed in breakfast as though she were a Scotchwoman (*Naval Treaty*). When the "Sea Unicorn" got to this country, the disappearance of the rescued man was easily hushed up—only Patrick Cairns had seen Captain Cary heave him overboard (*Black Peter*). Inspector MacDonald was brought up here (*Valley of Fear*).

SCOTLAND YARD. **H** was not greatly impressed with this institution's detective work (*Study in Scarlet*). Peter Jones of the Yard met **H** at Baker Street (*Red-headed League*). **H** took Mr.

Hatherley here to get help (*Engineer's Thumb*). This institution is mentioned in *Noble Bachelor, Resident Patient, Greek Interpreter, Solitary Cyclist* (by **W**), *The Hound, Cardboard Box,* and *Red Circle.*

The Yard sent Detective Forbes (*Naval Treaty*). The Yard owed **H** a good turn (*Norwood Builder*). Lestrade felt that all at the Yard would be proud of **H** (*Six Napoleons*). Stanley Hopkins of the Yard advised Cyril Overton to consult **H** (*Three-Quarter*). After the Yard had been notified, Stanley Hopkins was sent to Kent, and then **H** and **W** were called in (*Abbey Grange*). Inspector MacDonald of the Yard consulted **H** (*Valley of Fear*). Inspector Morton was on hand and made the arrest (*Dying Detective*). **H** felt that this organization was lonesome when he was away (*Lady Frances Carfax*). **H** came here to see Lestrade (*Lady Frances Carfax* and *Garridebs*).

**H** mentioned that this was where he was taking Von Bork (*Last Bow*). The Yard could not act in this case (*Illustrious Client*). In the event that **H** was murdered, he wished **W** to give a certain name to this organization (*Mazarin Stone*). **H** was about to go here from Isadora Klein's home (*Three Gables*). **H** went here to see Lestrade (*Garridebs*). Sergeant Coventry of the Winchester police would rather have **H** on the case than the Yard if he were to get any credit (*Thor Bridge*). **H** felt that he had been slow, and that *Cyanea* nearly avenged the Yard (*Lion's Mane*). Merivale of the Yard asked **H** to look into the St. Pancras case (*Shoscombe*). The Yard sent Josiah Amberley to consult **H** (*Retired Colourman*).

In the preceding twenty-seven cases Scotland Yard is cited as such, or as the Yard, or yarders are noted as such. Obviously many of the men with whom **H** worked were inspectors, sergeants, constables, detectives, or officials of Scotland Yard, but if this institution was not specifically mentioned or alluded to in a particular case, it was not included here. These twenty-seven case references do include the St. Pancras case, which, although not in the published series, was nevertheless one of **H's** collaborations with an official of Scotland Yard. Since there are sixty published cases, this summary reveals that in almost a third of them the existence of this institution is acknowledged.

SCOTLAND YARD MUSEUM. See air-gun.

**SCOTT ECCLES, JOHN.** Of Popham House, Lee. He wired **H** for a consultation from Charing Cross Post Office at the end of March, 1892. He had been affronted by the disappearance of his host, and he was afraid that he would be charged with the murder of Aloysius Garcia (*Wisteria Lodge*).

**SCYLLA AND CHARYBDIS.** **W** compared the two types of cases between which he would like to steer to these (*Resident Patient*).

**SEA OF AZOV FLEET.** See Admiral Green.

SECOND STAIN, ADVENTURE OF THE. The prime minister and secretary for European affairs consulted **H.** Later, Lady Hope consulted **H.** When **H** called on her, he prevailed, and Trelawney Hope found the missing letter in his case after all and had an assured diplomatic future. (Note that in the *Naval Treaty* case, it is reported that **H** demonstrated the true facts concerning the Adventure of the Second Stain to Monsieur Dubugue of the Paris Police and to Fritz von Waldbaum of Danzig. These officials were not mentioned in the *Second Stain,* but they belong to the saga.)

**SELDEN.** "Notting Hill murderer," escaped from Princetown prison. He was either killed or frightened to death by the Hound, and his body, clothed in Sir Henry Baskerville's clothes, was discovered by **H** and **W.** He was the brother of Mrs. Barrymore. (*The Hound*).

**SENEGAMBIA.** **H** recalled a parallel case from here (*Sign of Four*).

**SERGIUS.** To save his own life, he betrayed his wife, Anna, and her true love, Alexis, as well as others. Later Anna came to Yoxley Old Place to get the documents that would free Alexis. She killed Willoughby Smith (*Pince-Nez*).

**SERPENTINE, THE.** Lestrade donned a pea-jacket and, with more zeal than wit, dragged this water course for the body of Lady St. Simon (*Noble Bachelor*).

**SERPENTINE AVENUE.** Irene Adler's address in St. John's Wood (*Scandal in Bohemia*).

**SEVERN.** **H** and **W** en route to Boscombe Valley crossed this river (*Boscombe*).

**SHADWELL POLICE STATION.** Jim Browner, arrested for the murders by Lestrade, on evidence supplied by **H,** made a statement to Inspector Montgomery here (*Cardboard Box*).

**SHAFTESBURY AVENUE.** Mr. Melas and Mr. Latimer en route presumably to Kensington (*Greek Interpreter*).

**SHERMAN.** A taxidermist at No. 3 Pinchin Lane, Lambeth. He loaned Toby to **H** when the latter sent **W** after the dog (*Sign of Four*). Cf. dog.

**SHETLAND LIGHTS.** Before the "Sea

Unicorn" had sighted them, Neligan, Sr., was overboard (*Black Peter*).

"S.H. for J.O." This message was sent with five orange pips to Captain Calhoun by **H.** It meant: Sherlock Holmes for John Openshaw (*Five Orange Pips*).

*Shikari*. **H** mocks Colonel Moran with this appellation (*Empty House*).

SHIPLEY'S YARD. A hansom cab stand near Waterloo Station where John Clayton had his cab (*The Hound*).

SHIPPING OFFICE. James Mortimer could not recall if he had left his stick here or at 221B Baker (*The Hound*).

SHIPS AND BOATS.

- Alicia
- Aurora
- Bass Rock
- Esmeralda
- Friesland
- Gloria Scott
- Hotspur
- Matilda Briggs
- May Day
- Norah Creina
- Orontes
- Palmyra
- Rock of Gibraltar
- Ruritania
- Sophy Anderson

SHLESSINGER, DR. AND MRS. He was a South American missionary preparing a map of the Holy Land with special reference to the Midianites, on which subject he was writing a monograph. His left ear was jagged or torn. *Alias* of Holy Peters, or Henry Peters. His "wife" was actually Fraser. They tried to kill Lady Frances by burying her alive while under anaesthesia, but **H** intervened at the last possible moment to save her. They escaped capture by Lestrade. (*Lady Frances Carfax*).

SHOLTO, BARTHOLOMEW. Lived at Pondicherry Lodge, Upper Norwood. **H** and **W** found him murdered in his own room, with "Sign of Four" on a piece of paper and a stone-headed hammer by his body. He had been killed by a vegetable alkaloid poison on a thorn shot into his scalp by Tonga (*Sign of Four*).

SHOLTO, MAJOR JOHN. Father of twin sons, Bartholomew and Thaddeus. He was commander of the 34th Bombay Infantry Regiment, the same outfit to which Captain Morstan belonged (*q.v.*). On the latter's disappearance from the Langham Hotel in London, the captain's daughter, Mary, called on the major. Major Sholto was now retired at Pondicherry Lodge and professed ignorance of the fact that Captain Morstan had even been in London. This was a lie—cf. Captain Arthur Morstan.

Major Sholto had been in

command in the Andaman Islands, with Captain Morstan second-in-command. Cf. Lal Chowdar, and Thaddeus Sholto. He was about to tell Thaddeus where the Agra Treasure was kept (which he stole from Jonathan Small and his companions) when a face appeared at the window. His sons investigated, and on their return found their father dead. His death was reported in the April 28, 1882, edition of the *Times* (*Sign of Four*).

SHOLTO, THADDEUS. Brother of Bartholomew and son of John. He sent Williams to bring Mary Morstan and two friends (**H** and **W**) from a meeting-place at the Lyceum Theatre (cf. "Be at . . . etc."). They came to his home in Surrey, and he told them of his father's account of Captain Morstan's death (*q.v.*).

Thaddeus, **H, W,** and Mary went to Pondicherry Lodge to talk with his twin brother, Bartholomew. On arrival they found Bartholomew dead, and Thaddeus was arrested by Athelney Jones for his brother's murder. He was released because of an alibi, and his release was reported in the *Standard* and by Athelney Jones to **H** (*Sign of Four*).

SHOSCOMBE. A small village in Berkshire where **H** and **W** came, ostensibly for some fishing. They put up at the Green Dragon (*Shoscombe*).

SHOSCOMBE OLD PLACE. Property of Lady Beatrice Falder, widowed sister of Sir Robert Norbertson, who lived with her. Near the village of Shoscombe.

SHOSCOMBE OLD PLACE, ADVENTURE OF. Berkshire. When Lady Falder died of dropsy, her brother, Sir Robert Norbertson, hid her body and concealed her death until Shoscombe Prince won the derby to net him £80,000.

SHOSCOMBE PARK. This surrounded Shoscombe Old Place (*Shoscombe*).

SHOSCOMBE PRINCE. Colt belonging to Sir Robert Norbertson, which was entered in the Derby. His horse won the race, and Sir Robert picked up about £80,000—enough to pay his debts (*Shoscombe*).

SHOSCOMBE SPANIELS. A most exclusive breed, possibly the most exclusive in England, according to **W.** They were heard from repeatedly at dog shows (*Shoscombe*). Cf. dog.

SIAM. Mycroft Holmes disliked leaving his office, considering the state of this country, but he and Lestrade had to consult **H** (*Bruce-Partington*).

SIBERIA. Alexis slaved here while his true love, Anna, came to Yoxley Old Place to get the documents which would free him from her Russian husband (*alias* Professor Coram). She poisoned herself when **H** proved that she had killed Willoughby Smith (*Pince-Nez*).

*Sidelights on Horace.* Dr. Thorneycroft Huxtable's memorable work (*Priory School*).

SIERRA LEONE. This seemed best to Armitage, Evans, and the others cut adrift (*Gloria Scott*).

SIGERSON. An exploring Norwegian. *Alias* of **H** (*Empty House*).

SIGN OF THE FOUR, THE. July, 1888? Jonathan Small, Mahomet Singh, Abdullah Khan, and Dost Akbar were the Four. After they murdered Achmet, the Agra Treasure was buried. The Four were indicted and imprisoned. Small escaped and with Tonga got to England. Bartholomew Sholto was murdered. **H** solved the problem.

SILVER BLAZE. The favorite for the Wessex Cup vanishes. This Devonshire action involved **H's** being called in by Colonel Ross, owner of Silver Blaze, and by Inspector Gregory.

SILVESTER'S. Lady Frances Carfax banked here (*Lady Frances Carfax*).

SIMPSON. One of the Baker Street Irregulars. He kept watch on Henry Wood (*Crooked Man*).

SIMPSON, BALDY. Friend of Godfrey Emsworth. Killed near Buffelsspruit in the Boer War (*Blanched Soldier*).

SIMPSON, FITZROY. Arrested in connection with the disappearance of the favorite, Silver Blaze, for his cravat was found near the trainer's body. He was a genteel bookmaker in London (*Silver Blaze*).

SIMPSON'S. Restaurant where **H** proposed to break his fast of three days (*Dying Detective*). **H** and **W** ate here one evening and watched the Strand traffic. It was "our Strand restaurant," according to **W** (*Illustrious Client*).

SINCLAIR, ADMIRAL. Sir James Walter spent the evening with him (*Bruce-Partington*).

SINGH, MAHOMET. One of the Four, the others being Abdullah Khan, Dost Akbar, and Jonathan Small. Mahomet and Abdullah served under Jonathan at the Agra Fort (*Sign of Four*).

SIX NAPOLEONS, ADVENTURE OF THE. Six plaster busts of Napoleon were sold by Gelder & Co. at 6 shillings each. Pietro Venucci was murdered. Beppo was captured. **H** bought the last bust from Mr. Sandeford for £10 and thereby obtained the Pearl of the Borgias.

SKIBBAREEN. Altamont, *alias* of **H**, gave the Constabulary here much trouble and came to the attention of Von Bork (*Last Bow*).

SLANEY, ABE. "Most dangerous crook in Chicago," according to Wilson Hargrave. **H** sent Abe a message at Elrige's Farm, and Inspector Martin arrested him for murder (*Dancing Men*).

SLATER. A stonemason who saw someone else in Captain Cary's "cabin" at 1:00 A.M. (*Black Peter*).

SLATERS, HANDS OF. See Holmes, Sherlock, under Works.

SLEEPY QUARTERS. **H** said this of Chesterton, Histon, Waterbeach, and Oakington in his search of the countryside (*Three-Quarter*).

SLOANE, HANS. If Nathan Garrideb could find a third namesake, he could sell out for $5,000,000 and be a modern Hans Sloane (*Garridebs*).

SMALL, JONATHAN. One of the Four, the others being Mahomet Singh, Dost Akbar, and Abdullah Khan. He was middle-aged, small, active, sunburned, with a wooden stump for a right leg. He and an Andaman Islander murdered Bartholomew Sholto at Pondicherry Lodge. In the chase of the hired "Aurora" down the Thames by **H, W,** and Athelney Jones in a police launch, the Islander, Tonga, was shot and fell overboard. Jonathan Small was trapped when the "Aurora" grounded and his wooden leg became stuck in the mud.

He was born near Pershore, Worcestershire, received little education, and at eighteen joined the Third Buffs en route for India. A crocodile bit off his right leg in the Ganges, and he was saved by Sergeant John Holder and invalided out of service. Became overseer for Abel White. In the Great Mutiny when White was killed, he escaped to Agra. Joined the three Indians (to form the Four) in a plot to murder Achmet. He buried the Agra Treasure, was arrested and charged with the murder, and was sent to serve time in the Andaman Islands. He escaped with Tonga, an Islander, to follow and murder Major John Sholto, who had in turn stolen the Agra Treasure (*Sign of Four*).

SMITH, MR. CULVERTON. Of No. 13 Lower Burke Street. A Sumatra planter, he was the only person who could help **H**, or so **H** told **W. W** prevailed upon Smith to see **H. W** was on hand as an unseen witness, and Inspector Morton was on hand to arrest Smith when he was tricked into a confession that he had caused Victor Savage's death (*Dying Detective*).

SMITH, JAMES. Father of Violet. He had conducted the orchestra at the Imperial Theatre before his death (*Solitary Cyclist*).

SMITH, MORDECAI. He lived in a

small brick house with his wife and two sons (Jack being the younger and Jim the older), at water's edge at the end of Broad Street. Here he hired out boats, at least a barge and the fast steam launch "Aurora." Mordecai took Jonathan Small and Tonga aboard the launch at 3:00 A.M. **H** advertised for information on the whereabouts of the absent Smith and his launch in the *Standard.* **H** traced him and his boat to Jacobson's Yard. Later, after a wild chase down the Thames, his boat was captured. Cf. "Aurora"; also Jonathan Small (*Sign of Four*).

*SMITH-MORTIMER succession case, in 1894 (*Pince-Nez*).

SMITH, RALPH. Uncle of Violet. He did not write from Africa. On his death Violet inherited his fortune (*Solitary Cyclist*).

SMITH, VIOLET. Niece of Ralph. She was abducted and illegally married, but her tormentors were jailed on evidence supplied by **H.** She inherited her uncle's fortune and married Cyril Morton (*Solitary Cyclist*).

SMITH, WILLOUGHBY. Secretary to Professor Coram. His sound schooling was at Uppingham and Cambridge. He died from a carotid puncture made by his employer's sealing-wax knife. As he was dying he said, "The Professor—it was she." His killer, Anna, was the Professor's wife, and she took poison (*Pince-Nez*).

SOAMES, SIR CATHCART. His son was also sent to the Priory School.

SOAMES, HILTON. Tutor and lecturer at College of St. Luke's. He called on **H,** and the latter detected the guilty student (*Three-Quarter*).

SOLENT. Data supplied by Altamont, *alias* for **H,** would not be of much service to a German cruiser trying to escape mines in this area (*Last Bow*).

SOLITARY CYCLIST, ADVENTURE OF THE. Saturday, April 23, 1895. Violet Smith abducted, illegally married, but her tormentors jailed on the evidence of **H.** She inherited her uncle's fortune and married Cyril Morton.

SOMERTON, DR. A surgeon at Hope Town (*Sign of Four*).

SOMOMY STOCK. Silver Blaze was of this strain (*Silver Blaze*).

SOPHY. Paul Kratides embraced her. They were probably brother and sister. Reportedly she lived to kill her abductors (*Greek Interpreter*).

*"*Sophy Anderson.*" This British bark was lost at sea. **W** recorded it in 1887, but the case has not been published (*Five Orange Pips*).

SOTHEBY. As for Christie (*Illustrious Client* and *Garridebs*).

SOUTH AFRICA. Jack Woodley was a great bully here and known from Kimberley to Johannesburg (*Solitary Cyclist*). Gilchrist had decided to enter the Rhodesian Police (*Three Students*). Sir Charles Baskerville made a fortune here in speculation (*The Hound*). John and Ivy Douglas were on their way here when John was lost overboard (*Valley of Fear*). Philip Green made money at Barberton (*Lady Frances Carfax*). Mr. Dodd was in the Boer War here (*Blanched Soldier*). Cf. Africa; also West Africa.

SOUTH AFRICAN GOLD SHARES. Mr. Carruthers was deeply interested (*Solitary Cyclist*).

SOUTH AFRICAN SECURITIES. **W** was not going to invest in them (*Dancing Men*).

SOUTH AFRICAN WAR. **H** refused a knighthood shortly after the conclusion of this struggle, *circa* June, 1902 (*Garridebs*).

SOUTH AMERICA. This was the source of the arrow poison stolen by Jefferson Hope from York College (*Study in Scarlet*). According to John Barrymore, arrangements were made to get Selden here in a very few days (*The Hound*). Dr. Shlessinger was a missionary here, or so it was said (*Lady Frances Carfax*).

SOUTH COAST. Sir Henry Baskerville's father lived in a small cottage here, and as a boy in his teens Henry went from here to America (*The Hound*).

SOUTH DEVON. **H** retired here and kept bees (*Last Bow*).

SOUTH LONDON. T. Sholto lived here (*Sign of Four*).

SOUTHAMPTON. Alice Rucastle married Mr. Fowler here (*Copper Beeches*). Mr. Hargrave was reported from here (*Valley of Fear*). James Dodd had a letter from Godfrey Emsworth from here (*Blanched Soldier*).

SOUTHAMPTON HIGHROAD. It was by the *Copper Beeches.*

SOUTHERTON, LORD. His estate in Hampshire bordered on the residence of Jephro Rucastle (*Copper Beeches*).

SOUTHSEA. Watson yearned for it (*Resident Patient* and *Cardboard Box*).

SPANISH EMBASSY, LONDON. They could tell Mr. Scott Eccles nothing about Aloysius Garcia (*Wisteria Lodge*).

SPAULDING, VINCENT. *Alias* John Clay when he was assistant to Jabez Wilson at half-pay (*Red-headed League*).

SPECKLED BAND, ADVENTURE OF THE. April, 1883. **H** saved Helen Stoner.

*Spectator*. James M. Dodd told **H** that he thought that Mr. Kent could have been reading this journal (*Blanched Soldier*).

SPENCER-JOHN GANG. Barney Stockdale and Steve Dixie belonged (*Three Gables*).

Spender, Rose. She died of senility in the Poultney Square home of the Shlessingers (or Peters), and her death was certified by Dr. Horsom. She was to be buried by Stimson & Co., which furnished an extraordinary coffin (*Lady Frances Carfax*).

Splugen Pass. **H** felt that Baron Gruner killed his wife here (*Illustrious Client*).

Stackhurst, Harold. Head of coaching school, The Gables, about half a mile from **H's** home on the Sussex downs. His science master, McPherson, was killed, and fortunately **H** found that the killer was *Cyanea* before Harold lost his mathematics coach, Ian Murdoch, as well (*Lion's Mane*).

Stamford, young. **W's** dresser at Barts. After **W's** return from India, he introduced **H** to **W.** He suggested that **H** might start a paper entitled *Police News of the Past* in deference to **H's** phenomenal grasp of the historical aspects of crime (*Study in Scarlet*).

Stamford's. This firm sent **H** an Ordnance Map of the moor about Baskerville Hall (*The Hound*).

*Standard.* London newspaper, as for *Daily Telegraph, q.v.* Carried the news of the death of Bartholomew Sholto, giving acclaim to Athelney Jones; later noted the release of Thaddeus Sholto and Bartholomew's landlady, a Mrs. Bernstone. In same issue carried advertisement by **H** for information as to whereabouts of "Aurora" and her master, Mordecai Smith (*Sign of Four*).

Stangerson, Joseph. Private secretary to E. J. Drebber and staying at Madame Charpentier's boarding-house in Torquay Terrace, London. He was sought by Lestrade for murder of Drebber but was found murdered at Halliday's Private Hotel (*Study in Scarlet*).

Staples. Butler to Culverton Smith (*Dying Detective*).

Stapleton, Beryl. Passed as sister of Jack but in reality was his wife. It was she who sent the warning to Sir Henry in London. Earlier she was operating under the *alias* of Mrs. Vandeleur, *née* Beryl Garcia of Costa Rica (*The Hound*).

Stapleton, Jack. Naturalist, lepidopterist; two years in the Baskerville area; knew Grimpen Mire well; saw much of Sir Charles Baskerville. He lived at Merripit House nearby, with his "sister," Beryl. He objected to Sir Charles and Beryl falling in love—since she was really Jack's wife. At Black Tor **H** told **W** that Jack was their enemy. **H** recognized Jack's strong resemblance to a portrait of the infamous Hugo Baskerville. **H** killed his phosphoreted hound before it could kill Sir Henry Baskerville (cf. dog). Jack fled to the Grimpen Mire and probably died there. He was the only son of Rodger Baskerville, who went to Central America, where he died. Jack grew up in the region and married Beryl Garcia of Costa Rica. Jack Stapleton and Mr. Vandeleur are *aliases* therefore of this Baskerville (*The Hound*).

*Star*. London evening newspaper. As for *Globe* (*Blue Carbuncle*).

"STARR, DR. LYSANDER." He was mayor in Topeka, Kansas, in 1890, according to **H**, who invented this person on the spur of the moment. "John Garrideb" replied that his name was still honored there (*Garridebs*).

STARK, COLONEL LYSANDER. He consulted Victor Hatherley. Oddly enough, he was addressed as "Fritz" by his female companion at another time. He probably murdered Jeremiah Hayling, according to **H**, and he chopped off Victor's thumb. **H** and Inspector Bradstreet thought that the Colonel was the head of a large counterfeit organization. He escaped without trace (*Engineer's Thumb*).

STARS AND STRIPES. Mentioned in the *Noble Bachelor*.

STATES. See United States of America.

STAUNTON, ARTHUR H. A rising young forger (*Three-Quarter*).

STAUNTON, GODFREY. His disappearance probably caused his team, Cambridge, to lose the game with Oxford—although this is not assured by any means. His absence was a consequence of his concern for the young wife to whom he was secretly married. She lay dead in a cottage despite everything that Dr. Armstrong could do (*Three-Quarter*).

*STAUNTON, HENRY. **H** stated that his evidence helped to hang Henry, but this case is not available as yet (*Three-Quarter*).

STEILER, PETER, THE ELDER. Manager of the Englischer Hof in Meiringen, Switzerland. He was at the Grosvenor Hotel at one time (*Final Problem*).

STEINER. He was an agent of Von Bock, but he was in the Portsmouth jail (*Last Bow*).

STEPHENS. Butler to Lady Beatrice Falder of *Shoscombe* Old Place.

STEPNEY. Gelder & Company were in Church Street (*Six Napoleons*).

STEPS. **H** tells **W** that he sees but does not observe, that there are seventeen steps leading up from the hall to their consulting room at 221B Baker Street (*Scandal in Bohemia*).

STERNDALE, DR. LEON. Explorer. In love with Brenda Tregennis. When not on expeditions, presumably African, he lived in

Beauchamp Arriance near Brenda's house. He was recalled from Plymouth by Vicar Roundhay, and he killed Mortimer Tregennis on learning that Mortimer had destroyed his brothers and Brenda, their sister. **H** did not expose him; **W** did not expose him (*Devil's Foot*).

*STEVENS, BERT. **H** described him as "that terrible murderer." He wanted **H** to "get him off" in 1887 (*Norwood Builder*). No published report.

STEVENSON. He was on the Cambridge University rugger team (*Three-Quarter*).

STEWART, JANE. Housemaid to Mrs. James Barclay. She related to **H** that she had heard the Barclays quarreling (*Crooked Man*).

*STEWART, MRS. **H** felt that Colonel Moran was involved in her death in 1887 (*Empty House*).

STIMSON & CO. These Kennington Road undertakers were to bury Rose Spender, and, presumably, they did (*Lady Frances Carfax*).

STOCK-BROKER'S CLERK, THE. 1888. Shortly after **W** married Mary Morstan, Hall Pycroft went to work in Birmingham. He was impersonated in his absence by one of the Beddingtons. It was fortunate that **H** intervened in time.

STOCKDALE, BARNEY. Husband of Susan. He was a member of the Spencer John gang and was hired by Isadora Klein to obtain the Douglas Maberley manuscript (*Three Gables*).

STOCKDALE, SUSAN. Wife of Barney. She was planted as a "servant" in the home of Mary Maberley, probably to locate the Maberley manuscript wanted by Isadora Klein (*Three Gables*).

STOCKWELL PLACE. A four-wheeler carrying **H, W,** and Mary Morstan en route to Thaddeus Sholto (*Sign of Four*).

STONE, REVEREND JOSHUA. At Nether Walsling, near Oxshott. He too lived in a large house, but not the right one (*Wisteria Lodge*).

STONER, HELEN. Stepdaughter of Dr. Roylott of Stoke Moran, Surrey. She consulted **H** when her twin sister Julia died. **H** saved her life (*Speckled Band*).

STONER, JULIA. Stepdaughter of Dr. Roylott. Her death prompted her sister Helen to come to London to consult **H**. Her death was revenged (*Speckled Band*).

STONER, MAJOR-GENERAL. First husband of Mrs. Grimesby Roylott. He and his wife had twin daughters, Helen and Julia. He was in the Bengal Artillery, and after his death the young widow married Dr. Roylott, and the family came to England (*Speckled Band*).

STOPER, MISS. Manager of the West End agency, Westaway's, that specialized in governesses (*Copper Beeches*).

STRADIVARIUS VIOLINS. **H** discussed the difference between them and the Amati instruments (*Study in Scarlet*). Also, as for Miracle Plays (*Sign of Four*). **H** said that his Stradivarius was worth 500 guineas but that he had paid only 55 shillings for it in Tottenham Court Road (*Cardboard Box*).

STRAKER, JOHN. *Alias* Mr. Derbyshire. He led a double life and was killed by a horse (*Silver Blaze*).

STRAKER, MRS. She found her husband getting dressed at 1:00 A.M. **H** had a reason for asking whether he had met her at a Plymouth garden party (*Silver Blaze*).

STRAND, LONDON. **W** stayed in a private hotel here before the historic meeting with young Stamford (*Study in Scarlet*). The American Exchange was here (*Study in Scarlet*). **H** asked William Morris the way to the Strand (*Red-headed League*). **H** and **W** took a walk (*Resident Patient*). Godfrey Staunton ran in this direction (*Three-*Quarter). **H** and **W** ate there one evening at Simpson's, *q.v.* (*Illustrious Client*).

STRAND END OF THE LOWTHER ARCADE. **W** was to take a hansom and then run through here (*Final Problem*).

STRASBURG. **H** and **W** en route from Brussels to Switzerland (*Final Problem*).

STRAUBENZEE. His gunshop was in the Minories. He made the air-gun for Count Sylvius (*Mazarin Stone*). Cf. air-gun.

STREATHAM. **H, W,** and Toby on the trail of Bartholomew Sholto's murderers (*Sign of Four*). Mr. Holder, the banker, lived here (*Beryl Coronet*).

STREET ARABS. See Baker Street Division of the detective police force.

STROUD VALLEY. **H** and **W** en route to Boscombe Valley.

STUARTS, THE. Their ancient crown was hidden at Hurlstone Manor House (*Musgrave Ritual*).

STUDY IN SCARLET, A. **W** gave this name to the case of Jefferson Hope (*q.v.*) and was annoyed when **H** criticized the Watsonian ms. *Circa* 1881?

SUDBURY. Student at The Gables. He, with fellow student Blount, discovered the dead Airedale terrier that had belonged to his recently dead master, Fitzroy McPherson. Both master and dog were found dead at the same place (*Lion's Mane*).

SUEZ CANAL. The "Rock of Gibraltar" was south of this waterway (*Abbey Grange*).

*SULTAN OF TURKEY. **H** had to finish

a commission for this potentate before he could begin an investigation at Tuxbury Old Park (*Blanched Soldier*). As **H** narrated this case, and since **W** had moved out of their Baker Street chambers, one does not know if the Turkish affair was concluded. The case notes should be in one of **H's** receptacula.

SUMATRA. **H** told **W** that he had contracted a deadly coolie disease which was only contagious by touch (*Dying Detective*).

*SUMATRA, GIANT RAT OF. According to **H**, "the world is not yet prepared" to know the details of this rat case (*Vampire*). So far (with excessive caution?) **W** has respected **H's** prohibition.

SUMNER. Shipping agent, Ratcliff Highway. "Send three men on, to arrive ten to-morrow morning.—Basil." This was the wire that **H** sent Sumner. Captain Basil was an *alias* of **H** in certain quarters (*Black Peter*).

SURREY. **H** felt the four-wheeler that was carrying Mary Morstan, **W**, and himself to the unknown T. Sholto was making for the "Surrey Side" when the hansom crossed the Vauxhall Bridge (*Sign of Four*). Jonathan Small compared Surrey to India before the Mutiny (*Sign of Four*). On their return trip from the Cedars in Kent **H** and **W** passed through a part of Surrey (*Twisted Lip*). **H** and **W** to Stoke Moran in Surrey, home of Dr. Roylott (*Speckled Band*). Colonel Hayter lived near Reigate (*Reigate Puzzle*). **H** had breathed thirty miles of Surrey air and was hungry (*Naval Treaty*). Miss Violet Smith taught music near Farnham (*Solitary Cyclist*). Inspector Baynes was interested in John Scott Eccles, and in turn this led to Aloysius Garcia, Mr. Henderson, and participation by **H** and **W** (*Wisteria Lodge*). Mr. Barker, a competent amateur detective on the Surrey shore, had several good cases to his credit at the time he and **H** collaborated (*Retired Colourman*).

SUSSEX. Elias Openshaw lived near Horsham (*Five Orange Pips*). The Musgraves lived in this county (*Musgrave Ritual*). Captain Peter Cary lived near Forest Row (*Black Peter*). The John Douglas home was at Birlstone (*Valley of Fear*). Cheeseman's, Lamberley, was the scene of action (*Vampire*). **H** retired to his home in this county and narrated the case of the *Lion's Mane*.

SUSSEX DOWNS. **H** retired here for study and bee-keeping, with a small amount of agriculture (probably light gardening).

His farm was about five miles from Eastbourne (*Last Bow*). This retirement was in **H**'s thoughts for some time. As early as September, 1903, he was thinking of such a life, here or elsewhere (*Creeping Man*). **H** was settled in and apparently adjusted when he narrated the case of the *Lion's Mane,* which had its scene of action quite near **H**'s place on the southern slope of the downs and the Channel coast.

SUSSEX VAMPIRE, ADVENTURE OF THE. November 19. **H** established the view that vampires are not operational in Sussex, proved Robert Ferguson's wife was innocent, and suggested that their older boy, Jack, spend a year at sea.

SUTHERLAND, MARY. **H** referred to her case (*Red-headed League*) as related to the *Case of Identity*.

SUTRO, MR. Mary Maberley's lawyer. He objected to the terms of the sale of the *Three Gables.*

SUTTON. One of the Worthingdon bank gang. He informed on Cartwright and was murdered by the gang. *Alias* Mr. Blessington (*Resident Patient*). Cf. Worthingdon Bank gang.

SWAN & EDISON. Sir Henry Baskerville intended to brighten up the Hall with their electric lamp-bulbs (*The Hound*).

SWINDON. **H** and **W** lunched in this village en route to Boscombe Valley.

SWITZERLAND. **H** felt that he and **W** should come to this country, secretly if possible, to avoid Professor Moriarty's vengeance (*Final Problem*). Cf. Reichenbach Falls. **W** investigated the disappearance of Lady Frances. Her last letter to Miss Dobney was from the Hotel National in Lausanne (*Lady Frances Carfax*). Cf. Shlessinger.

SYDENHAM. The Randalls had done a burglary job here a fortnight ago, according to Inspector Stanley Hopkins (*Abbey Grange*).

SYDNEY. Australia. Armitage and Evans arrived here via the "Hotspur" (*Gloria Scott*).

SYLVIUS, COUNT NEGRETTO. Of 136 Moorside Gardens, N.W. He came to 221B Baker Street to bluster, and **H** deprived him of his liberty as well as the *Mazarin Stone.*

SYRIA. Professor Coram's treatise dealt with the Coptic monasteries of this country (*Pince-Nez*).

# T

**Tangey, Mr.** Commissionaire at the Foreign Office where Percy Phelps worked. He lived at 16 Ivy Lane, Brixton, and was formerly in the Coldstream Guards (*Naval Treaty*).

**Tangey, Mrs.** She had trouble with a tradesman and ran away (*Naval Treaty*).

***Tankerville Club Scandal.** Major Prendergast told John Openshaw how **H** had saved him in this affair. This led John to consult **H** (*Five Orange Pips*), but the case concerning the major has not been published.

**Tapanuli fever.** **W** had never heard of it (*Dying Detective*).

***Tarleton Murders.** These were referred to by **H** as one of his former cases. No record of its subsequent publication (*Musgrave Ritual*). Since this was prior to **W's** collaboration, we know only of the notes of the affair that **H** showed to **W**. They may be difficult to locate now.

**Tarlton, Susan.** Maid in Professor Coram's household (*Pince-Nez*).

**Tavernier, M.** Accomplished French modeler who made a bust of **H** (*Mazarin Stone*).

**Tavistock contractor.** He built some houses for those wishing to enjoy pure Dartmoor air (*Silver Blaze*).

**Teddy.** Henry Wood's mongoose (*Crooked Man*).

**telegram.** There are many of these. For example: **H** deduced that **W** had dispatched one from the Wigmore Street Post Office; **H** wired Athelney Jones to await him at 221B Baker Street and signed himself Poplar; **H** wired for the Baker Street Irregulars from the Great Peter Street Post Office (*Sign of Four*). Cf. "The old man is dead" (*Solitary Cyclist*); also Sumner (*Black Peter*).

*Telegraph*. Newspaper that gave an account of the murder of John Straker and the disappearance of *Silver Blaze*.

**telephone.** **W** called from the Railway Arms, Little Purlington, to **H** in London (*Retired Colourman*). XX.31 was a private number which **H** could call to reach Sir James Damery (*Illustrious Client*). **H** and **W** called

Nathan Garrideb (*Garridebs*).

TERAI. Victor Trevor was said to be doing well in tea-planting here (*Gloria Scott*).

THAMES. **W**, **H**, and Mary Morstan crossed this river by the Vauxhall Bridge in a four-wheeler en route to see Thaddeus Sholto; later, **H**, **W**, and Athelney Jones chased the "Aurora" and captured Jonathan Small (*Sign of Four*). Dr. Barnicot had a large practice south of the river (*Six Napoleons*). **W** recalled the pursuit of the "Aurora" in *Pince-Nez.* Sir James Walter's villa had lawns on the river side (*Bruce-Partington*).

"THE OLD MAN IS DEAD." Telegram sent to Mr. Carruthers, in Farnham, from South Africa (!), supplying the information that Ralph Smith was dead (*Solitary Cyclist*).

THEOLOGICAL COLLEGE OF ST. GEORGE'S. Elias Whitney, D.D., was Principal (*Twisted Lip*).

"*the* WOMAN." See Irene Adler.

THIRD BENGAL FUSILIERS. They fought near Agra in the great Indian Mutiny and achieved a local success at Shahgunge early in July, then fell back on Agra (*Sign of Four*).

THIRD BUFFS. Jonathan Small's regiment that went to India (*Sign of Four*).

THOR BRIDGE. A stone span over a long and reedy pool at Thor Place. Mrs. Gibson's body was found in the water near the bridge (*Thor Bridge*).

THOR BRIDGE, THE PROBLEM OF. October. Suicide of Maria Gibson was proved by **H**, despite the fact that she had arranged her death to appear to be a murder committed by governess Grace Dunbar.

THOR PLACE. Hampshire estate of J. Neil Gibson, near Winchester (*Thor Bridge*).

THOREAU. **H** quoted this author about a "trout in the milk" (*Noble Bachelor*).

THREADNEEDLE STREET. Hugh Boone begged here every day (*Twisted Lip*). Holder & Stevenson banking firm was here (*Beryl Coronet*).

THREE GABLES. Harrow Weald area, and the home of Mary Maberley (*Three Gables*).

THREE GABLES, ADVENTURE OF THE. Isadora Klein hired Barney Stockdale to obtain the Douglas Maberley manuscript. He did, and she burned it, but she ended up by giving **H** a check for £5,000 so that Mary Maberley, mother of Douglas, could take a trip around the world.

THREE GARRIDEBS, ADVENTURE OF THE. June, 1902. As in *The Red-headed League,* the criminal, this time a supposititious John Garrideb maneuvering to decoy Nathan

Garrideb away so that he could get at the money left by forger Rodger Prescott, runs afoul of **H**. *En passant,* Nathan Garrideb ended in a Brixton nursing home.

*Three Months in the Jungle.* By Colonel Sebastian Moran. 1884 (*Empty House*).

THREE-QUARTER POSITION. Godfrey Staunton was missing from this position on the rugger team (*Three-Quarter*).

THREE STUDENTS, ADVENTURE OF THE. In 1895 **H** and **W** were at St. Luke's College, and **H** saved tutor Soames from an awkward situation in the examination in Greek for the Fortescue Scholarship.

THROGMORTON STREET. James M. Dodd was a stockholder here (*Blanched Soldier*).

THURSTON. He was the only person that **W** played billiards with, according to Holmes (*Dancing Men*).

TIBET. **H** spent two years here and visited Lhassa and talked with the head lama. He conducted explorations here under the Norwegian *alias* of Sigerson (*Empty House*).

*Times,* LONDON. In this newspaper on May 4, 1882, there was an advertisement asking for the address of Miss Mary Morstan. Mrs. Cecil Forrester, in whose home Mary was governess, advised Mary to publish her address in this paper; later, **H** found that Major Sholto had died on April 28, 1882. This datum was back-filed in the *Times* (*Sign of Four*). Countess of Morcar's lost jewel was advertised for here (*Blue Carbuncle*). **H** was reading its agony column when *W* brought in Mr. Hatherley (*Engineer's Thumb*). Then there was the advertisement as to the whereabouts of Violet Smith and her mother (*Solitary Cyclist*). **H** had read this paper prior to the arrival of Cyril Overton (*Three-Quarter*). The warning to Sir Henry Baskerville had been pieced out of an article in this paper (*The Hound*). Von Herling felt the German purpose (in 1914) was as clear as if it had been advertised here (*Last Bow*).

*TIRED CAPTAIN, ADVENTURE OF THE. This is an unrecorded case which was investigated by **H** in the July following the Watson-Morstan nuptials (*Naval Treaty*).

TIRE IMPRESSIONS. See Holmes, Sherlock, under Methods.

TOBIN. Caretaker at the Worthingdon Bank. He was murdered by one of the five burglars during their entry. Cartwright was hanged for the crime, on evidence supplied by Sutton (*Resident Patient*).

TOBY. See dog.

"TO JAMES MORTIMER, M.R.C.S.,

FROM HIS FRIENDS OF THE C.C.H." This was engraved on the visitor's stick (*The Hound*).

TOKAY. Thaddeus Sholto offered Mary Morstan a glass of this wine and was refused (*Sign of Four*). According to Von Bork, Altamont favored this wine (*Last Bow*).

TOLLER. He was described as a servant of the Rucastles. He was addicted to alcohol and took "care" of Carlo (*Copper Beeches*).

TOLLER, MRS. She helped Mr. Fowler to rescue Alice Rucastle (*Copper Beeches*).

TONGA. An Andaman Islander who murdered Bartholomew Sholto with a poisoned dart and was later shot by **H** and **W** in their chase of the "Aurora." He disappeared in the Thames (*Sign of Four*).

TOPEKA, KANSAS. "John Garrideb" was said to be in law practice here (*Garridebs*).

TORONTO. Canada. Henry Baskerville bought a pair of black boots here (*The Hound*).

TORQUAY TERRACE. In Camberwell. E. J. Drebber was a lodger here (*Study in Scarlet*).

TORRINGTON LODGE. Mr. McFarlane lived here (*Norwood Builder*).

*TOSCA, CARDINAL. **H** investigated his sudden death "at the express desire of His Holiness the Pope" (*Black Peter*).

TOTTENHAM COURT ROAD. The late Mr. Sutherland had a profitable plumber's business here. When Mr. Windibank married Mrs. Sutherland, he had her sell the business at a poor figure (*Case of Identity*). Peterson was coming home and, *en passant,* got a used hat and a fine Christmas goose (*Blue Carbuncle*). **H** bought his Stradivarius here for 55 shillings (*Cardboard Box*), probably at a pawn shop. Mr. Warren was the timekeeper for Morton & Waylight here (*Red Circle*).

TRAFALGAR SQUARE. John Clayton, cabby, picked up some one who gave his name as "Sherlock Holmes." His passenger had him drive to the Northumberland Hotel, then to 221B Baker Street, and finally to the Waterloo Station. John was asked to come to 221B Baker and tell his story, and **H** was impressed by the passenger who had used his name. This incident alerted **H** as to the character of his adversary (*The Hound*).

TRAFALGAR SQUARE FOUNTAIN. **H** twitted Lestrade about dragging this water for the body of Lady St. Simon (*Noble Bachelor*).

TRANSYLVANIA. In **H's** index under "V" there was an account of vampires in this area (*Vampire*).

**Tredannick Wartha.** Home of Brenda, George, and Owen Tregennis. Brother Mortimer visited them. Next morning Brenda was dead, and George and Owen were insane. Dr. Richards too was partially overcome when he called. **H** decided to investigate (*Devil's Foot*).

**Tredannick Wollas.** A village in Cornwall (*Devil's Foot*).

**Tregellis, Janet.** Daughter of head gamekeeper at Hurlstone Manor House. She was receiving the attentions of Brunton, the butler, while the latter was engaged to Rachel Howells. This was a mistake for Brunton (*Musgrave Ritual*).

**Tregennis, Brenda.** Sister of Mortimer, George, and Owen. She was found still seated at the table, dead (*Devil's Foot*).

**Tregennis, George.** Brother of Mortimer, Owen, and Brenda. He was found seated beside Brenda, demented (*Devil's Foot*).

**Tregennis, Mortimer.** Brother of Brenda, George, and Owen. He had rooms in the Vicarage, apart from his kith and kin. He and the Vicar, Mr. Roundhay, came to consult **H.** Mortimer later met his sister's fate when Dr. Sterndale learned of the peculiar circumstances (*Devil's Foot*).

**Tregennis, Owen.** Brother of Brenda, George, and Mortimer. As for George (*Devil's Foot*).

**Trepoff murder.** See Odessa.

**Trevelyan, Dr. Percy.** Physician who won the Bruce Pinkerton Prize for his monograph on obscure nervous lesions. He lived at 403 Brook Street and in the end needed **H** rather badly (*Resident Patient*).

**Trevor, Senior.** He was Justice of the Peace and father of Victor. Lived at Donnithorpe, near Langmere in the Broads, Norfolk. Trevor was an *alias* for James Armitage who was chained in the "Gloria Scott" bound with other convicts for Australia. He escaped (*Gloria Scott*).

**Trevor, Victor.** Son of Trevor, Senior. Victor was **H's** best friend in two years at college. His bull terrier bit **H** on the ankle. In the end Victor did well in tea plantings at Terai (*Gloria Scott*). He invited **H** to the Trevor establishment, and this had a deep bearing on **H's** future. Cf. Holmes, Sherlock.

**Trichinopoly cigar.** **H** said that the murderer of E. J. Drebber had smoked one, producing characteristic dark gray ashes (*Study in Scarlet*). See Holmes, Sherlock, under Works.

**Trincomalee.** See Atkinson brothers.

**Trinity College.** Of Cambridge University. Cyril Overton went here (*Three-Quarter*).

**Triple Alliance.** The gray roll of paper defined the position of Great Britain toward the Alliance and bore on naval affairs (*Naval Treaty*).

TRUMPINGTON. Godfrey Staunton's dead wife lay in a cottage nearby, and here **H**, **W**, and Dr. Armstrong finally understood each other (*Three-Quarter*).

TUNBRIDGE WELLS. In Kent, about ten miles from Birlstone, Sussex (*Valley of Fear*). Patrick Cairns took a train from here to London (*Black Peter*).

TURKEY, SULTAN OF. See Sultan.

TURKISH BATH. **W** had one (*Lady Frances Carfax*). **H** and **W** had a weakness for them (*Illustrious Client*).

TURNER, ALICE. Daughter of John Turner. She was in love with James McCarthy (*Boscombe*).

TURNER, JOHN. Father of Alice. Largest landed proprietor in the Boscombe Valley area. He had made his money in Australia (*Boscombe*).

TURNER, MRS. At one period at least, she was landlady at 221B Baker Street for **H** (*Scandal in Bohemia*). Cf. Mrs. Hudson. The substitution of Turner for Hudson might be a *lapsus calami* on the part of **W**, as chief narrator. On the other hand, Mrs. Hudson might have needed a well-earned rest from her exacting patrons and asked in a friend to take over for a while.

TURPEY STREET. John Clayton lived at No. 3 (*The Hound*).

TUSON, SERGEANT. He captured Beddington, with the aid of Constable Pollock (*Stock-broker's Clerk*).

TUSSAUD, MADAME. Merton felt she could take a lesson from Tavernier (*q.v.*), but in all fairness, the dummy was substituted for **H**, and **H** substituted for the dummy (*Mazarin Stone*).

TUXBURY OLD PARK. Near Bedford, in Bedfordshire. Home of Colonel Emsworth, V.C. (*Blanched Soldier*).

TYBURN TREE, of evil memory. Little Ryder Street was nearby (*Garridebs*).

# U

UBANGHI COUNTRY. In West Africa, where Dr. Sterndale obtained a sample of *Radix pedis diaboli,* or Devil's Foot.

UFFA, ISLAND OF. See Grice Patersons.

UNDERGROUND, THE. London subway system. **H** and **W** went as far as Aldersgate (*Red-headed League*). Cadogan West was dead on the tracks on Tuesday morning, his body being near the Aldgate Station (*Bruce-Partington*).

UNDERWOOD, JOHN, & SONS. 129 Camberwell Road, London. They had sold a hat to E. J. Drebber (*Study in Scarlet*).

UNION JACK. Mentioned in the *Noble Bachelor.*

UNITED STATES OF AMERICA. See Cleveland, Ohio; Chicago, Illinois; New York, New York; Philadelphia, Pennsylvania; Topeka, Kansas; San Francisco, California, and various of the states. Cleveland noted in *Study in Scarlet.* In three days Baron Gruner was to leave on the "Ruritania" from Liverpool bound for this country, but **H** intervened (*Illustrious Client*). "A. H. Garrideb" was said to have made a will which caused John Garrideb (*alias* for "Killer" Evans) to scour this country (*Garridebs*).

*Upon the Distinction between the Ashes of the Various Tobaccos.* One of **H**'s monographs, in which 140 forms of cigar, cigarette, and pipe tobacco ashes are discussed (*Sign of Four*). See Holmes, Sherlock, under Works.

UPPER NORWOOD. Major John Sholto retired here, and after his death, one of his twin sons, Bartholomew, occupied the house, known as Pondicherry Lodge (*Sign of Four*).

UPPER SWANDAM LANE. The Bar of Gold opium den was located in this vile alley on the north side of the Thames and to the east of London Bridge (*Twisted Lip*).

UPPINGHAM. As a boy Willoughby Smith went here to prepare for Cambridge University (*Pince-Nez*).

*UPWOOD, COLONEL. He was exposed

by **H** in connection with the card scandal at the Nonpareil Club (*The Hound*).

Uriah and Bathsheba. **H** explained that when Mrs. Barclay called her husband "David" it referred to his betrayal of Henry Wood in India. **H** told **W** he could find the reference in the first or second chapter of Samuel (*Crooked Man*). (Samuel II:11 is the correct reference).

Utrecht. Van Jensen died here (*Study in Scarlet*).

# V

VALLEY OF FEAR, THE. January 7, at the end of the 1880's. Professor Moriarty was involved according to **H. H** solved the "death" of John Douglas, but later Douglas was lost overboard en route to South Africa, and **H** knew that Moriarty had triumphed once again. Cf. Vermissa.

*VAMBERRY, THE WINE MERCHANT. This was a pre-Watsonian case, but the records of the affair had been exhibited to **W** by **H** (*Musgrave Ritual*).

VAMPIRES. **H** demonstrated that they were inoperative at Cheeseman's, Lamberley, Sussex, despite circumstantial evidence (*Vampire*).

VANDELEUR, MR. AND MRS. They operated St. Oliver's school, and **H** discovered that they were at Merripit House under the *alias* of Jack and Beryl Stapleton, "brother" and "sister" (*The Hound*).

VANDERBILT AND THE YEGGMAN. This case was in **H's** index under "V" (*Vampire*).

VAN JENSEN. **H** recalled his death in Utrecht in 1834 having been reported (*Study in Scarlet*).

VAN SEDDAR. He was in Lime Street and could take the jewel to Amsterdam and have it cut in four pieces before Sunday (*Mazarin Stone*).

*VATICAN CAMEOS. **H** was so preoccupied by this case that he had not heard of the death of Sir Charles Baskerville (*The Hound*). Since **H** was alert to such events, especially those in which death was associated with the English countryside, his preoccupation suggests that the cameo affair would be of interest.

VAUXHALL BRIDGE ROAD. **H, W,** and Mary Morstan crossed the Thames here en route to Thaddeus Sholto. Much later in the case **W** was to be let out here with the Agra Treassure and was to bring it to Mary Morstan (*Sign of Four*).

VEGETARIAN RESTAURANT. Next to the city and Suburban Bank on the Strand (*Red-headed League*).

VEHMGERICHT. On the occasion of the death of E. J. Drebber, the *Daily Telegraph* alluded to the operations of this secret tribunal, among other agencies (*Study in Scarlet*).

VEILED LODGER, ADVENTURE OF THE. 1896. The wife of Ronder, and his strong man, Leonardo, murdered her husband and blamed the crime on the lion Sahara King. The lion mauled the wife, and Leonardo went away. Some seven years later Mrs. Ronder confessed her crime to **H**, with **W** as witness. **H** persuaded her not to take her own life.

VENEZUELAN LOAN. It ruined Coxon & Woodhouse (*Stock-broker's Clerk*).

VENNER & MATHESON. An engineering firm of Greenwich. Cf. Hatherley (*Engineer's Thumb*).

VENUCCI, LUCRETIA. Maid to Princess Colonna. She probably aided Pietro Venucci and Beppo in the theft of the black pearl of the Borgias (*Six Napoleons*).

VENUCCI, PIETRO. Of Naples and London. He had a connection with the Mafia, according to Inspector Hill. Pietro was found dead on Horace Harker's doorstep (*Six Napoleons*).

VERE STREET. A brick fell from a building and would have killed **H** if it had struck him. **H** wondered whether Professor Moriarty was at work (*Final Problem*).

VERMISSA. A flourishing town at the head of a coal and iron valley in the United States. V.V. = Vermissa Valley = *Valley of Fear.*

VERNER, DR. A young physician who purchased **W's** general practice in Kensington. He paid **W's** first suggested price without demur. Years later **W** discovered that **H** had found at least part of the money. The young physician was a distant relative of **H** (*Norwood Builder*). The incident not only is evidence of **H's** generosity and of his desire to have **W** live with him again, but it also bears out his French grandmother's family name of Vernet. Cf. Holmes, Sherlock, under Pre-Watsonian.

VERNET. French artist. His sister was a grandmother of **H.** See Holmes, Sherlock, under Pre-Watsonian; also Dr. Verner.

VERNON LODGE. Near Kingston. Baron Gruner lived here (*Illustrious Client*).

VIBART, JULES. One of the head waiters at the Hotel National in Lausanne. He was engaged to Lady Frances Carfax' maid, Marie Devine (*Lady Frances Carfax*).

VICTORIA. Australia. John Turner made his money here in gold-mining and knew Charles McCarthy (*Boscombe*).

VICTORIA STATION. **H, W,** and Colonel Ross en route to London arrived here in less than ten minutes (*Silver Blaze*). Mr. Melas en route from Clapham Junction to London (*Greek Interpreter*). **W** was to send his luggage unaddressed to this station (*Final Problem*). **H, W,** and Inspector MacDonald en route to Birlstone Manor (*Valley of Fear*). **H, W,** and Robert Ferguson en route to Cheeseman's, Lamberley (*Vampire*).

*Vie de Bohème.* By Henri Murger. It was read by **W** (*Study in Scarlet*).

VIEW-HALLOA, THE. **H** responded to the opening of a case like an old hound to this (*Devil's Foot*).

VIGOR, THE HAMMERSMITH WONDER. The citation is from **H's** index under "V" (*Vampire*).

VINCENT SQUARE. **H, W,** and Mary Morstan in a four-wheeler en route to Thaddeus Sholto (*Sign of Four*).

VIOLINS. Cremona, Stradivarius, and Amati were discussed (*Study in Scarlet*). **H** and **W** went to hear the violinist Sarasate (*Red-headed League*). **H** played his violin in the *Noble Bachelor* and in the *Norwood Builder.* On another occasion, a case was not going well and **H** played snatches of this and that (*Second Stain*). Again, **H** played his violin to postpone thought (*The Hound*). **H** talked about violins and violinists one afternoon to **W** (*Cardboard Box*). Charlie Pease was both a violin virtuoso and a great criminal (*Illustrious Client*). This musical instrument was an essential item of equipment in the art of detection in one case. **H** told Count Sylvius and Merton that he wanted them to think the matter over and would give them privacy by going into another room to play Hoffman's *Barcarole* on his violin. Soon they heard the strains of music behind the closed door. **H** had put a record of the *Barcarole* on a gramophone instead and then, taking the place of the dummy, was in a position to grab the *Mazarin Stone.* Cf. Stradivarius for the price of **H's** instrument; also Norman Neruda for his appreciation of a fellow artist.

VITTORIA. A circus belle. In **H's** index under "V" (*Vampire*).

VIXEN TOR. As for Belliver Tor.

VON BISCHOFF. He would have been hung at Frankfort, *circa* 1877, if **H's** test for haemoglobin had been known then (*Study in Scarlet*).

VON BORK. Chief German espionage agent in England prior to World War I. Captured August, 1914, by **H,** operating under the *alias* of Altamont, and **W** (*Last Bow*).

Von Herder. The blind German mechanic who made the air-gun ordered by Professor Moriarty and used by Colonel Moran (*Empty House*).

Von Herling, Baron. Chief Secretary of the German legation in London. He worked hand in glove with Von Bork (*Last Bow*).

Von Kramm, Count. Pseudonym of the King of Bohemia. He stayed at the Langham Hotel while consulting **H** in London (*Scandal in Bohemia*).

von Ormstein. Wilhelm Gottsreich Sigismond von Ormstein, Grand Duke of Cassel-Felstein and hereditary King of Bohemia. He consulted **H** under the pseudonym of Count Von Kramm (*Scandal in Bohemia*). Cf. von Saxe-Meningen.

von Saxe-Meningen, Clothilde Lothman. Second daughter of the King of Scandinavia and betrothed to the King of Bohemia (*Scandal in Bohemia*). Cf. von Ormstein.

*Von und Zu Grafenstein, Count. Uncle of von Ormstein. **H** saved his life from the Nihilist Klopman (*Last Bow*).

von Waldbaum, Fritz. Of Danzig. He was on the wrong track entirely in the adventure of the *Second Stain* (cited in *Naval Treaty* only).

voodoo. **H** had studied the subject at the British Museum and was able to interpret the significance of the remains of a white cock and kid bones in the kitchen of Aloysius Garcia's home near Esher, in Surrey (*Wisteria Lodge*).

*Voodooism and the Negroid Religions.* By Eckermann. **H** quoted a passage pertinent to the case (*Wisteria Lodge*).

"V.V.–341." This was on a card by the body of a murdered man reputed to be John Douglas. V.V. stood for Vermissa Valley. 341 was the lodge number (*Valley of Fear*).

# W

WAGNER NIGHT. There was an unspecified Wagnerian opera at Covent Garden, and **H** wanted **W** to hurry. This was after the successful conclusion of the case of the *Red-headed League*.

WAINWRIGHT. He was both a great criminal and no mean artist (*Illustrious Client*).

WALDRON. *Alias* Rodger Prescott, *q.v.* (*Garridebs*).

WALLENSTEIN. His death in Egria was cited by **H** (*Scandal in Bohemia*).

WALLINGTON. Sarah Cushing lived on New Street here at the time her sister Susan received Jim Browner's package of human ears (*Cardboard Box*).

WALSALL. Violet Hunter became head of a private school here (*Copper Beeches*).

WALTER, COLONEL VALENTINE. Brother of Sir James, he was crushed with grief when Sir James died of shock over the theft of the submarine patents. Later, the colonel answered **H's** message in the *Daily Telegraph* and went to jail (*Bruce-Partington*).

WALTER, SIR JAMES. Brother of Colonel Valentine Walter. He was the official guardian of the highly classified submarine patents at Woolwich Arsenal. He kept one of the two keys, and Sidney Johnson had the other. Sir James died of shock a few hours after the patents, or some of them at least, were discovered to be missing (*Bruce-Partington*).

WALTERS. Constable left on duty at Wisteria Lodge. He was happy to see Inspector Baynes again (*Wisteria Lodge*).

WANDSWORTH COMMON. Mr. Melas was a long way from home (*Greek Interpreter*).

*WARBURTON, COLONEL. This case, involving the colonel's madness, was one of only two cases that **W** brought to the attention of **H**. The other was the severed thumb of engineer Hatherley. The latter has been published, but not the former (*Engineer's Thumb*).

WARDLOW, COLONEL. His horse, Pugilist, ran in the Wessex Cup race (*Silver Blaze*).

WARNER, JOHN. Gardener at High

Gable. He helped protect Miss Burnett from Mr. Henderson and his secretary Mr. Lucas. He was dismissed (*Wisteria Lodge*).

WARREN, MRS. She consulted **H** about her strange lodger, on the strength of the recommendation of a former lodger, Fairdale Hobbs. Her odd lodger was really Emilia Lucca, although no one knew this at the time. **H** cautioned Mrs. Warren against telling Emilia she must leave (*Red Circle*).

WARSAW. King of Bohemia met Irene Adler, Prima Donna of the Imperial Opera, in this city (*Scandal in Bohemia*).

WARSHIPS OF THE FUTURE. As for miracle plays.

WATCH. One had been given recently to **W**, and as a jest he asked **H** to examine it and give him his deductions. **H** was delighted to do so, to **W**'s chagrin. This small diversion prevented **H** from taking a second dose of cocaine (*Sign of Four*).

WATERBEACH. **H** searched here also (*Three-Quarter*).

WATERFORD. Browner's ship stopped at this port (*Cardboard Box*).

WATERLOO. **H** told **W** that the case was not their Waterloo but their Marengo, *i.e.*, it began in defeat and ended in victory (*Abbey Grange*).

WATERLOO BRIDGE. John Openshaw met his death nearby (*Five Orange Pips*).

WATERLOO BRIDGE ROAD. **H** and **W** en route from the Cedars in Kent to London (*Twisted Lip*).

WATERLOO ROAD. "Killer" Evans shot and killed the coiner-forger, Rodger Prescott, here. Both men were from Chicago (*Garridebs*).

WATERLOO STATION. John Openshaw planned to take a train from here to his home in Horsham (*Five Orange Pips*). Helen Stoner took the first train from Leatherhead to this station (*Speckled Band*). **H** and **W** off to Aldershot on the 11:10 A.M. (*Crooked Man*). **H** and **W** off to Woking (*Naval Treaty*). **W** caught the 9:13 A.M. for Farnham (*Solitary Cyclist*). John Clayton's hansom was nearby from Shipley's Yard. Henry Baskerville was arriving shortly, according to James Mortimer (*The Hound*).

WATSON, JOHN H., M.D. *Pre-Holmesian:* Doctor Watson received his medical degree in 1878 from the University of London.

Shortly after, he went to Netley to take the prescribed course for Army surgeons. He was then attached to the Fifth Northumberland Fusiliers as Assistant Surgeon. This regiment was in India at the time. He followed, landing at Bombay, and eventually caught up with his outfit at Candahar in time to take part in the Second Afghan war. He was transferred to the Berkshires and at the battle of Maiwand was struck in the shoulder by a Jezail bullet. Murray, his orderly, saved him from capture, and he was removed to the base hospital at Peshawur for rehabilitation.

Recuperating from his shoulder wound, John contracted enteric fever and was returned to England on the troopship "Orontes." He landed at Portsmouth with a nine-month furlough from the British Government and his health "irretrievably ruined."

At this time he had no living relative and depended on an income of 11 shillings sixpence per day. He went to London and for a time stayed at a private hotel in the Strand. This soon became too expensive, and he began casting about for cheaper quarters. It was at this period that he ran into young Stamford at the Criterion Bar.

Stamford had been John's dresser at Barts hospital in the early days. On impulse, pleased to be looking at a familiar face again, Watson invited him to lunch, and they went on by hansom to the Holborn restaurant. In the course of the conversation John told Stamford that he was looking for reasonable chambers. Stamford then remembered that a chap he knew, Holmes, had found himself in the same boat—at least, he wanted to move.

*Historic Meeting and Settling-in at 221B Baker:* After lunch Stamford took Watson to meet Holmes. This meeting has been described elsewhere (cf. Holmes, Sherlock, under Historic Meeting).

Sherlock's choice of chambers seemed good to John. The two young men were attracted to each other apparently from the first. In an exchange of candor, John gave his worst points as being lazy, getting up all hours of the day or night, disliking raucous noises, and keeping a bull pup. Oddly enough, both this pup and young Stamford disappear from sight in subsequent published accounts of the doings of Holmes and Watson. So, fortunately for the cases, does Watson's objection to noise and excitement. Holmes then stated his bad points, and both John and Sherlock decided to visit the proposed quarters of joint occupancy the next day.

They went to 221B Baker Street and concluded the bargain. Early in this period they were involved in the investigation of two deaths, and near the end of the affair Watson was asked to give a professional opinion on the state of health of Jefferson Hope—an early bit of medical assistance in the budding collaboration. He diagnosed an aortic aneurism. This precipitated Hope's account of the twin killings—one could hardly call them murders—to Holmes, Watson, and Inspectors Gregson and Lestrade of Scotland Yard.

At the conclusion of this strange case Sherlock summed up the situation while Watson listened in rapt attention, his mystification gradually giving way to admiration. After this explanation Holmes assured Watson that Lestrade and Gregson would have all the credit. Watson countered this pessimistic view with a statement of great future significance: "I have all the facts in my journal, and the public shall know them" (*Study in Scarlet*).

Even in these early days Watson reflected that Holmes might be partially addicted to the use of some narcotic. He dismissed this hypothesis in view of Holmes's general temperance and cleanliness (*Study in Scarlet*). Unfortunately, Holmes did use cocaine or morphine to calm himself in periods of dull inactivity when there were no problems to engage his keen mind. Watson remonstrated bitterly when Holmes gave himself a deliberate injection of a seven-per-cent solution of cocaine and at the end of the case was reaching for more (*Sign of Four*). Through the long years of collaboration, with Holmes detecting and Watson later narrating, Watson's opinion apparently prevailed. Thus, only an occasional dose was used by the time the case of the *Yellow Face* was investigated. This weaning of Holmes, with such a sensitive temperament, must be recorded as one of Watson's unobtrusive achievements in their long association (*Three-Quarter*).

*John and Mary:* In July, 1888, a Miss Mary Morstan (*q.v.*) called on Holmes, on the advice of Mrs. Cecil Forrester (*q.v.*). She was a young lady in rather indifferent financial circumstances who had gone to meet her father Captain Morstan (*q.v.*) by appointment, but he had vanished. Thereafter, over a period of six years, she had been receiving valuable pearls, and now there was an invitation to meet someone who, apparently, could assist her (Cf. "Be at . . . etc."). Would Mr. Holmes please advise?

Watson had risen to go, at the beginning of this recital but Mary had asked him to remain —that he might help her. Watson sat down with alacrity, and that was that. Watson was greatly impressed by her: "She was a blonde young lady, small, dainty, well gloved, and dressed in the most perfect taste." Though she fell considerably short of beauty, "her large blue eyes were singularly spiritual and sympathetic." When she walked away down Baker Street, with Watson watching her from the window, Holmes had virtually lost his roommate.

The writer of the note allowed Mary to bring two friends. Holmes decided to undertake the case, and Mary happily accepted Holmes and Watson in the role of friends. The three were to go to a certain spot by the entrance of the Lyceum Theatre at 7:00 P.M. about July 7, 1888. From there, they were taken by a four-wheeler to the home of Thaddeus Sholto (*q.v.*). Here Thaddeus made it clear how rich Mary was going to be, and Watson was depressed at the thought (cf. Agra Treasure). Nevertheless, a few hours later John and Mary were holding hands on the grounds of Pondicherry Lodge, where they had all gone to visit Bartholomew Sholto and had found him murdered.

The case progressed, chiefly as a consequence of the efforts of Holmes, and Watson went along when he was invited, but in the meantime he dreamed of Mary Morstan. He took to calling on her, and Mrs. Forrester of course, to give them news of the case—which none of them understood at the time. Later, after the chase of the "Aurora," the Agra treasure chest was recovered and Watson was delegated to take it to Mary Morstan. There, in Mrs. Forrester's home in Camberwell, they forced the lid of the chest. The chest was empty, and, except for Mary's six pearls, she was no wealthier. Both John and Mary seemed relieved, and John asked Mary to marry him. She accepted at once (*Sign of Four*).

Watson may have been too preoccupied with his medical practice and with his collaborations with Holmes to intercalate these with his marital life—or he may have felt that such matters were outside the purview of his writing. At any event, he is distressingly vague about his domestic affairs.

John and Mary did get married, but when? In the *Sign of Four* Mary told Sherlock and the much-interested John that an advertisement in the *Times* appeared about six years ago, or exactly May 4, 1882. This would make the conference in 1888. At the conclusion of this celebrated case John and Mary were engaged. Yet in the *Scandal in Bohemia* John and Mary were not only married but well settled into married life, with an incorrigible maid, Mary Jane, about to get her notice, John obviously in general medical practice—and the date is given specifically as March 20, 1888. Both dates cannot be right. In addition there are scant references in other cases that they were married for a few months, or "shortly after" their marriage, or a few weeks before the marriage. Suffice it to say that they did get married, sometime between 1888 and 1890.

This confusion about time is one of the oddities of Watson's account. Whereas in describing the investigation of a case he is concise and pertinent, when he deals with dates, there may be some doubt as to which date to accept. An example is pertinent here anent his domestic affairs. It seems clear that the events narrated in the *Sign of the Four* occurred in 1888, a date derivable from two internal circumstances: the receipt of pearls by Mary and her father's strange disappearance. In this case she stated categorically to Holmes and Watson that her mother was dead when she went to school in Edinburgh, indeed that she had no relative in England. Nevertheless, in the *Five Orange Pips,* listed by Watson with five other cases in 1887, Watson states, "My wife was on a visit to her mother's, and for a few days I was a dweller once more in my old quarters at Baker Street."

The fact that Watson had forgotten the exact year of his marriage may not be even remarkable, but it is more difficult to believe that he had forgotten that his mother-in-law was deceased before he became engaged. Furthermore, it could not have been Watson's mother whom Mary was visiting, since Watson tells us in the fourth paragraph of the first published collaboration, the *Study in Scarlet,* that he had "neither kith nor kin in England, and was therefore as free as air." At any rate, confused or not, Watson was settled with his bride.

By at least 1888 he held a general practice in the Paddington District. His practice was quite small. He purchased it from old Mr. Farquhar, with the suggestion that it had fallen off considerably prior to the transfer. This was at the time of the case of the *Stock-broker's Clerk*, shortly after the wedding. John worked rather hard at his medical practice, and what with his collaboration with Holmes and, presumably, his attentions to his young bride—of which little to nothing is said—he must have been very much occupied. We do know that by the summer of 1889, not long after his marriage, his medical practice was increasing steadily (*Engineer's Thumb*). In fact, he was responsible for bringing the case of Mr. Hatherley to the attention of Holmes, via his surgery.

By June, 1890, the Watsons had found a home in Kensington (*Red-headed League*). From here on, for some time, there came the succession of cases in which Holmes was usually triumphant. Watson went with Holmes on most of them, and Mary urged him to do so. A few months after their marriage the case of the *Crooked Man* arose, and Dr. Jackson took over Watson's practice while he went to Aldershot with Holmes for a few days in connection with this unhappy affair. Again, in the *Boscombe Valley Mystery,* Mary urged John to go with Sherlock, assuring him that Dr. Anstruther could take his practice for a few days. In a situation where grave public matters were at stake, Mary rose to the occasion. For example, she felt that not a moment should be lost in getting Holmes to go to Briarbrae (*Naval Treaty*).

Mary and John apparently had a happy life together but their marriage was of short duration. Mary was alive and presumably well as late as April 24, 1891 (*Final Problem*). Nothing definite is known of their marriage from this date until the spring of 1894. During this period, while Sherlock was on his long journey and everyone except Mycroft Holmes thought that he had fallen into the Reichenbach abyss, Mary died. Somehow Holmes had learned of Watson's bereavement and quietly comforted him. This was in the spring of 1894 (*Empty House*). At most the marriage could have lasted six years, and apparently they had no children.

For the next six to seven years Watson was a widower. In September, 1902, he was living in his own rooms in Queen Anne Street, and he was glad to join Holmes in the case of the *Illustrious Client.* By January, 1903, Watson has married for the second time (*Blanched Soldier*). There are no data on this second marriage; we do not even know her name.

From 1903 on, there is little to report. By July, 1907, Holmes had retired to his farm on the Sussex downs, and the two old friends seldom saw each other except for a rare week-end visit (*Lion's Mane*).

Their last recorded association was a brief reunion in August, 1914, when Watson joined Holmes in the capture of Von Bork (*Last Bow*).

*Disposition and Personality:* John Watson is easier to understand than Sherlock Holmes. He lacks the incandescent genius of his old friend, and combines many of the simple virtues one hopes for in mankind with some of its shortcomings.

One imagines that in the pursuit of his medical practice he was calm, friendly, practical, and rather old-fashioned. When Victor Hatherley came to his surgery hysterical and with a thumb chopped off, Watson gave him brandy, cleaned and dressed the wound, and sympathetically took him to the one man who could look into his case, Sherlock Holmes (*Engineer's Thumb*). He was not keenly alive to medical research, and though he did glance over the *British Medical Journal* (*Stock-broker's Clerk*) and a new treatise upon pathology (*Study in Scarlet*), his conversation as reported did not deal with his profession or its technological advance to any extent. One felt that he was much more at home reading a good sea story (*Five Orange Pips*).

He told Holmes on the first day of their acquaintance (*Study in Scarlet*) that he was lazy, that this was one of his bad points, at any rate during his convalescence. One cannot agree with Watson's interpretation of himself. Instead, a more justified view is that he had no strong personal ambition. Certainly he showed willingness to exert all his efforts on behalf of Holmes's cases over a long period of time, and his wooing of Mary Morstan was not a placid affair (*Sign of the Four*). No, John could not be described as lazy in any sense.

He was fond of sports, both as a participant and as a spectator. In his youth he played rugby for Blackheath (*Vampire*). He played billiards with Thurston (*Dancing Men*). He knew much about dogs and horses. For example, he explained to Holmes that the Shoscombe spaniels were possibly the most exclusive breed in England and that they were heard of frequently from the dog shows (*Shoscombe*). He was equally up on horses and horse racing. He had the philosophy that people who control either horses or boys have a firm and austere expression, and he told Holmes that he spent about half of his wound pension on the races (*Shoscombe*).

Watson had a fondness for the expensive and relaxing Turkish bath, probably more so than Holmes, although both patronized such establishments (*Lady Frances Carfax* and *Illustrious Client*).

This easy-going day-by-day attitude could give way to quick emotional disturbance, as when he fainted on seeing Holmes after he had thought him dead (*Empty House*) and had to be revived with strong spirit. Too, it will be remembered that it was Watson who first fought off the effects of the deadly fumes and saved Holmes and himself (*Devil's Foot*). Also, there was a kind of foolhardy courage about Watson that does not fail to cause admiration, even though one feels that he is on the wrong track, as when he accuses the formidable Philip Green (*Lady Frances Carfax*).

Neither scientific investigation nor precise observation was Watson's forte. He could not tell Holmes how many steps led up from the hall to their consulting room at Baker Street and was gratified to learn from Holmes that there were seventeen steps. He saw but did not observe (*Scandal in Bohemia*). His mystification over Holmes's conclusions, usually followed by an explanation from Holmes as to how the conclusions were reached, began in the *Study in Scarlet* and continued throughout their long association of seventeen years (*Veiled Lodger*). Certainly, in a patient willingness to listen and try to learn, Watson had no peer.

Still, it is obvious that Watson would have made a poor detective; the record is clear on this point. For one reason or another, Holmes occasionally asked Watson to investigate a case. Invariably he did all the wrong things, or almost all, as

Holmes pointed out to him with acerbity. Such misinvestigations included (1) the whereabouts of the principal figure in *Lady Frances Carfax;* (2) the whereabouts of Mrs. Josiah Amberley and Dr. Ernest (*Retired Colourman*), and the comical sequel of Watson and Josiah Amberley decoyed in the wilds of Essex while Holmes and Mr. Barker investigated the matter. This humorous episode is one of the few such interludes in the long history. (3) Watson's investigation of Violet Smith's case was misguided (*Solitary Cyclist*). Then there were (4) Watson's investigations about Dartmoor and his pathetic distress when he thought that Holmes had not read his long October reports (*The Hound*).

Though he never begrudged such humble services, John seemingly could never learn to be a detective. Usually he was at sea in a case from its inception to the moment when the identity of the wrongdoers was revealed. One instance will suffice here. In the *Creeping Man,* although the pieces were falling into place rapidly for Holmes, John did not see the relationship between an angry wolfhound and a visit to Bohemia. He says of Holmes's enthusiasm, "Thank goodness that something connects with something."

Through it all Watson was loyal. This seems to be the central fiber of his personality. Loyalty to England, to his wife, and to Holmes. Even when he objected to breaking into a house (*Bruce-Partington*), he brought the burglar tools, and when Holmes decided to crack a safe (*Milverton*), he stood watch.

*Watson's Reports:* Sherlock Holmes had a true appreciation of the situation when he called John Watson his "Boswell" (*Scandal in Bohemia*). Had it not been for John's enthusiasm in recording Holmes's numerous cases, the latter would be unknown except to a select coterie of Scotland Yard inspectors and hardened criminals. Loyalty, once more, was a strong motivation for Watson. He was determined to see that his comrade had justice. If the professional police took the credit at the time, at least, he told Holmes, the public would have the true facts sooner or later. This is stated prophetically in their first joint case, *Study in Scarlet,* where John comforted Sherlock: "Never mind . . . , I have all the facts in my journal, and the public shall know them." John lived up to this promise as well as could be expected. If he did not have all the facts and if he confused a few dates, the record of Holmes's adventures is nevertheless well told.

Watson states (*Veiled Lodger*) that of the twenty-three years in which Holmes was in active professional practice, he was with Holmes for seventeen. In this long period of collaboration sixty cases were published. These included fifty-six short accounts and four much longer records, *viz., Study in Scarlet, Sign of Four, Hound of the Baskervilles,* and the *Valley of Fear.* Of these sixty reports, John Watson certainly narrated fifty-six, including two which preceded his meeting with Holmes, *i.e., Gloria Scott* (Holmes's first case) and the early *Musgrave Ritual.*

Two cases were narrated by Holmes: *Blanched Soldier,* when Watson was away with his second wife, and *Lion's Mane,* which was an adventure on the Sussex downs after Holmes had retired. The other cases, namely, *His Last Bow,* and the *Mazarin Stone,* are told more or less in the third person and to this extent are anonymous. An oddity in the series of cases narrated by Watson is that in the *Resident Patient* and the *Cardboard Box* paragraphs three to nineteen are identical.

Watson frequently refers back to former cases, as did Holmes. Among these backward glances are the following: (1) in the *Final Problem* he thinks of the *Naval Treaty* and a *Study in Scarlet;* (2) in the *Naval Treaty* he notes the adventure of the *Second Stain;* (3) in the *Second Stain* he thinks of the *Abbey Grange.* (4) The *Resident Patient* evokes a memory of the pre-Watsonian *Gloria Scott* and the first collaboration, *Study in Scarlet.* (5) *Black Peter* recalls the *Solitary Cyclist,* where Watson did not do as good a job as Holmes thought that he should. (6) In the *Mazarin Stone,* which Watson may or may not have written since it is in the third person initially, the *Empty House,* with its happy opening, is noted. (7) In the *Bruce-Partington Plans,* in which John faithfully brings burglar tools, the *Greek Interpreter* is mentioned. The suggestion is that both Holmes and Watson lived for their cases.

Perhaps the extreme eagerness for new cases and absorption in the cases already under way accounted for Watson's failure to record more. One appreciates his care in composition —he himself speaks at one point of the "pains and the pride" with which he wrote (*The Hound*)—but it was evidently a most time-consuming exercise. He completed the four long accounts and the fifty-two short adventures; but this effort, along with his medical practice and marital commitments, seems to have left him insufficient time to prepare others.

Certainly there is a tremendous amount of unreported material. Not only did Watson have a shelf full of yearbooks (*Veiled Lodger*), but there were boxes of notes, records, and mementos. Holmes too had quantities of organized and unorganized case-histories that were pre-Watsonian (*Musgrave Ritual*), and in a vault of the Cox & Company bank at Charing Cross is another box full of cases that are largely unpublished (*Thor Bridge*).

Listed in this guide are at least seventy-eight cases, or possible cases, which have not been published. These added to the sixty known to have been given to the public make a minimum of 138 cases. Put more bluntly, published cases account for not more than 43%, whereas unpublished cases account for at least 67% of a possible total. This is a great loss to the thinking public, and there are resentful moments when one feels that John might have done better, even if it came to giving up a sea story or so, or even a Turkish bath.

WATSON, MARY. *Née* Morstan. Not a great deal is known of her after she married. For her early life, cf. Mary Morstan, and for her romance, cf. Watson, John, under John and Mary.

She was a devoted and thoughtful wife, ever wishing her husband to be happy, *i.e.*, to take off a few days and work on a case with Holmes (*Boscombe* and *Naval Treaty*, for example).

The Watsons lived in Kensington (*Red-headed League*), and Mary herself was away from home at least twice, once in the *Five Orange Pips*, and again in late April, 1891 (*Final Problem*). In neither instance do we know where she went.

She died between this date and the spring of 1894, when Holmes returned to a bereaved Watson (*Empty House*).

WATT STREET CHAPEL. At Aldershot, where the Guild of St. George met to supply the poor with cast-off clothing (*Crooked Man*).

Weald Forest. The Birlstone area was on its fringe (*Valley of Fear*).

Weald Station. Mary Maberley lived but a short walk from here (*Three Gables*).

weavers, hands of. See Holmes, Sherlock, under Works.

Weiss & Company. London. Straker's knife, which **W** identified as a cataract knife, was made by this firm (*Silver Blaze*).

Welbeck Street. **H** was nearly run down here. Was Professor Moriarty at work behind the scene? (*Final Problem*).

Wellington Street. **H** and **W** en route from the Cedars in Kent to London (*Twisted Lip*).

Wells, Artesian. A dead giveaway in "Howard Garrideb's" advertisement (*Garridebs*).

Wessex Cup. The favorite for this race had disappeared, and **H** was asked to investigate (*Silver Blaze*).

West Africa. Dr. Sterndale obtained a sample of *Radix pedis diaboli* here in the Ubanghi country (*Devil's Foot*). Cf. Africa; also South Africa.

West, Arthur Cadogan. Twenty-seven years old, married, clerk in the Woolwich Arsenal. He was discovered dead beside the Underground tracks on Tuesday morning. This brought Mycroft Holmes to 221B Baker for a second time. **H** took the case, was triumphant, and again saved England from a difficult situation (*Bruce-Partington*).

Westaway's. A well-known agency for governesses in the West End (*Copper Beeches*).

Westbury House Festivities. Hatty Doran was much admired at them (*Noble Bachelor*).

Westbury, Violet. Fiancée of Arthur Cadogan West. She had faith in Arthur, and after he was not only murdered but his memory liable to be reviled, she too asked **H** to investigate. He cleared the young man of being accused of selling his country's secrets (*Bruce-Partington*).

West End. **H** went there to continue the investigation of the missing jewels (*Beryl Coronet*). Westaway's Agency for governesses was here (*Copper Beeches*). Mr. Blessington was unduly alarmed at a burglary (*Resident Patient*), or so it seemed. At some place here the Underground was free of the tubes (*Bruce-Partington*). Grosvenor Square, where Isadora Klein lived, was in this area (*Three Gables*).

*Western Morning News*. See *Leeds Mercury*.

Westhouse & Marbank. Claret importers in Fenchurch Street (*Case of Identity*).

West India Docks. As for pool.

West Indies. Rear-Admiral Baskerville served under Rodney here (*The Hound*).

WESTMINSTER. Morton & Kennedy, electricians, had a firm here (*Solitary Cyclist*). It was only a few minutes walk from here to Whitehall Terrace (*Second Stain*). Bevington's pawnshop was here (*Lady Frances Carfax*). Adolph Meyer lived at 13 Great George Street (*Bruce-Partington*).

WESTMINSTER BRIDGE. **H** and **W** en route to Shlessinger's house in Poultney Square (*Lady Frances Carfax*).

WESTMINSTER STAIRS. **H** told Athelney Jones to have a fast police steam-launch here at 7:00 (*Sign of Four*).

WESTMINSTER WHARF. The police launch was waiting for **H, W,** and Athelney Jones and ready to chase the "Aurora" (*Sign of Four*).

WESTMORELAND. James Desmond lived here (*The Hound*).

WESTPHAIL, MISS HONORIA. Sister of Mrs. Stoner and aunt to the twins, Julia and Helen Stoner (*Speckled Band*).

WESTVILLE ARMS. At Birlstone, Sussex. **H** and **W** had a room here while they investigated the murder of "John Douglas" at the invitation of both White Mason and Inspector Alec MacDonald (*Valley of Fear*).

*Whitaker's Almanac.* Fred Porlock's cipher message referred to this volume (*Valley of Fear*).

WHITE, ABEL. An indigo planter who hired Jonathan Small as overseer of his plantation at Muttra, near the border of the Northwest Provinces. Abel was killed and his house burned down in the great Indian Mutiny (*Sign of Four*).

WHITE EAGLE TAVERN. It was just before one came to the timberyard of Broderick & Nelson on Nine Elms Street (*Sign of Four*).

WHITE HALL (WHITEHALL). Percy Phelps worked in the Foreign Office here (*Naval Treaty*). Mycroft Holmes worked in the area (*Bruce-Partington*). **H** had the cabman who took Count Sylvius to this area (*Mazarin Stone*).

WHITEHALL TERRACE. Trelawney Hope lived here (*Second Stain*).

WHITE HART. London pub in which there was a fight at 11:00 P.M. and in which Constable Rance officially restored order (*Study in Scarlet*).

WHITNEY, ELIAS, D.D. Late of the Theological College of St. George's, where he was Principal (*Twisted Lip*).

WHITNEY, ISA. Brother of Elias Whitney. He was addicted to opium. Rescued by **W** and sent home in a cab (*Twisted Lip*).

WHITNEY, KATE. She asked help from John and Mary Watson. Her husband, Isa, had been away for two days. **W** found and rescued him from the Bar of Gold and sent him home in a cab (*Twisted Lip*).

WHITTINGTON, LADY ALICIA. She was of the St. Simon–Doran wedding party (*Noble Bachelor*).

WIGGINS. Leader of the Baker Street division of the detective police force. It was he who brought up the cabman (really Jefferson Hope) to 221B Baker Street, where, in the presence of Gregson and Lestrade, **H** snapped handcuffs on Hope by a ruse of having him help with some boxes (*Study in Scarlet*). Later, **H** wired Wiggins from the Great Peter Street Post Office (*Sign of Four*).

WIGMORE STREET. **H** and **W** en route to inquire about the goose (*Blue Carbuncle*).

WIGMORE STREET POST OFFICE. **W** got a bit of reddish mould on his instep about here (*Sign of Four*).

WILD, JONATHAN. A master criminal who lived about 1750. **H** thought that he would have been an earlier Moriarty (*Valley of Fear*).

WILDER, JAMES. Duke of Holdernesse' secretary and his illegitimate son. He was jealous of his young brother, Lord Saltire, and got in touch with Reuben Hayes. They plotted to kidnap young Lord Saltire (Arthur), but the matter ended by James's going away to Australia and Reuben's being arrested. Holmes picked up £6000 (*Priory School*).

WILLESDEN. An outlying junction of the London Underground (*Bruce-Partington*).

WILLIAMS. Thaddeus Sholto's "man." He inspected the party and then, satisfied, drove **H**, **W**, and Mary Morstan to talk with Thaddeus (*Sign of Four*).

WILLIAMS, JAMES BAKER. He lived at Forton Old Hall, near Oxshott. It was a large house, but not the right one (*Wisteria Lodge*).

WILLIAMSON, MR. He rented Charlington Hall. He was an unfrocked clergyman and unmitigated ruffian who solemnized the false marriage of Violet Smith to Jack Woodley. His recompense was seven years in prison (*Solitary Cyclist*).

WILLOWS, DR. He was John Turner's physician (*Boscombe*).

WILSON. He liberated Delhi in the Indian Mutiny (*Sign of Four*).

WILSON. Constable on duty at Yoxley Old Place (*Pince-Nez*).

*WILSON. A notorious canary-trainer. His arrest on information supplied by **H** in 1895 rid London's East End of "a plague-spot" (*Black Peter*). No public report.

WILSON. Manager of a district messenger office in Regent Street. He provided young Cartwright for **H**. Cartwright was to look into the wastepaper of twenty-three Charing Cross hotels for a cut-up center page of the London *Times* and report by wire to **H** on this quest (*The Hound*).

WILSON, JABEZ. Pawnbroker in Coburg Square. He became the dupe of John Clay (*Red-headed League*).

WILSON, SERGEANT. Of the Sussex Constabulary. He came to Birlstone Manor at the invitation of Cecil Barker (*Valley of Fear*).

WILSON. Sham chaplain of the "Gloria Scott." It was he who murdered the ship's captain (*Gloria Scott*).

WIMBLEDON. The Ronder show was on its way here, and the caravan stopped at Abbas Parva for the night (*Veiled Lodger*).

WIMPOLE STREET. **H** and **W** en route to inquire about the goose (*Blue Carbuncle*).

WINCHESTER. Jephro Rucastle lived at the Copper Beeches nearby. Neil Gibson's affair was in the hands of the Assizes here (*Thor Bridge*).

WINDIBANK, JAMES. Stepfather of Mary Sutherland. A traveler in wines for Westhouse & Marbank, claret importers in Fenchurch Street. To keep control of Mary's small income, he impersonated a fictitious Hosmer Angel and became engaged. Home: No. 31 Lyon Place, Camberwell. He was foiled by **H** (*Case of Identity*).

WINDIGATE. Presumably the owner of the Alpha Inn (*Blue Carbuncle*).

WINE. Beaune, Chianti, Port, and Tokay are mentioned in the *Sign of Four*. Francis Hay Moulton had sherry at an expensive hotel (*Noble Bachelor*). Tokay was favored by Altamont (*alias* of **H**), according to Von Bork (*Last Bow*). **H** recalled that the Chequers in Camford served an above-average port (*Creeping Man*). **H** and **W** had a bottle of Montrachet with a cold partridge (*Veiled Lodger*). Westhouse & Marbank were claret importers in Fenchurch Street, and James Windibank was one of their travelers (*Case of Identity*). Cf. also Vamberry.

WINTER, JAMES. *Alias* "Killer" Evans, *q.v.*

WINTER, KITTY. She threw vitriol in the face of Baron Gruner (*Illustrious Client*).

WISTERIA LODGE. Between Esher and Oxshott, home of Aloysius Garcia in Surrey (*Wisteria Lodge*).

WISTERIA LODGE, ADVENTURE OF. The San Pedro population overthrew its dictator, Don Juan Murillo. The latter, with his secretary, Lopez fled. Finally the dictator and his secretary were killen in Madrid. Mr. John Scott Eccles was innocently involved. **H** and Inspector Baynes solved the case in so far as England was concerned. This case opened in the Baker Street chambers and **W** assigns it to the end of March, 1892.

This date is not possible, since at this time all the world, except Mycroft Holmes, believed that **H** was dead. However, the case has to fall after October, 1890, since the *Red-headed League* is recalled. A more feasible date for the adventure would be March, 1895.

Woking. Percy Phelps lived at Briarbrae (*Naval Treaty*).

Wombwell. His circus was in competition both with Sanger's and with Ronder's (*Veiled Lodger*).

Wood, Dr. He pronounced "John Douglas" dead (*Valley of Fear*).

Wood, Henry. Cripple who had not seen Mrs. James Barclay (*née* Nancy Devoy) for thirty years. He talked with her in Hudson Street, Aldershot. Henry was formerly Corporal in the old 117th in the Indian Mutiny. He was betrayed, tortured, and escaped (*Crooked Man*).

Wood, J. G. Author of *Out of Doors,* in which reference **H** found a description of the giant medusa, *Cyanea capillata,* the killer of both McPherson and his dog (*Lion's Mane*).

*Woodhouse. One of fifty men who had reason to kill **H**, according to **H** (*Bruce-Partington*). The suggestion is that among these fifty people who might kill **H** a considerable number of them might have tried, or at the least there are a number of cases involved, some of which might be complete enough for reporting.

Woodley, Edith. She came from Carstairs and at one time was engaged to Robert Adair (*Empty House*).

Woodley, Jack. He was home from Africa with Mr. Carruthers with the news about Violet Smith's uncle (he did not tell Violet the whole story). En route from Africa he won the right to court Violet from Carruthers in a card game. Violet repulsed him. He then abducted and illegally married Violet; was caught by **H** and jailed for a ten-year sentence; and Violet married her true love (*Solitary Cyclist*).

Woodman's Lee. Near Forest Row, Sussex. Home of the retired sealer, Captain Peter Cary (*Black Peter*).

Woolwich Arsenal. The plans of the secret submarine were stolen from here, but **H** recovered them and saved England from a serious naval loss (*Bruce-Partington*).

Woolwich Branch. Of the Capital & Counties Bank. Cadogan West had a checking account here (*Bruce-Partington*).

Woolwich Theatre. Cadogan West

and his fiancée, Violet Westbury, were to attend a performance here, but his death intervened (*Bruce-Partington*).

WORCESTERSHIRE. Jonathan Small was born here (*Sign of Four*).

WORDSWORTH ROAD. H, W, and Mary Morstan en route to Thaddeus Sholto (*Sign of Four*).

WORTHINGDON BANK GANG. Comprised of Biddle, Hayward, Moffat, Sutton (*alias* Blessington), and Cartwright. They killed Tobin, the bank caretaker and stole £7000 in 1875 from the Worthingdon Bank. Sutton informed on Cartwright, who was hanged. Biddle, Hayward, and Moffat each got fifteen years for the crime. When the three got out of prison, they tried three times to kill Sutton, and the third time succeeded (*Resident Patient*).

WRIGHT, THERESA. Lady Brackenstall's maid at *Abbey Grange*.

# X

XX.31. This was the private telephone number which **H** was to call to reach Sir James Damery (*Illustrious Client*).

# Y

"YARD, THE." See Scotland Yard.

YELLOW FACE, THE. Mr. Hebron and only child were said to have died of disease in Atlanta, Georgia. In this case **H** was wrong and asked **W** to whisper "Norbury" if he ever appeared too confident.

YORK. **H** showed Mrs. Lyons a photograph taken here four years ago of Jack and Beryl Stapleton but endorsed by Mr. and Mrs. Vandeleur (*The Hound*).

YORK COLLEGE. An American school where Jefferson Hope was janitor. Once he was about when a professor was lecturing to a class on poisons and showed a deadly poison to the students. This poison was an alkaloid that he had extracted from a South American arrow poison. Jefferson stole some of the poison, worked it up as a pill, and put it in a box with a second pill, similar in appearance but harmless (*Study in Scarlet*).

YORKSHIRE. Mr. and Mrs. Vandeleur established a private school here, St. Oliver's (*The Hound*).

YOUGHAL. Of the C.I.D. **H** sent **W** with a message to him, to say that he was to come to 221B Baker Street to arrest Count Sylvius and Sam Merton (*Mazarin Stone*).

YOXLEY OLD PLACE. Home of Professor Coram, seven miles from Chatham, in Kent (*Pince-Nez*).

# Z

**Zamba, Signor.** He was an invalid and a partner in the firm of Castalotte & Zamba (*Red Circle*).

**Zeppelin.** Von Herling felt that if Zeppelin made good his promise, the air would not be so peaceful (*Last Bow*).

**zoo.** H compared Charles Augustus Milverton with one of the serpents kept here (*Milverton*).